O9-CFT-574

Making Peace with
Your Office Life

Also by Cindy Glovinsky

Making Peace with the Things in Your Life

One Thing at a Time

Making Peace with Your Office Life

End the Battles,

Shake the Blues,

Get Organized,

and

Be Happier at Work

Cindy Glovinsky, L.M.S.W., A.C.S.W.

St. Martin's Griffin　New York

MAKING PEACE WITH YOUR OFFICE LIFE. Copyright © 2010 by Cindy Glovinsky. All rights reserved. Printed in the United States of America. For information, address St. Martin's Press, 175 Fifth Avenue, New York, N.Y. 10010.

www.stmartins.com

"Harlem (2) ['What happens to a dream deferred . . .']" from *The Collected Poems of Langston Hughes* by Langston Hughes, edited by Arnold Rampersad with David Roessel, Associate Editor, copyright © 1994 by the Estate of Langston Hughes. Used by permission of Alfred A. Knopf, a division of Random House, Inc.

"Dolor," copyright 1943 by Modern Poetry Association, Inc., from *Collected Poems of Theodore Roethke* by Theodore Roethke. Used by permission of Doubleday, a division of Random House, Inc.

Arlie Russell Hochschild, *The Managed Heart: Commercialization of Human Feeling.* © 1983 by the Regents of the University of California. Published by the University of California Press.

"Walls," © Bruce Bennett, reprinted with permission.

Book design by Phil Mazzone

Library of Congress Cataloging-in-Publication Data

Glovinsky, Cindy.
    Making peace with your office life : end the battles, shake the blues, get organized, and be happier at work / Cindy Glovinsky.—1st ed.
        p. cm.
    Includes bibliographical references.
    ISBN 978-0-312-57602-8
    1. Job satisfaction.   2. Quality of work life.   3. Interpersonal conflict.
4. Interpersonal relations.   I. Title.
    HF5549.5.J63G58 2010
    650.1—dc22

                                                            2009040014

First Edition: March 2010

10 9 8 7 6 5 4 3 2 1

For all my office coworkers, past and present,
and for office workers everywhere, with love

Contents

Acknowledgments

This is the product of countless conversations with all sorts of people, not all of whom realized that they were helping me to write a book. I especially want to thank Yu Xie, Catherine Thibault, James Jackson, and the members of the Survey Research Center's Professional Advisory Committee and the Director's Advisory Committee on Diversity at the Institute for Social Research, University of Michigan. A number of generous and insightful readers provided comments on portions of the manuscript, including Marie Campbell, Chris Greene, Jane Dutton, Howard Kimeldorf, Erik Kreps, Mary Vardigan, and David O. Williams. Thanks also to Robert Addison, Sue Budin, Marilyn Churchill, Kathy Edgren, Jay Harter, Jeanetta Housh, Chris Lord, Lisa Madden, Andrea Pedolsky, and Ken Salaman for their help in brainstorming when this project was in its infancy.

I'm grateful to my editor, Alyse Diamond, for all her excellent work, and to all the staff at St. Martin's Press who were involved in the production of this book or in supporting their efforts.

Most of all, I want to thank my husband, Ira Glovinsky, for his great ideas, patience, humor, and loving support.

As minute changes can result in great discoveries, so small adjustments can turn a routine job one dreads into a professional performance one can look forward to with anticipation each morning.

—*Mihaly Csikszentmihalyi,* Finding Flow

Only connect!

—*E. M. Forster,* Howards End

Making Peace with
Your Office Life

Introduction

W e gotta get out of this place . . . if it's the last thing we ever do!"
The words of the old Animals song wail through your mind after a particularly unpleasant conversation with one of your co-workers. Retreating to your cubicle, you imagine yourself magically entering the green pastures of your screen saver and dancing off toward the bright blue sky, away from here, imprisoned in a job that suits you about as well as a doghouse suits a canary. But instead, you start clicking your way through the forty-odd e-mails that accumulated while you were having the unpleasant conversation.

Meanwhile, you brace yourself for the next attack. What will it be? Someone from Accounting calling to say you did your expense report wrong and must do the whole thing over? Your boss's partner demanding information ASAP for a project that doesn't have to be done for at least another six months? Or that neat-freak colleague making sardonic remarks about the piles of papers on your desk?

You glance around your cubicle for comfort, but your eyes meet only an inorganic desert of gray, white, and beige—they yearn for something green, natural hardwood floors, or a colorful painting. Machines beep and arguments buzz beyond the flimsy half walls.

There's a crick in your neck that refuses to go away no matter what you do, your legs itch for a good run in the park, and you can feel your brain cells dying in your head. Why did you bother to go to college if this was where you were going to end up? Most of all, you long for good old unconditional love, for someone in your workplace with whom you can share your joys, gripes, and great ideas who won't ever give you that I-can't-believe-how-unprofessional-you're-being look.

Oh, yes, you know you're lucky to have work at all in today's economy, that millions of unemployed would love to have your job, but the fact remains: You'd give anything not to have to flush away enormous chunks of your life typing nonsense into a plastic box when your real passion is playing the saxophone, quilting, writing novels, climbing rocks, or taking care of your own kids. So far, you've managed to survive by telling yourself that you just have to "get through the day," but you wonder how much longer you can go on this way, living always for five o'clock, for Friday night, for the day when you can go back to school, marry someone rich, retire, or do whatever else will take you out of the office world once and for all.

The weird thing is, everyone around you seems perfectly happy. Your coworkers smile and make squeaky-clean small talk, never say no to the boss, rarely take lunch breaks, and seem to find filling out forms in an online system that constantly spits out error messages fascinating. At times you suspect that you're working with some new, updated brand of Stepford wives who've been adjusted to fit the office scene rather than the home and come in both genders. Don't they realize that there's a whole wonderful world out there that they're missing? Is there something the matter with them, or something the matter with you?

In truth, it's probably neither. Human beings are an extremely variable species, and just as some people are made healthier and others sick by eating shellfish, individuals have different levels of tolerance for an office world that was not designed for human health or happiness but for productivity. That world has never been ideal for *Homo sapiens*, who didn't start out in cubicles. And in the early twenty-first century, twisted out of shape by the unregulated, runaway market forces of what former secretary of labor Robert B. Reich calls supercapitalism, that world has become increasingly hazardous to the mental and physical health of all of us, sometimes in ways we're not even aware of.

While some folks love their jobs, countless others experience the office situation as unnatural, undemocratic, ungenerous, and unrelenting. Unnatural because office work involves confinement to a closed, mostly inorganic environment; the wearing of neckties and high heels instead of clothes made for human comfort; and superficial interchanges instead of genuine conversations. Undemocratic because there are no elections for those in charge, and exercising any of the freedoms guaranteed by the Bill of Rights may put one's "pursuit of happiness" in jeopardy. Ungenerous because today's lower-status office job provides the employee with only mediocre pay and benefits, minimal job security, insufficient vacation time, and little genuine food for the senses, intellect, emotions, or ego. Unrelenting because demands on office workers have become ever more unrealistic as organizations have downsized personnel without downsizing their missions. In such formidable circumstances, how you feel about your own office job may depend mostly on how well you're able to tolerate artificiality, tyranny, deprivation, and stress.

For as long as offices have existed, some folks have fit more comfortably into them than others. Some people are naturally orderly, compliant, attentive, goal-driven, detail-oriented, uncritical, even-tempered, and conforming. Office work, especially clerical or administrative work, suits these people pretty well, though some aspects may still affect them more negatively than they realize. Others are programmed to think for themselves, daydream, feel feelings, look at the big picture, question authority, empathize, love the outdoors, and create big paper piles and big ideas. These people are almost guaranteed to hate office work. Still others—probably most of us—have some traits of both types.

As professional organizer Julie Morgenstern points out in *Never Check E-mail in the Morning*, when problems occur, workers tend to ask themselves, "Is it me or is it them?" In many cases, I believe that it's neither. Instead, the problem is *it*—the bizarre fun house of distorting mirrors that I call the office world, though *they*, most of whom are unaware of *it*, will often try to make you think it's *you*. Don't let them succeed. If you dread coming to work every day, it's most likely because present-day offices can be tough places for human beings to be, especially sensitive, intelligent, creative, freedom-loving people like you.

While the obvious solution if you're an office misfit is to get yourself onto a different career track, this may not always be possible, at least not right now, when the economy is hurting and unemployment rates are high. During hard times, along with unemployment goes "misemployment," people having to take whatever jobs they can get even if they don't suit their particular talents, interests, education, or experience. Some misemployed office workers may be just starting out, waiting for their "real" careers to begin, while others may be grieving the loss of a more rewarding profession or a business they owned and loved. While unemployment causes pain, so does misemployment, though workers lucky enough to have a decent-paying job may feel they have no right to complain.

If you're one of the millions of office misfits struggling to adapt to life in a cubicle, this book is for you. If you find "how to succeed" books superficial and feel that there's more to life than outsmarting someone into giving you a corner office and a longer, more stressful workday, you're in the right place. The focus of this book is not success but well-being, though obviously if you feel better, you're likely to also be more successful if you want to be. My purpose is not to show you how to do more faster so as to climb higher and higher, but to show you how to feel healthier, happier, and more connected in the job you have right now, for however long you stay in it. You may be looking for an escape route, but meanwhile, learning to make the best of your current job will help you to enjoy future, more satisfying work situations all the more.

Office Blues and Office Battleshock

When individuals feel trapped in a job, over time their mental and even physical health may begin to suffer. When your environment has a negative effect on your mental health and well-being, causing you to become depressed or anxious or both, psychotherapists call this an adjustment disorder. I believe many office workers suffer from a kind of eight-to-five adjustment disorder that is confined mainly to their working hours, though it may sometimes progress into full-blown depression or anxiety. When depression is the dominant symptom, I call this the office blues. When anxiety is more salient, I call it office battleshock. Many workers experience some of both conditions.

The office blues is a mildly depressive state that is mostly a result of deprivation and loneliness. It's characterized by dread before going to work (for many of us, on Sunday night), a sinking feeling when you walk in the door of your office building, sadness, and a sense of unreality—of merely existing rather than really living during working hours. The office blues is nothing new. Among creative artists, the office blues has long been a source of pathos and humor, from Herman Melville's *Bartleby* to Scott Adams's *Dilbert* cartoons, the popular TV series *The Office*, and the movie *Office Space*, in which the character Peter provides a textbook example of someone with the office blues. Poet Theodore Roethke, writing in the 1940s, describes his version of the office blues in "Dolor":

> *I have known the inexorable sadness of pencils,*
> *Neat in their boxes, dolor of pad and paper-weight,*
> *All the misery of manilla folders and mucilage,*
> *Desolation in immaculate public places,*
> *Lonely reception room, lavatory, switchboard,*
> *The unalterable pathos of basin and pitcher,*
> *Ritual of multigraph, paper-clip, comma,*
> *Endless duplication of lives and objects.*
> *And I have seen dust from the walls of institutions,*
> *Finer than flour, alive, more dangerous than silica,*
> *Sift, almost invisible, through long afternoons of tedium,*
> *Dropping a fine film on nails and delicate eyebrows,*
> *Glazing the pale hair, the duplicate grey standard faces.*

Roethke's poem illustrates the type of office misery that was most common in the mid-twentieth century, when office life tended to be fairly undemanding, but workers were forced to do a lot of mindless, repetitive work. In the twenty-first century, routine office work can still be dull—though in general it requires more thought than it used to—but meanwhile it has become far more taxing. According to Princeton Survey Research Associates, three-fourths of all employees believe their work to be more stressful than it was a generation ago, and the World Health Organization has recognized workplace stress as a worldwide epidemic. The result is a different variant of office un-happiness characterized by high levels of anxiety and overwhelm that in severe cases may even have some characteristics of post-traumatic stress, such as flashbacks, hypervigilance, dissociation, and nightmares. I call this condition office battleshock.

People with office battleshock feel that they're living in a war zone in which they're constantly under attack from hostile forces, like rats in a psychology experiment who are in continual danger of being shocked. They often wake up in the middle of the night with their minds racing, wondering what they forgot to do at work. Ever on the alert, they find it almost impossible to relax. At work they feel disconnected from those around them and may experience others' legitimate requests or corrections as personal attacks. These workers are usually struggling with unrealistic workloads and/or managerial perfectionism and bullying on the job, and they may be wrestling with problems at home as well. Overwhelmed by e-mails, frustrated by interruptions, constantly multitasking, and thrown into a panic by technological breakdowns, they're never able to step off the tread-mill long enough to get organized. Instead, they try to solve every-thing by working faster and longer in a world that feels ever more nightmarish and unreal. In clinical terms, they dissociate. If un-treated, they may eventually become either mentally or physically sick and be forced to go on medical leave.

Office Challenges to Health and Well-being

Just because you feel blue at the office, this doesn't necessarily make you a blue person. Just because you feel embattled, this doesn't mean you're a natural-born victim. It may just be that the following chal-lenges affect you more adversely than they do some workers.

Confinement

Although telecommuting has altered this challenge for a few folks, most employees still spend their workdays confined to a single building, often a single room and even a single chair, for hours at a time. Confinement to a building means that all office workers are more at risk than outdoor workers for seasonal affective disorder (SAD), a type of depression that results from insufficient sunlight. Beyond that, workers inclined toward claustrophobia may feel anxious, restless, and imprisoned. Finally, the types of spaces where workers are confined carry a message about their relative importance to the organization—often a negative, depressing one, as in the case of the infamous cubicle, which *Dilbert*'s creator, Scott Adams, compares to a livestock-fattening pen, a child's playpen, or a prison cell.

Inactivity

It is a known fact that aerobic exercise benefits not only physical health but mental health as well, and that without it, both tend to deteriorate. People who drive to work and sit in offices all day get exercise, if at all, only outside of their working hours. Thus, they may be more susceptible to depression and obesity than people with more active jobs. In addition, workers who are naturally more active may feel stressed by the necessity of sitting still for long periods and may not concentrate well in such a situation. Finally, sitting at a keyboard for hours on end can result in eye strain; headaches; carpal tunnel syndrome; and neck, back, and shoulder pain, and it's hard to be happy when you're hurting.

Deprivation

Much has been written about the stresses office workers experience, but little about the equally harmful effects of sensory, emotional, and intellectual deprivation on the job. Traditionally, the cardinal rule for those making decisions about office decorating has been "Less is more," partly to minimize costs and partly out of the misbelief that all workers concentrate best in a state of sensory deprivation. Thus, many sources of comforting stimulation are visibly absent from most office environments, including color, natural fabrics, wood, water, plants, animals, children, music, art, antiques, comforting textures, and pleasing aromas. Arts and humanities types may also be frustrated by the absence of creative language and ideas, wistfully remembering college days filled with philosophy, history, and literature now that "job enrichment" means nothing more than taking another class in Excel. Where the brain is concerned, according to modern neuroscientists, the rule is "Use it or lose it." Thus, restricting the activities of a gifted mind for many hours per day may result in the loss of neurological connections and the wasting of resources that, properly fed, could be taking organizations in exciting new directions. As for emotions, office workers are expected to check those at the door, fearing accusations of whining if they tell anyone how they really feel. At the same time, workers may also feel deprived of adequate recognition and financial compensation for their labors.

Disconnection

The creators of office life as we know it mistakenly assumed that humans are most productive when unhampered by emotional ties. This makes as much sense as assuming that babies develop best if they're never touched or held. Of course, as children grow, they need emotional space in which to venture out and explore the world; likewise, adults often do need to pull away from their connections when on some type of mission. As conservative managers are fond of saying, "Work is work." But not all adults are emotional camels designed to thrive in a state of disconnection for eight or more hours at a time before returning to those people and activities that emotionally feed them. Shut away in buildings that are often far from their homes, office employees may feel disconnected from nature, families and loved ones, communities, cultural groups, religious practices, hobbies, and interests. Inside the workplace, competitive cultures of toughness forbid the open expression of feelings and thus also keep workers emotionally disconnected from one another and even from awareness of their own emotions.

While it's an established fact that positive relationships can have a powerful protective effect in dealing with anxiety, depression, trauma, and grief, office workers are often denied this protection, to the detriment of their mental and physical well-being. Psychiatrist Edward M. Hallowell, in *CrazyBusy: Overstretched, Overbooked, and About to Snap!*, hypothesizes that social disconnection is at the root of most of the psychiatric problems for which patients visit his office, including depression, anxiety, substance abuse, low frustration tolerance, violence, and poor work performance. Hallowell adds that disconnection can also have a negative effect on the immune system and can even lower life expectancy.

To try to counter the negative effects of disconnection, many office workers, especially those of low status, turn to the only source of comfort and connection available to them at work: food. Alas, the abundance of high-calorie foods available in many office workplaces, along with the extreme inactivity of office life, makes obesity a serious health risk to office workers as well as a source of sluggishness and underproductivity.

Frustration

When you try to accomplish a goal and your progress is continually blocked, frustration results. This can happen in any type of job, but for most office workers, experiences of frustration from multiple sources are continuous. Efforts are blocked by technological breakdowns, interruptions, the unavailability of information or authorization, communication problems, lack of proper training, lack of aptitude for a particular task, and rigid bureaucratic rules and regulations. High levels of frustration, in addition to other stresses, put workers at risk for angry outbursts and even violence. According to a survey conducted by the Society for Human Resource Management, nearly 10 percent of employers can expect some type of violent altercation to break out in their offices each year.

Overwhelm

Today's office employees, along with their bosses, are frequently challenged by unrealistic workloads, the combined result of technological advances that saved far less time than expected and downsizing in response to market pressures. Many office workers struggle with overly diverse task arrays after taking on not only their own duties but also those of positions that have been eliminated from the workplace. Meanwhile, most office tasks now require electronic training that continually has to be updated. Thus, instead of performing a few types of tasks frequently enough to master them, workers have to continually relearn many different types of tasks that they perform only rarely, and are more likely to make mistakes for which they may be held accountable. As workloads have become more unrealistic, errors have multiplied, to which many managers respond with demands for perfection, becoming unrealistic about quality as well as quantity.

Some overwhelmed employees react to their situations by working overtime or taking work home, thus giving up badly needed restorative personal time, while others refrain from taking breaks and struggle to do everything at an unhealthy pace during their workdays. According to financial writer Jill Andresky Fraser in *White Collar Sweatshop*, almost 12 percent of all U.S. workers (about 15 million people) spend forty-nine to fifty-nine hours per week at the office, and 8.5 percent (about 11 million) work over sixty hours. Although the overworked consist mostly of white-collar professionals such as corporate managers, investment bankers, lawyers, editors, and accountants, the secretaries, programmers, and others who support their activities are often expected to overwork right along with their bosses. And while white-collar professionals receive emotional benefits of high status and financial compensation that may partially—though not totally—offset the psychological hazards of time poverty, their support staffers do not, placing these workers at higher risk for stress-related illnesses. A well-known 2002 study at Kyushu University in Fukuoka, Japan, looked at 705 men and found that those working sixty hours a week were *twice* as likely to have heart attacks as those working forty hours a week. In Japan they even have a special word for death by overwork: *karoshi*.

Toxicity

For a few workers, the confinement of office life is solitary—a type of punishment prisoners fear more than any other—while for most it's shared with other human beings, any one of whom may either provide support and connection or engage in toxic behaviors (i.e., those that can be detrimental to the mental health of their subordinates, bosses, or coworkers). The social situation of office workers, especially those working a lot of overtime, is, in reality, not much different from that of astronauts confined together in a space station. Daily contact in such circumstances—especially in a sterile, isolated building—has the potential to intensify both positive connections and the toxic effects of others' psychopathologies.

But disturbed individuals are not the only source of workplace toxicity. Sometimes otherwise-nice people can become involved in dysfunctional workplace patterns comparable to those of dysfunctional families, and those from traditionally underrepresented groups, such as women, minorities, or the disabled—and others as well—may fall prey to forces of discrimination, harassment, and bullying, which is as serious a problem in the workplace as it is in the schoolyard. In a 2002 study of workplace aggression and bullying, the U.S. Department of Veterans Affairs surveyed almost five thousand employees and found that 36 percent reported "persistent hostility" from coworkers and supervisors, experiencing at least one aggressive behavior per week for a period of a year. Another study at Arizona State University in 2006 showed that office bullies affect 25–30 percent of employees at some time in the course of their careers.

Powerlessness

The more control you have over your situation, the less likely you are to become depressed. While even CEOs may sometimes feel that they have little control over what goes on, the lower you are on the totem pole, the more likely you are to succumb to feelings of powerlessness. Employees whose best efforts continually go unrewarded often fall into a pattern of "learned helplessness," feeling that there is no point in trying to do their jobs well or feel better.

An employee in an assistantship position who is forced to jump each time the boss snaps his or her fingers may be particularly susceptible to the adverse effects of powerlessness. This may explain why a study by R. Garrison and W. W. Eaton at Johns Hopkins University found that women employed as secretaries are more likely to be depressed than other women, more likely to have missed work in the last three months, and more likely to have used mental-health services. The authors of this study, published in *Women's Health* in 1992, conclude, "We believe our findings warrant further investigation into the work environment of secretaries."

Uncertainty

Strangely enough, even office workers who loathe every minute of their jobs are often tied up in knots with fear of losing them—for several reasons:

1. The recommendation system of hiring means that if you're fired from your present job, you may find it impossible to get another one, especially during periods of high unemployment.
2. In a society in which health insurance is linked to employment, keeping your job may well mean the difference between you or someone you love living and dying.
3. In today's recessed economy, good jobs are becoming more and more difficult to get.
4. Failing at anything, especially when you've really tried to succeed, can leave you feeling wounded and worthless.

But the possibility of getting fired isn't the only type of uncertainty you have to contend with at the office: You may also be unsure whether your coworker is a friend or a competitor, whether it's okay to take a lunch break, whether to call someone by his or her first name, whether your clothes are right, and a host of other matters in a world in which change is the name of the game and rules are often unspoken rather than spelled out.

Office Benefits to Health and Well-being

By now, you're probably thinking about quitting your job even if you don't have someplace better to go. Stop! Before you walk out, you need to consider that, along with the crazy-making aspects of office work, there are some real benefits that you may be less aware of than your happier coworkers. These factors may at least partially compensate for the negatives and are probably why you took the job in the first place. They include, among others, the following.

Salary and Benefits

While a consistent salary and benefits don't buy happiness, doing without them can be a major cause of misery and ill health, which is why most of us are willing to put up with a lot of slings and arrows at the office in order to keep getting them.

Structure

If you've ever had your own business, worked as a homemaker, or experienced a period of unemployment, you know how challenging the burden of structuring your own time can be. While some people are pretty good at self-structuring, many slide into getting up later each morning and ending their days feeling that they've done little or nothing. A regular job from eight to five, or whatever hours you work, gives you a reason to get up. And once you're at work, you usually have at least some sense of what you're supposed to do throughout your workday, relieving you of some of the burden of decision making.

Comfort

You're not crawling around gasping for air at the bottom of a mine. You're not straddling a steel beam hundreds of feet above the ground. Your back isn't breaking from hour upon hour of shoveling or vacuuming. And although the temperature in your office might not be exactly ideal, you're probably not having to worry about frostbite or heat exhaustion. Sitting in front of a computer may have its health hazards, but they're minimal compared to those of doing physical labor. For the most part, you can rejoice in the fact that you're warm, dry, and relatively safe. And if peace and quiet are what you crave, you're more likely to find them in an office than in a restaurant filled with clattering dishes or a schoolroom filled with rebellious kids.

Order

In most offices there is a place for everything, though not all of us keep everything in its place. Manuals are arranged in a row on the shelf, supplies are in their niches in the supply cabinet, the hole puncher lives next to the printer. To many of us, order tends to be soothing.

Alphabetically arranged files, logically arranged e-mail directories, and numerically arranged spreadsheets offer us a haven, reassuring us that in this crazy, violent, unpredictable world there are at least some pockets of order.

Connection
Despite the forces that serve to disconnect office workers from one another, many do find true friends who share their interests and with whom they can talk honestly. This can make an enormous difference in workers' health and well-being. Those in assistantship positions may enjoy the intimacy with their bosses that is one of the perks of their situation, taking pride in working for people whose accomplishments they respect. Workers in organizations, although sometimes frustrated by bureaucratic roadblocks and rigidities, may also enjoy the sense of being part of something larger than themselves.

Learning
There are many things you can learn even in a routine clerical job, not all of which are computer programs or online systems. You can also learn to manage time more efficiently, to communicate more clearly, and to deal with different types of people. You can learn about your organization and the work it does. You can learn about the people you work with and their languages and cultures. Most of all, you can learn about yourself and how you respond to various situations.

Achievement
Nothing is better for your health and well-being than experiencing a sense of accomplishment for a job well done. You may feel particularly empowered if the task is something you thought you couldn't do. Every day in the office world, new opportunities arise to test your capabilities, and sometimes you find that those capabilities are greater than you thought. You might believe, for example, that you're a language person who isn't great at math, and be surprised to discover that you're actually good at reconciling accounts. Such discoveries may come in handy even if you end up in a nonoffice career.

Opportunities

Routine office jobs may often serve as stepping-stones to other careers that creative, independent thinkers may find more satisfying. The secretary with strong English skills who works for a publishing company may end up as an editor. The financial assistant may end up as an accountant. The administrative assistant with strong computer skills may end up in technical support or Web designing. Making the jump from one field to another requires careful strategizing, but it does happen.

Flow

When you forget about what time it is and become fully engaged with the task at hand, you may be experiencing what positive psychologist Mihaly Csikszentmihalyi calls flow. While it might be more difficult to achieve this heightened state of awareness doing routine office tasks than playing the violin or looking for a cure for cancer, it's not impossible. Even with routine office work, employees can become fully engrossed in what they're doing and manage to enjoy tasks for their own sake. Even fleeting moments of this can hugely benefit one's health and well-being.

From Blues and Battleshock to Peace

If you want to look forward to coming to work instead of dreading it, all you need to do is find ways to cope with the challenges and tune in more fully to the benefits. This requires conscious effort. Your first task is to get a better sense of how your office job is affecting your happiness right now by using the OCAB Ratio Form to figure out your Office Challenges and Benefits (OCAB) ratio. This is a simple ratio showing how strongly affected you feel by emotional challenges versus benefits at the office. A worker with an OCAB of 80/40, for example, is experiencing twice as much misery from challenges as happiness from benefits—in other words, this person has office blues and/or battleshock. If someone's OCAB is 40/80, on the other hand, he or she probably feels pretty good at work, though there's almost always room for improvement.

OCAB RATIO FORM

Your OCAB ratio will give you a baseline from which to chart your progress. As you begin to implement some of the ideas in this book, and refigure the ratio from time to time, the challenges side of the ratio should decrease, and the benefits side should increase. Note that this score is a function not simply of what challenges or benefits exist in your specific work situation but of how you *experience* them. You can change your OCAB ratio either by reducing a particular challenge or by finding a way to be less bothered by it; likewise, you can either find ways to add new benefits or learn to experience more fully those benefits already in place.

Instructions: To find your OCAB ratio, rate the degree to which you feel negatively affected by each challenge on a scale of 0 (not affected) to 10 (extremely affected). Then rate the degree to which you feel positively affected by each benefit on a scale of 0 (not affected) to 10 (extremely affected). Then total up each list. Your OCAB ratio is a ratio of challenges/benefits.

Note that your ratings should reflect your *feelings* in response to a particular challenge or benefit, not just how much of that challenge or benefit you're being exposed to in

Dealing with the challenges of the office workplace requires problem solving. Too often, however, this is not what happens. Instead, employers and employees alike tend to act as though the challenges don't exist, failing to pinpoint and address the specific causes of employee unhappiness and ill health while superficially cultivating a "positive attitude." The result is that employees may experience a vague sense of malaise but feel powerless to do anything about it.

The heart of the problem lies in what neuroscientist Antonio Damasio calls Descartes' error, the artificial separation of thinking and feeling, which informs the structure of our workplaces. In the traditional world of work, offices are supposed to be places where only thinking your job. You could, for example, have a job in which you're highly confined in space, but if this confinement doesn't bother you, your rating for the challenge of Confinement should still be low. Likewise, if you have a job in which you can leave the building whenever you like but still feel trapped, your rating should be high.

Challenge Effects
___Confinement
___Inactivity
___Deprivation
___Disconnection
___Frustration
___Overwhelm
___Toxicity
___Powerlessness
___Uncertainty

___**Challenge effects total**

Benefit Effects
___Salary and benefits
___Structure
___Comfort
___Order
___Connection
___Learning
___Achievement
___Opportunities
___Flow

___**Benefits effects total**

OCAB ratio
(challenge effects total/benefits effects total): _____
Date: _____

goes on, while feelings, regarded as an impediment to thought, are to be left at home with the spouse and kids, and physical action takes place on the factory floor. This worldview predates the discovery that neurologically, thoughts and emotions aren't actually separate at all but constitute two interwoven strands, and that feelings provide the mind with data about problems it needs to solve for the organism to survive and thrive.

Believing that feelings only get in the way of logical thought, un-enlightened employers often deprive themselves of valuable data by discouraging employees from expressing negative emotions at work, which office cultures have been quick to label as whining. The result is that serious misery-creating problems have gone unsolved for decades, leading to worker burnout, absenteeism, illness, high job turnover, violence, white-collar crime, and other negative effects, though some more emotionally intelligent managers, disturbed by these effects, are now beginning to pay more attention to employees' feelings.

Meanwhile, office workers, whose livelihoods may depend on their ability to please their employers, often buy into Descartes' error themselves, treating their own feelings as irrelevant distractions instead of valuable sources of data about problems they need to solve. If you have a history of suppressing or ignoring your feelings at work, your first priority must be to reconnect with them, including the negative ones, so you can use them to figure out what changes you need to make to feel better. This book will help you. It contains a four-part program that guides you through the journey from blues and battleshock to peace and happiness in the workplace.

My goal in part 1 of this book, "Thinking Outside the Cubicle: What's Really Going On?" is to provide you with a fresh view of the office world as well as all the equipment you need for a healthy, happy office journey. This equipment includes various types of knowledge and insight plus the assessment tools for determining what specific factors are contributing to your office blues and battleshock. We'll begin with an overview of the office world and the global contexts and constraints within which we all operate. Then we'll jump back in time and look at how offices became the way they are. In doing so, you'll discover that even professions that the office world now trivializes, such as clerk and secretary, actually have a long, distinguished history, and that office life did not spring into the world in its present form but has reached it through a long process of evolution to which all kinds of people have contributed. The lesson of history is that if office life doesn't work well for human beings now, it doesn't have to stay that way—we can change it.

From there, the next four chapters will examine several possible factors that may be mixed up in an individual employee's office blues and battleshock. We'll look first at the place where you work—your organization, its culture, and the dynamics of your particular work group. Then we'll talk about the many individual differences that can make workers more interesting to one another but can also create conflict and the mislabeling of some workers as "difficult people." After that, we'll look at the truly difficult people, those who have what therapists call personality disorders, people who are dangerous to the health and well-being of those around them, and with whom you need to use special coping strategies. Finally, we'll talk about you, examining the baggage you may bring into the office workplace.

Once you've got all the equipment you need to remake your life at the office, you'll be ready to get started. Part 2, "Starting Fresh in the Office: The First Big Steps," will help you. First, you'll learn how to make a "Work Companion," a tool that you'll use to gather information about your work life as it unfolds and process feelings that come up in the course of your workday. Next, you'll use the data you collected to put together a "Job Transformation Plan" for creating more quality in your workplace life. Finally, we'll talk about ways you can optimize your energy by taking better care of yourself, not only at the office but outside it as well.

Part 3, "From Blues and Battles to Peace: One Change at a Time," consists of nuts-and-bolts suggestions for dealing with specific problems in the office workplace relating to place, time, information, technology, tasks, culture, people, and reward systems. You'll learn things like how to cope with being boxed up, how to keep from being buried by e-mail, or how to deal with a micromanaging boss. Rather than reading this section straight through, many readers may want to skim over the chapters while making their Job Transformation Plans, making use of only those sections that are relevant to their specific situations. For this reason, I've put checkboxes next to each issue discussed, enabling you to check off those items to which you can best relate. As you begin to put a few of these suggestions into effect, you'll be surprised by how much difference even small changes can make.

Finally, part 4, "Beyond Peace: Working Together for Quality of Life in the Office," will help you to expand your focus from your own individual health and well-being to that of all workers, both within and beyond your own workplace. You'll learn how even workers at the bottom of the organizational pyramid have the power to become change agents and to work with others to create community, break down walls, and improve the quality of office life for everyone.

A Note on How This Book Came About

Although as a clinical social worker and professional organizer, I've helped many clients to deal with office workplace issues, I've also struggled with these issues myself. Like many permanent residents of university towns, I have a career history consisting of alternating periods of going back to school to get another not-very-practical degree and, between career flights, doing support staff work for professors and researchers to make money. Altogether, since 1970, I've spent a total of over fifteen years doing various kinds of office work at a major university, holding jobs as a clerk, secretary, administrative assistant, and associate editor.

The last time I left the office world behind—in 1995—I believed I was leaving it forever. Having received my M.S.W. the previous year, I went from my university editorial job to a small-town psychotherapy clinic, where I worked for low wages for a few years to gain experience and credentials, then spent some wonderful years establishing a private practice and organizing business. During this time I also published two successful books, *Making Peace with the Things in Your Life* and *One Thing at a Time*. Then 9/11 happened, and business slowed. When Michigan's economy started to tank, business slowed even more. Meanwhile, the premiums for the Blue Cross health insurance policy my husband and I had purchased through the Detroit Chamber of Commerce went from a little more than $400 to more than $1,400 a month in about six years, with no end to the escalation in sight. Eventually, I had to face the fact that the party was over: I could no longer afford to have my own business. Although I might have gotten a state social worker's job that would have given me good benefits, such jobs typically involve heavy caseloads, and I wanted to continue writing, which I'd come to love. Thus, by process of elimination, I decided to return to office work at the university one last time.

This proved harder than I'd anticipated. Even with an impressive résumé and some excellent references, it took me over six months to land a position as an administrative assistant at a large research center. When my boss—a world-class social scientist, excellent administrator, and supportive friend—called to offer me the job, I was delighted. It was wonderful not to have to pay huge health-insurance premiums every month, the pay was good, and the university campus was a great place to work. However, as the novelty of the new job wore off, I became progressively more grief-stricken. Before I'd gotten this job, I'd had the luxury of doing work that I loved, being my own boss, and, as a professional and an author, feeling that I was somebody. Now here I was, relieved of financial stress but spending eight hours a day on work that was about as much fun as doing taxes, having to jump when someone else snapped his fingers and, as a low-ranking support-staffer among Ph.D.s, suddenly invisible. This was going to take some getting used to.

To make matters worse, I discovered that the office world had changed since I'd left it ten years earlier. It was as though someone had turned up a movie to high speed, making the characters zip around the screen and chatter like chipmunks. The worst part was that people expected me to act like a chipmunk too, to eagerly scamper from task to task when all I wanted to do was shut my door and have a good cry. As the weeks went by, I found myself succumbing more and more to office blues and battleshock. (Retrospectively figuring what my OCAB ratio would have been at that time, I come out with a score of 86/46—in other words, I had about twice as much job-related misery as job-related happiness.)

I struggled to make sense of what was happening. I knew that I'd come to this job with some baggage, but as a social worker, I'd been taught to use a "person-in-situation" approach, taking environmental as well as biological and psychological factors into account in thinking about why people feel and behave the way they do. This helped me to see that the problem wasn't all me. I began to take stock of the various causes, both internal and external, of my unhappiness. In doing this, I was struck by how many serious challenges not just this job but any office job presented to workers' health and well-being, though I later came to see that there were also some benefits.

Fortunately, I'd just spent ten years in a profession where most workers take good care of themselves, because if they don't, they burn out. One form of self-care that I'd found particularly valuable in the past was journaling, and I soon began making use of this tool in my job, gradually developing a type of abbreviated journal that was especially suited to office work, which I called the Work Companion, a tool you'll learn to use in chapter 7. Reading back through what I'd written in my Work Companion led me to think seriously and to talk with coworkers about what it means to work in an office, which, in turn, led to my spending whole evenings reading about office workplace issues. What was it about office work, I wondered, that made it such a downer for some people but not for others? I was determined to figure this out.

Thus it was that what began as "just a job" turned into research for a book on how to improve and preserve one's health and well-being in the office. So much for my office blues—I now looked forward to coming to work so I could experiment with new strategies to put in the book! The beauty of this was that the more I experimented and learned, the more my work performance also improved, and my boss was happy too.

As I began to adjust to my own individual workplace circumstances, I found better ways to connect with the people around me. I invited coworkers to lunch, started a book discussion group, joined committees, and wrote stories for our office newsletter. Working on a university campus, I also had the luxury of attending various workshops, lectures, exhibits, and conferences on topics such as project management, ergonomics, stress, mental health in the workplace, and "work-life balance," and of meeting experts in a host of relevant fields who proved a rich source of ideas and inspiration.

Eventually, when my boss decided to hire a second administrative assistant to share my workload, I was able to cut my hours back to part-time and thus make time to finish this book. While I still spend twenty hours a week in the same job I was in three years ago, for me it has become quite a different job in almost every respect, both because of my employer's generous accommodations and because I worked hard to change the way I looked at and approached my time at the office. At present, although I can't say that I'm happy every moment at work, I can say that I'm living just as fully there as anywhere else and that the black cloud of dread that used to descend on me on Sunday nights is now a thing of the past. (My most recent OCAB ratio came out as 31/64, with happiness now outweighing misery two to one—the opposite of my ratio three years ago.)

If I could accomplish this, so can you. Whatever your work situation, and wherever you are in your own personal office journey, know that as you work through this book, I'll be traveling with you. As our journey progresses, you'll learn new ways of looking at things and new coping skills so that one day, blues and battleshock free, happier and healthier, you'll feel as proud as I do of the quality you've created in your workplace life.

PART I

Thinking Outside the Cubicle:
What's Really Going On?

1

The Office World Has Walls

If someone put you in a pitch-black room, your first action would probably be to start feeling your way around its walls. You'd want to know how big the room was and, more important, whether there was an open door or a working light switch somewhere. Once you'd finished, assuming you didn't find a light or a way out, you could settle down and explore the interior. Perhaps you'd find water, furniture, blankets—things that might make your stay more comfortable. Eventually, if you were unable to escape from your prison, you'd begin to adapt to it.

Every situation human beings find themselves in has its walls, those limits within which daily life takes place. Occasionally some heroic person or group manages to shift the limits, but this takes tremendous effort, and it happens only when people are solidly in touch with the realities of their world. Thus, most of the time life goes better if we focus on exploring the parameters we have to operate within and getting to know exactly where they are.

In this chapter, we'll feel our way around the walls of the office world, the constraints within which you, your colleagues, and your organization conduct your daily affairs. It is a world that, as we shall see in chapter 2, has taken many centuries to reach its present form. Although it's constantly changing, it normally does so only in response to larger forces in the world, not to the whims of individuals, or even single organizations. This is good to keep in mind if you feel frustrated when you push against them to no avail, as we all do from time to time.

This book is about how to feel better at work. However, because of external constraints, there are certain things you simply can't do to make yourself feel better. For example, you probably can't bring in your own plumber to install a Jacuzzi in your cubicle, even though it might feel great to spend your afternoons there. Nor can your boss give everyone a six-month paid vacation, no matter how much happiness might result from this. Even your CEO operates within certain limits: It might make the chief feel great to build a building twice the size of the current one, but if the money and politics aren't there, it's not going to happen.

Just because there are limits to what you can do in your office situation, this doesn't mean you should quit your job. Should you do so, you'd only find yourself trapped within a new set of walls, either the constraints of having no money in your bank account, the challenges of a new job somewhere else, or, should you win the lottery, the moral quandaries and family pressures experienced by the suddenly rich. Even if you can't build your own office Jacuzzi, having a good sense of where the walls of the office world are should make it easier for you to live comfortably within them. Armed with such an understanding, you won't be constantly bumping up against barriers by trying to do things that are unrealistic or by blaming yourself, your associates, or your organization for problems that are simply the result of the global realities we all operate within.

What fundamental realities, then, make up the outer limits of your happiness in the office world? Here are some of them.

The office world is not a democracy.

Forget life, liberty, and the pursuit of happiness. Forget the Bill of Rights. None of it applies when you walk through your office door, at least not in the United States.* You can be fired for saying or writing the wrong things, conducting unauthorized meetings, or just being one more mouth for your employer to feed. The recommendation requirement for job applications means that your boss has power over you not only while you work for him or her, but, to some extent, for the rest of your working life. Even when benevolently ruled and tempered by such management tactics as "quality circles," "climate surveys," and "360 evaluations" by employees appraising their bosses, the typical American workplace is, in reality, a dictatorship, in response to which the worker's one freedom is to walk away, though often with no place better to go. Consequently, people in offices—and other types of workplaces as well—often act less like citizens of a democracy than like subjects of a tyrannical regime, self-censoring words and even thoughts that might get them into trouble, flattering and manipulating the powerful, and engaging in forbidden behaviors on the sly.

The office world is governed by economics and technology.

Offices evolved within the context of competitive market economies in Europe and America, necessitating, at least in private businesses, that costs be kept down in order to maximize profits. Until recently, the level of competition in America between large corporations was moderate and regulated, but in recent decades, according to Robert B. Reich in *Supercapitalism: The Transformation of Business, Democracy, and Everyday Life*, technological changes have resulted in global, unregulated competition on an unprecedented scale.

The result of this runaway competition is that organizations of all sorts, especially but not exclusively corporations, have become ever more ruthless in their efforts to cut costs. Mostly they've done this by cutting some jobs and adding to the workloads of the remaining employees, resulting in greatly increased levels of stress,

---

* The European Union has a social contract protecting the rights of working people as part of its 1991 charter, and many non-European governments also guarantee workers' rights.

competitiveness, uncertainty, fatigue, and illness among all workers, including office workers. Furthermore, in the United States the expectation that employers will cover health-insurance costs for employees motivates them to hire fewer and fewer workers to work longer and longer hours, in contrast with most European countries, where national health care covers these costs, and hours of work can thus be more equitably shared. Meanwhile, hypercompetition and economic recession have also affected working conditions as money-saving initiatives have resulted in smaller cubicles, fewer frills, and more rigid policies about how employees spend their time.

The office world doesn't exist for the sake of its workers.

Rather, it exists to serve the interests of its owners—individuals, stockholders, voters, taxpayers: whoever they might be—and, to a lesser extent, its clients or customers. If CEOs ever do things that make workers happier, it's only because someone has convinced them that happier workers will result in greater profits—or, in the case of nonprofits, greater productivity—for their organization. Thus, the happiness of workers will never be at the top of any CEO's list, though a wise CEO will always make sure it's somewhere on the list, given that it's been shown that positive human relationships are conducive to an organization's health and well-being and that toxic ones lead to higher rates of job turnover, absenteeism, strikes, crimes, lawsuits, and other effects that threaten to undermine the CEO's overarching goal of getting as much work as humanly possible out of the labor force.

The office world wasn't designed to meet
the needs of a diverse workforce.

It's no secret that in Western democracies the vast majority of executives who originally made the decisions that created office work as we know it—from building skyscrapers to hiring secretaries to dividing large rooms up into cubicles to replacing typewriters with PCs to extending the length of the office workday—were drawn from a single demographic group: Almost all were heterosexual white males with stay-at-home wives and intellectual backgrounds in business or engineering. Furthermore, they were men who, according to William

H. Whyte in his 1956 sociological classic, *The Organization Man*, were unusually comfortable being disconnected from their roots. "Almost by definition," Whyte writes, "the organization man is a man who left home and, as it was said of the man who went from the Midwest to Harvard, kept on going."

These people created institutional lifestyles that worked well for people like themselves. If you're different from them, chances are you're going to be less than 100 percent comfortable with some aspects of the world they created, whether it's the gray-white-beige color scheme, the prohibition of touching others while conversing, or the expectation that you'll be available for overtime hours even if your children are waiting to be picked up.

The office world is affected by political movements.

Three major political movements during the last half of the twentieth century have had a huge effect on office life as we know it. The first of these was the civil rights movement, which began with African Americans and spread to other nondominant groups claiming their rights to equal opportunity in schools, neighborhoods, and workplaces. Over time, this has created an ever more diverse office workforce, especially in the lower ranks, and has led to nondominant groups gradually moving up the status ladder, which has benefited not only them but their organizations as well.

The second movement, most likely inspired by the American civil rights movement, was the movement of second-wave feminism that began in the late 1960s and 1970s, which focused mainly on the right of women to enter and move up in the workplace. While large numbers of women had already been working in offices since the typewriter was introduced around 1900, the vast majority held low-status clerical and secretarial jobs, which they quit once they married and had children. This began to change in the 1970s, when numerous women with children began returning to the workplace, many of them single mothers. Before long, it had become the norm for women to work outside the home for most of their adult lives. Women were thus able to build careers and work their way up to higher positions in office hierarchies, sometimes even to the top, though until President Obama signed the Lilly Ledbetter Fair Pay Act in 2009, women were often denied equal pay for doing the same jobs men did. Meanwhile, women continued to do most of the housework and serve as primary caregivers to children, as revealed in Arlie Hochschild and Anne Machung's 1989 sociological classic, *The Second Shift*, and by more recent research as well. Thus, the excessive hours that office workers have been expected to work in recent years have had the effect of discriminating against women, who are most likely to experience the emotional stress of being torn between attachments to work and to family.

One by-product of both the civil rights movement and second-wave feminism has been political correctness, the trend toward people becoming ever more careful not to say anything even slightly offensive to one another. While this has served to protect individuals from racism, sexism, and other forms of abuse, the fear of being unjustly accused because of some casual slip of the tongue may have also created more distance between workers.

The third political movement to have an effect on the office world was the conservative movement that began in the 1970s and blossomed during the 1980s in the United States with the election of Ronald Reagan as president. Although cost cutting at the expense of workers' interests had already begun in response to runaway global competition, the total subordination of rank-and-file workers' human needs to corporate goals became standard management practice during the conservative era. In countless organizations, what began as bracing discipline in pursuit of excellence and profit eventually crossed the line into heartlessness. Harsh new attitudes invaded the office world, not only in corporations but even, to a lesser extent, in traditionally kinder institutions such as social service agencies and university departments. While prior to that time offices had been relatively laid-back places, suddenly everyone began talking about "accountability"—i.e., blame—and the need to "get tough." Corporate CEOs were given huge salaries not only for their managerial skills but for their ability to harden their hearts in making "tough choices," and were immortalized with names such as Neutron Jack and Chainsaw Al. In this "lean and mean" workscape, employees naturally learned to keep their emotions hidden and their relationships superficial.

These conservative excesses, along with extremes of political correctness, have resulted, in our own time, in a prevailing climate of mistrust, isolation, and emotional deprivation in many office workplaces. Now, however, change is in the air. As I write this, cataclysmic economic and political shifts are under way that may affect the office workplace as dramatically as the three previous movements did, though it's too soon to predict in what ways. One can only hope that the end result will be a more humane work environment than employees have experienced in recent years.

The office world is not, in most cases, ruled by social workers.

Or psychologists or nurses or anyone likely to possess particularly strong people skills. These are often regarded as "soft" skills and therefore dangerous to cultivate in a competitive marketplace that rewards toughness, despite plenty of research that shows that many soft skills can benefit companies. Often people get to be bosses by having strengths in areas that have nothing to do with people, such as engineering, accounting, or computer technology. Some do have business degrees that require psychology courses, but writing papers and passing tests does not necessarily guarantee that you know how to deal with human beings. "A moment's reflection," writes psychologist Robert Hogan, a major authority on personality assessment, leadership, and organizational effectiveness, "reveals that it is possible to climb a hierarchy without ever demonstrating talent for leadership."

Tragically, therefore, many people running organizations have little idea of what makes people tick, and the effects of their ignorance can be costly to workers' health and well-being, as well as to the health and well-being of whole companies. When employers commit errors such as blaming a worker with a learning disability for not being able to perform a certain type of task, failing to refer a depressed worker for counseling, or forbidding workers from listening to music on headphones, they themselves may end up paying a price in the form of reduced employee health and well-being and a negative workplace climate that drives quality workers away.

The office world is influenced by institutional fads.

In *Flavor of the Month*, sociologist Joel Best talks about how institutional fads can sometimes have highly negative consequences for organizations, causing them to waste millions of dollars and implement policies that are harmful to their workers. In business, fads usually begin with a book by a "management guru," someone chosen not for business expertise or writing ability but for public speaking and workshop-presenting potential. These gurus give colorful, dynamic, and outrageously expensive presentations to get managers excited enough to adopt uncritically their "revolutionary" (often old wine in new bottles) approaches, without looking at what actual research shows about their results. Managers then jockey for higher positions by throwing themselves wholeheartedly into implementing the new impressive-sounding fads, spewing forth the gurus' newly coined jargon, and spending large amounts of money on staff trainings and materials that could have been used more profitably. Each of the fads thus circulated has a limited lifespan before vanishing in the wake of the next year's fad.

In recent decades, many institutional fads have made life difficult for both white- and blue-collar employees, who often grow to detest them. A lot of these fads have had something to do with perfectionism, as in "zero defects," "continuous improvement," "100 percent excellence," or "total quality management," all of which translate into added stress for employees, who may fear being fired for making a single, minor mistake.

The office world is minimally unionized, especially in the United States.

Unlike their blue-collar brothers and sisters, office workers have often accepted without protest management policies that worked against their interests, and have rarely joined forces to bargain collectively with their employers. There are a number of possible reasons for this. First, clerical and administrative employees, unlike factory workers, often work closely with the people who sign their paychecks. In doing so, they may develop emotional attachments that lead them to overidentify with their bosses' interests at the expense of their own, or comply with unreasonable requests out of fear of losing their bosses' approval. Second, many lower-status office workers see their jobs as stepping-stones to managerial positions for which they must prove their loyalty by accepting the unacceptable. Third, American trade unions grew up in response to industrial workers' needs, which were somewhat different from those of office workers, and thus unions were slow to recruit them. Fourth, large multinational office employers often have strict antiunion policies reinforced by cults of individualism and professionalism among their employees. Last, in the hypercompetitive economy of the previous four decades, unions of all sorts—whose gains often benefited non-union as well as union workers, including office employees—have been seriously in decline, as some corporations have found ways of circumventing labor laws in order to fire those who tried to organize, especially in the United States. While in Europe white-collar unions are widespread, in America they're confined mainly to the public sector and are much less common.

Government in the United States offers minimal protection to workers in the office world, especially where workers' time and mental health are concerned.

The Fair Labor Standards Act, passed in 1938, established the forty-hour workweek as the standard beyond which "nonexempt" (those to whom the act applied) workers were to be paid time-and-a-half for overtime. The FLSA doesn't, however, limit the number of mandatory overtime hours employers can require, and since it's generally cheaper for employers to pay fewer employees overtime than to hire more workers and pay for their benefits, the law has failed to limit the number of hours individual employees work. Instead of a forty-hour week for everyone, what we have is huge numbers of unemployed workers working zero hours while countless employed workers are forced to work up to eighty hours per week and beyond, despite devastating effects to their health, safety, work quality, family life, and communities. Furthermore, since salaried professionals are considered "exempt," they can be worked beyond the breaking point without their employer having to pay them a penny extra.

In addition, the U.S. government is the only government in the developed world that fails to guarantee workers a certain amount of paid vacation time. Nor does it protect workers from being laid off or otherwise penalized for taking vacation days their employer agreed to pay them for. Consequently, many workers don't even bother to take the time off that they're entitled to. According to a study commissioned by Expedia.com, American workers in 2002 gave back 175 million days of paid vacation to their employers, a $20 billion gift to business, and 26 percent take no vacation at all. The combined result of all these regulatory failures is that American employees work, on average, a full nine weeks more than their European counterparts.

Time, however, is not the only issue on which the U.S. government fails to protect workers: Its oversight of workplace relations is also seriously inadequate by international standards. If a worker can prove discrimination, sexual harassment, or physical injury, he or she may receive compensation or even win the occasional lawsuit; but subtler forms of bullying and intimidation that, repeated on a daily basis, can lead to serious mental-health problems mostly go unpunished. The workers' compensation system and courts still fail to recognize depression as a work-related disability, despite abundant evidence that a hostile environment can trigger a depressive episode: If a worker becomes clinically depressed due to working conditions and tries to sue, American juries tend to blame the worker, not the employer.

The office world is constantly changing.

An office job now means something quite different from what it did a hundred or two hundred years ago, as will most likely be the case in another hundred years. Over the centuries, and especially in recent decades, the pace of change has accelerated, and sometimes it can be difficult for workers to keep up with all this change, both technological and social. On the other hand, if you don't like the way things are now, all you need to do is wait a little and they're sure to be different. And it's important to remember that every bit of change in the office world is the result of human decisions, not some irreversible law of nature. If humans can decide that men have to wear neckties or that secretaries get paid less than accountants, they have the power to decide differently any time they like, though some options will always be more practical than others.

Blues and Battleshock Busters

1. Ask yourself how free you feel in your own workplace. What do you feel safe doing or not doing? Who, specifically, has power over you? Do those who have power over you use this power responsibly, or do they abuse it? Do they give workers control over some aspects of their situations? How genuine is this control?

2. Find out what you can about your management's priorities. Whom do those in charge have to please? Do they seem to believe that keeping workers happy is important? How has this affected life in your workplace?

3. Talk to some of your coworkers and ask them what their ideal workplace would be like. Compare the visions of people from different groups. How much influence have women and minorities had in creating your own office workplace and its policies?

4. Talk to some of the old-timers in your workplace—assuming there are any—and ask them how things have changed since they've been there. How have the civil rights and second feminist movements played out in your organization? What effects have political correctness and conservatism had? How have more recent political and economic changes affected people's expectations in the workplace?

5. Go to the business section of a bookstore and browse through some of the books on the shelves. What fads or would-be fads do you see described? How do the books emotionally appeal to their readers? Are you aware of any institutional fads that your own organization has adopted? Ask the old-timers if they remember anything about fads that are now passé.

6. Consider what effect, if any, collective bargaining has had on your workplace. Do office workers there belong to a union? If so, how effective has it been in serving workers' interests? If not, are other parts of your organization's workforce unionized? If they are, has their bargaining had any effect on nonunionized workers?

7. Find out what government regulations, if any, affect how your organization deals with workers. Is there something you would like to see regulated? What would it be? Have there been any

lawsuits between workers and management in your organization? What were the outcomes?

8. Check out the Web site for the group Take Back Your Time, (www.timeday.org), described as "a major U.S./Canadian initiative to challenge the epidemic of overwork, over-scheduling and time famine that now threatens our health, our families and relationships, our communities and our environment." This group is currently working to support a bill in Congress that would guarantee more vacation time to many workers.

2

The Office World Has a History

In the beginning, there were no offices. People worked a lot less than they do now and when they did, they worked in unspecified locations, hunting and fishing, or gathering berries, logs, flax, or whatever else they needed to survive. Their work was with plants, animals, people, weapons, or cooking tools, not with pens and paper, much less typewriters or computers. As long as people worked for their own families or tribes and shared everything they acquired, there was little need to keep track of fish, berries, or logs—they just brought them home and consumed them as needed. But as time went on, people began to grow crops, to gather and create material possessions in ever larger quantities, to designate certain things as their own, and to trade their things with others. They also began working for other people, either as slaves or as paid employees. Eventually, they started using a new technology—writing—not only to communicate but also to keep track of the flow of things and workers, as one can see in those Egyptian hieroglyphics that contain rows of fish, servants, sheaves of grain, etc., which were an early form of record keeping on behalf of the pharaoh.

Meanwhile, the activity we call work started out almost universally divided by gender. Women stayed home and prepared food, made clothes, and raised children, crops, or livestock while men ventured out to conquer nature, to reap its bountiful harvest in the form of valued natural resources, wildlife, and even other humans, who became their slaves. While to women, nature was just nature, to men, charged with the responsibility of providing for and protecting their families, it was a dangerous enemy that required continual conquest. Whether they were hunting animals, harvesting wheat, sawing lumber, digging for gold, or filling a hostile human body with arrows, men's whole purpose was to dominate that natural world, which was hard to do if you were looking over your shoulder at your loved ones. The result was that men—and eventually women as well, as they began to take on men's roles—have been divided ever since between the desire to connect with significant others and the need to disconnect so as to venture out, battle nature and other humans—whom they had to compete with in times of scarcity—and bring home needed resources. This is true in today's offices and elsewhere.

As history unfolded, whole economies evolved from hunting and gathering to agriculture to feudalism to industry and present-day capitalism, communism, and other economic systems. These changes were driven by two basic realities:

1. Some people are stronger than others, either physically or mentally or both.
2. Collectively, human beings can accomplish things they couldn't accomplish by themselves, including protecting the weak from the strong.

As we shall see, both dominance struggles and cooperation are still fundamental to an office world operating within a competitive market economy, locked in perpetual conflict.

Somewhere along the line, the office was born. The word "office" comes from the Latin *officium*, which, according to *Merriam-Webster's 11th Collegiate Dictionary*, originated from a combination of *opus*, or "work," and *facere*, or "to make or do." Thus, the original meaning of the word, "to do or make work," had nothing to do with place. This is fitting, because the first offices were not places at all, but groups of workers with certain skills. When place-type offices did appear in antiquity, they were not usually self-contained but located within larger complexes of palaces or temples. The typical office consisted of a room where scrolls were stored, on which scribes recorded and copied information. In Roman times as well as in Byzantium, ancient China, and elsewhere, elaborate bureaucracies—hierarchies of offices—evolved for keeping accounts and engaging in correspondence.

Medieval government buildings and churches in Europe contained chanceries, rooms in which letters were written and laws, in an age before printing presses, were copied out by hand as part of administering the kingdom or the church parish. These rooms often had walls with pigeonholes for rolled parchments covered with Latin officialese.

Since relatively few people—even aristocrats—could read or write in those days, nobles, churchmen, and tradespeople often hired assistants—almost always male—to handle their correspondence as well as keep their records and accounts. These helpers were known as clerks—relating to the word "cleric," as clergymen were the most literate group during the Middle Ages and often performed these functions. For many centuries, the title "clerk" carried with it a high level of prestige that continued until the Industrial Revolution, though in the present day it is often regarded as an insult. If you were a clerk for a tradesman, you worked closely with the boss and might marry his daughter and thus inherit the business.

Meanwhile, another, related profession had originated during classical times and continued on: that of the secretary, a word derived from the Latin *secernere*, which came to mean "confidential" or "private." In other words, a secretary is a person who keeps secrets, the first secretaries being men who worked for powerful figures such as emperors, kings, or popes. In the twentieth century, this meaning was often preserved in titles such as "private secretary" or "personal secretary." Even now, the dignified history of the secretarial profession is reflected in the title's use for members of the American president's cabinet, but like "clerk," in other contexts the title has declined in status, such that in recent decades, many employers have replaced the title with "administrative assistant." Whatever you call it, the profession of assisting others with correspondence and finances has a high-class history, so if you're one of those people who says, "I'm just a clerk/secretary/administrative assistant," you should stop that and start taking pride in what you do!

The Evolution of the Modern Office

Human history took a bizarre turn in Britain in the mid-1700s. For some strange reason that scholars haven't yet agreed upon, in that place and at that time, people began inventing all sorts of machines and using them to perform tasks that only human or animal labor had been able to accomplish before that point. The results were a giant leap in the production of goods, and massive social changes as people flocked into the cities to work in the newly created factories. This unexpected turn is known as the Industrial Revolution. It was followed by the Second Industrial Revolution, which occurred in the late nineteenth and early twentieth centuries with the advent of mass production methods, particularly the assembly line, accompanied by mass marketing and mass distribution. While the primary locus of change in both revolutions was the manufacturing of goods, the dramatic changes also had the effect of creating office work as we know it.

For one thing, more goods produced meant more things—as well as more workers, managers, and customers—to record, plan, reckon, and correspond about, requiring far more office workers than ever before. It also meant that more banks, insurance companies, legal firms, and other associated businesses were needed to provide services for the new manufacturers and their employees, and these businesses all hired clerks, secretaries, accountants, managers, and administrators. In order to accomplish tasks that required higher levels of literacy and math skills, whole bureaucracies of offices were created, for which business and secretarial schools, such as the famous Katharine Gibbs Schools on the eastern seaboard—whose female graduates were famous for wearing white gloves—began training workers.

While in the past, large bureaucracies had been associated mostly with governments, now private corporations developed bureaucracies of their own. Instead of clerks and bookkeepers working in a wing attached to a workshop, the office staff might take up a whole building, sometimes a very big building. The two rivals for the status of first American skyscraper—the ten-story Home Insurance Building in Chicago, built in 1884–85, and Louis Sullivan's Wainwright Building in St. Louis, built in 1891—were both office buildings, not factories or apartment buildings.

These rectangular boxes filled with office workers sprang up in every big city, spreading all around the globe. Each new skyscraper was a city in itself, hermetically sealing in workers for hours at a time, regulating their lives by the clock, and cutting them off from their surrounding communities. Architecturally, the new Chicago School meant simplicity, which unfortunately also often meant bland uniformity, fostering conformist attitudes in all who walked through the revolving doors of the skyscraper, where jobs were organized into military-style hierarchies that employed a variety of subtle and not-so-subtle tactics to suppress individual differences.

While mechanization began in the factory, by the late nineteenth century, machines had begun to invade the office as well with the introduction of the typewriter, the telephone, and the adding machine. Typewriters began to be used on a widespread basis in the 1880s. Since men hadn't used the new machines before, management, struggling to deal with a shortage of office workers as business exploded, found it relatively undisruptive to hire women to use them, though not without some trepidation. When, in 1878, the YWCA started offering training in typing, its staff asked doctors to certify that women were physically and mentally capable of using the new machines. As time went on, more and more women began to be hired as clerks and secretaries until, by the 1930s, relatively few men occupied these jobs. By 1960, of the 1.4 million secretaries in the United States, only 42,000 were men.

Typing and its companion, shorthand, became the staples of secretarial work. Both were subjected to the fanatical emphasis on speed that had invaded the factory floor with the creation of the assembly line and a movement called scientific management, fathered by Frederick Winslow Taylor and by Frank and Lillian Gilbreth, whose children Frank Gilbreth Jr. and Ernestine Gilbreth Carey wrote the popular book *Cheaper by the Dozen*. As the Gilbreth children describe in their book, the proponents of scientific management invented "motion study," which involved timing the performance of different tasks with stopwatches and analyzing movies of workers frame by frame. Workers hated this, but it did enable them to produce a lot more widgets more quickly—and thus more cheaply—for the rest of us to purchase. One of the by-products of scientific management for the office was the QWERTY keyboard on the typewriter, on which keys were supposedly placed according to how frequently the letters were used (though the letters from the top row were actually chosen because all but "Q," "U," and "O" were used to spell "typewriter," enabling salespeople to more efficiently type the name of the new machine for their customers).

In some of their more extreme moments, scientific managers also timed the minute movements of clerical workers and published their findings, recording that it takes .04 minutes to pull out a file drawer or folder, .033 minutes to get up or sit down in a chair, .009 minutes to turn in a swivel chair, and so forth. While to my knowledge no one today resorts to such measures, the general attitude that office workers should be "efficient" and constantly hurry to cram as much work into as little time as possible may hearken back to the days of scientific managers evaluating secretaries based on their shorthand and typing speeds.

As the clerical and secretarial workforce became feminized and the number of qualified applicants increased, the status and pay of these professions declined, eventually to pay levels below those of many factory workers. Until second-wave feminism emerged in the 1970s, however, women secretaries, schooled from the cradle to regard themselves as second-class citizens, made little protest, meekly making coffee for their male bosses and contenting themselves with the emotional connection and vicarious lives that service to their particular power figures gave them.

Nevertheless, some secretaries did begin to professionalize their field, creating the National Secretaries Association in 1942, later renamed the International Association of Administrative Professionals

(IAAP), an organization that now has approximately fifty thousand members. Although the IAAP sets standards for the profession and enables members to share information that can be useful in advancing their careers, its Web site states plainly that it is not a labor union, and that its members believe in working with employers rather than in opposition to them.

In the prosperous post–World War II years, office jobs in large bureaucracies—corporate and otherwise—provided security and comfort to millions of the white male workers by and for whom they were designed. As time went on, however, even some members of that group began to question the conformity, lack of autonomy, and stress that office life entailed. Critiques such as Sloan Wilson's *The Man in the Gray Flannel Suit* and William H. Whyte's *The Organization Man* became bestsellers in the 1950s. Wilson's novel traces the office career of a World War II veteran, Tom Rath, who advances quickly up the corporate ladder under the mentorship of a supportive CEO, but ultimately rejects the opportunity to become a CEO himself, putting family ahead of the corporate rat race:

> I'm not the kind of person who can get all wrapped up in a job—I can't get myself convinced that my work is the most important thing in the world. I've been through one war. Maybe another one's coming. If one is, I want to be able to look back and figure I spent the time between wars with my family, the way it should have been spent. Regardless of war, I want to get the most out of the years I've got left. Maybe that sounds silly. It's just that if I have to bury myself in a job every minute of my life, I don't see any point to it. And I know that to do the kind of job you want me to do, I'd have to be willing to bury myself in it, and, well, I just don't want to.

Wilson's and Whyte's books were about men, however, not about the women who worked for them. While they treated male office types as bland conformists, strangely enough, during the same period, the media version of the organization man's secretary was much more glamorous. The secretary that I grew up viewing on TV, in movies, and in office cartoons in the 1950s was a cagey young woman with platinum blond hair and an hourglass figure, dressed in a beautifully tailored suit and high heels, who spent her afternoons filing her nails, manipulated her boss into doing as she saw fit, and was destined to wind up married to the man who hired her.

In the real world, most secretaries, though not necessarily blond bombshells, probably *were* young, since the majority of middle-class women quit their jobs when they married or had their first child. My mother, a valedictorian of her high school class who, after she decided to marry my father, dropped out of Grinnell College to learn typing and shorthand at a business school, did secretarial work only until she had her first child, except for a brief stint working for the navy during World War II while my father was at sea. As soon as he returned from the service, she was back in the home, like all of her friends. To her generation, office work was something you did for a man, either while you were waiting to get a man or because you were stuck without a man. It wasn't something you did permanently if you could help it, and thus it was a waste of time and energy to either put much into it or try to get more out of it than was offered. This attitude that office work was supposed to be temporary—something you did on your way to marriage—may have led these women's baby boomer daughters to also regard office work as temporary, though they replaced the ultimate goal of marriage with a "real" career in a more highly respected profession. This sense of temporariness may, in some women, contribute to the sense of unreality that is part of office blues.

Office Work and the Electronic Revolution

Although to many in the 1950s the rigid structures of the office world seemed destined for permanence, beneath the surface, a new revolution was brewing. The electronic computer had already appeared during World War II, and in 1954 General Electric became the first private corporation to acquire a computer, which the company used for payroll processing. By the mid-1960s, computers, which initially took up whole buildings, led to the hiring of large numbers of people, not only to write programs—a new profession for which bright young office workers might receive training and extremely good raises—but also to do keypunching, which involved typing on a machine that punched patterns of holes in cards for mainframe computers to read.

Keypunching was a highly frustrating job—I keypunched a few cards for a friend once in the 1970s and found it infuriating that if you made a single mistake, you had to do the whole card over—and much less intrinsically satisfying than typing manuscripts, which also involved editing and formatting. Keypunchers were generally paid close to the minimum wage and were the closest thing to factory workers that ever appeared in the office. By the 1980s, however, networked personal computers had begun to replace the mainframes for which keypunch cards were intended, and the keypunchers disappeared.

Now every office worker had an IBM or a Mac on his or her desk, though most people still used a typewriter for at least some tasks. When I became a secretary in the mid-1980s, the typical desk had a computer in the center and a typewriter off to one side. By the mid-1990s, the typewriters were gone. Around that time, a whole new team of workers appeared on the scene: computer support people, eventually housed in a separate "information technology" unit. These folks had to have both excellent communication skills and high emotional intelligence, as their jobs often involved dealing with frustrated individuals. Today, in a world in which every large organization has a basement filled with computer staff, it's hard to believe that there was a time when the basements were used for storage, while technical support meant nothing more than a call to the local typewriter repairman.

Socially, computers were a great equalizer. Since you had to be intelligent to use them, they provided a means by which women and minorities were able to move up the corporate ladder on the basis of merit. This was just at the point when the civil rights movement and second-wave feminism were taking off in the workplace, with dramatic consequences for office cultures that are still playing out.

Meanwhile, in the early nineties, one last technological development occurred that was destined to have a bigger effect on human history than all the others put together: the creation of the World

Wide Web, also known as the Internet. For office professionals, the Internet has been both a plus and a minus, not so much because of the technology itself as because of how management has chosen to use it. The instantaneous communication and access to information that the Internet provides saves office workers hundreds of hours. However, it is not human, face-to-face communication but communication bereft of gestures, voice tones, and facial expressions other than the ridiculously inadequate little icons some people use ☺. This is not always bad; at times it may actually be a plus, as it saves sensitive souls from too much intensity. But at other times it leaves workers feeling isolated and disconnected. Furthermore, ease of communication has meant that people tend to be a lot less choosy about what they communicate, resulting in the enormous black hole known as e-mail, into which hundreds of work hours disappear each day.

Finally, the Internet has also had major effects on the types of tasks office professionals perform. One effect has been that tasks have been broken down into smaller and smaller parts, resulting in less satisfying work for workers, who may feel like cogs in the wheel. Another effect has been an increase in the amount of training most jobs require. In many large organizations, much of today's office work now involves entering information into online systems that require extra training and are continually being updated, resulting in frequent technical problems. Although technical support staff can help employees to deal with such problems, they also must continually update their skills. There was a time when a secretary learned to type and take shorthand or a bookkeeper learned to keep books and that was that, but in the new, networked office world, the need to acquire and update skills is constant, diminishing the gains in efficiency that the Internet provides. Some organizations tout all this learning as "job enrichment," and it does keep the worker's mind occupied, but it's unlikely to be as satisfying as substantive learning to educated workers.

The Internet is also having a huge effect on where and when work can be done, with all sorts of consequences, again both plus and minus. Work can be done from more than one workstation within an organization, resulting in workers losing ownership of individual offices. It can be done from home, allowing workers to telecommute, saving them fuel costs and keeping them near their families while also saving their organizations office space. It can done from vacation resorts, intruding upon workers' leisure time. It can be done from the other side of the world, resulting in outsourcing, resulting in layoffs in the home country.

Some people, especially corporate managers, have a habit of blaming "technology," an entity that they personify, for policies they have chosen to institute that are harmful to office professionals. In *Windows on the Workplace*, information systems expert and environmental psychologist Joan Greenbaum maintains that from the beginning, it has not been the machines but the people who have made decisions that hurt workers. "If this book were a murder mystery," she writes, "we would discover that it wasn't technology that 'did it,' but the people who make the decisions about what technology is designed for and how it is used."

The main thing corporate management has used technology for, Greenbaum goes on to show, is to cut costs so as to maximize profits, and benefit themselves and their stockholders. If managers had so decided—or if the government officials who were supposed to set the rules of the game had chosen to make them—the time-saving advantages of technology could have resulted in a shortened workweek and higher quality of life for everyone (in the 1930s, economist John Maynard Keynes even predicted the two-day workweek and expressed concern about what people would do with so much leisure time), but that was not what managers chose to do. Instead, they used the technology to justify laying off some workers and forcing those who remained to work faster and longer hours than ever before. Like so much of what went on in industry in the 1980s and 1990s, this has had a hidden, long-term cost: the detrimental effect on the health and happiness of office workers, upon which the quality and continuity of work ultimately depends.

The New Managers

The good news is that lately some employers have become interested in making things better for their workers, though whether that will prove to be a passing fad or genuine change remains to be seen. Frustrated by escalating rates of illness, absenteeism and job turnover, poor product quality and/or customer service, lawsuits, white-collar crime, and workplace violence, enlightened managers have had to face the fact that harsh policies either don't work at all or work only in the short run. "Study after study," writes Peter J. Frost in *Toxic Emotions at Work*, "has shown a distinct correlation between a harmonious workplace and a company's profits." One study of 136 companies by Jeffrey Pfeffer and Jack Veiga, published in the *Academy of Management Executive*, showed that companies that valued human resources were 20 percent more likely to still be around after five years.

The result of such findings is that more and more books on "emotional intelligence"—a concept developed in the late 1980s by psychologists Jack Mayer and Peter Salovey and later popularized by Daniel Goleman—have begun to appear in the business sections of bookstores. Managers are beginning to realize that feelings are not, as previously thought, irrelevant distractions from work, but valuable data receptors that are essential for creative thinking, and that positive emotions and interactions can make the difference between an organization thriving and failing. In business schools, whole new departments are springing up to study these connections, such as the Center for Positive Organizational Scholarship at the University of Michigan's Ross School of Business.

Many employers have conducted climate surveys to try to ascertain workers' real feelings, with varying degrees of success, depending on whether their surveys ask the right questions and how safe the workers feel being truthful. Too often, however, efforts to improve conditions in response to negative findings have consisted of window-dressing initiatives, such as setting up task forces without granting them power to change anything, or providing workers with workshops in stress management rather than creating the type of stress-prevention program that is recommended by the National Institute of Occupational Safety and Health (NIOSH). NIOSH suggests that employers take the following stress-reducing steps, which originally appeared in the journal *American Psychologist*:

- Ensure that the workload is in line with workers' capabilities and resources.
- Design jobs to provide meaning, stimulation, and opportunities for workers to use their skills.
- Clearly define workers' roles and responsibilities.
- Give workers opportunities to participate in decisions and actions affecting their jobs.
- Improve communications—reduce uncertainty about career development and future employment prospects.
- Provide opportunities for social interaction among workers.
- Establish work schedules that are compatible with demands and responsibilities outside the job.

Yet even employers with the best of intentions can do only so much to make their workers happy. Research on job satisfaction shows a high degree of consistency among individual workers from one job situation to another. This doesn't mean that the challenges of office life are imaginary, but it does mean that workers vary in how well they cope with them.

The Office of the Future

Is working in an office likely to become healthier and pleasanter for employees in the future than it is now? This is not an easy question to answer. One problem is that people who try to predict future trends tend to assume that things will just continue farther down the same road they're already on, forgetting that roads can sometimes fork off in entirely new directions, often when technology takes a sudden, unexpected leap.

In a large survey titled "Office of the Future: 2020," conducted by the temporary staffing agency OfficeTeam, respondents predicted that future workers will have greater spatial and temporal flexibility, particularly in allowances for more telecommuting, but will also be working longer hours. Perhaps this is how events will unfold, but perhaps not. Just because more workers are currently telecommuting, does that mean this trend will continue until everyone is? Eventually some management guru might make a fortune reinventing the "centralized workplace" in response to managers' frustrations over never being able to see their employees in person and the resulting lack of synergy. And just because the workday has gotten progressively longer in recent decades, does that necessarily mean it will continue until people are working twenty-five hours out of every twenty-four? At some point, workers are likely to say "Enough!"

Technological predictions are more likely to be accurate than those about people's behaviors. These are some of them from the "Office of the Future" survey:

- More sophisticated miniature wireless communication tools and other wireless technologies
- Instant "plug and play" offices that can be set up anywhere, as well as more fully wired commercial spaces that make this quick and easy
- Self-healing software that makes it possible for computers to detect and repair problems before users discover them
- Interactive office spaces equipped with sensors that monitor and maintain the temperature, humidity, and lighting of an environment in response to the user's needs
- Chairs that detect tension in your body and give you a massage!

Of course, no one can really know what the office—or non-office—of the future will look like, but these are some general changes that I believe need to occur along the way:

A total rethinking of work and time: Workers should no longer be imprisoned in an office for X number of hours whether they have anything to do or not, but instead should be required to accomplish certain tasks and be evaluated on results rather than attendance. Whenever possible, workers should be able to set their own schedules and vary them as their circumstances change. Workloads need to be reevaluated, taking the realities of information overload, technological breakdown, and constant retraining into account. Government needs to relieve employers of the expense of providing health insurance so that organizations can hire more permanent workers for fewer hours. As technology takes over more tasks, the six-hour day should become the norm so as to allow fuller employment and to provide workers with more time to spend with families and on activities outside of work, many of which benefit society.* Overtime should be a rare event in a worker's life, not an everyday occurrence, and more than a certain amount should be forbidden even if it's voluntary, as too much overtime is hazardous to the worker's health and is likely to affect the quality of work. Mandatory overtime should be outlawed, and vacation time comparable to that in European workplaces should be guaranteed.

A total rethinking of work and space: The skyscraper and the cubicle should become the exception rather than the rule, and new types of spatial arrangements should be created that take workers' mental-health needs into account. Workers should be able to do most jobs from anywhere, including their own homes, though face-to-face interactions will probably always need to be part of the mix. Whatever office buildings continue to exist need to be smaller and better connected to neighborhoods and communities where homes are affordable on the salaries employees earn, not cut off from the rest of society, and where workers can walk or bike to their offices if they choose. Children need to be able to visit their parents daily at work, day-care facilities for preschool children should be available in workplaces, and workers should be near enough to elderly relatives to be able to visit them during their lunch breaks.

Workplaces reconnected with nature: New buildings need to be designed with courtyards so that more workers can have access to windows, and workers should be allowed and encouraged to go outside at least twice a day. Inside, lighting should be natural, and

---

* During the 1930s, the Kellogg Corporation in Battle Creek, Michigan, adopted the six-hour workday so as to allow more workers to keep their jobs, and studies showed that not only were employees more productive, family and community life also improved. The arrangement was so successful that it continued on for several decades after the Depression ended.

decorators should make more liberal use of color, natural woods and fabrics, plants, terrariums, waterfalls, and arts and crafts by different ethnic groups or that feature nature themes and motifs.

More ergonomic office workplaces: All workers should have ergonomic chairs, desks that can be raised to allow them to stand as well as sit, and, whenever possible, treadmills to allow them to walk while working. Exercise facilities should be available in office buildings, and workers should be provided sufficient break time to use them. The negative effects of insufficient sunlight need to be corrected with special lighting, thermostats need to be adjustable to suit workers' individual temperature needs, and individual stimulation thresholds need to be taken into account in dividing up work spaces to allow for optimal noise levels for each worker.

A total rethinking of office cultures: Individual differences as well as differences between cultural groups should be acknowledged and respected. Workers should feel free to express themselves by means of creative language, clothing choices, or office decorations without fear of disapproval. Training in diversity issues should be required of all employees and supervisors, and cultural groups should be allowed to create displays honoring their arts and contributions. Workers should receive support in creating office nests that fit with their individual sensory, intellectual, cultural, and emotional needs rather than being forced to conform to a sterile, "professional" ideal. The word "professional" should be redefined to focus exclusively on quality performance of one's duties, not willingness to project a company image. Activities should be organized that encourage workers to build positive relationships, and services should be available to help workers resolve conflicts.

A more enlightened view of neurological diversity, mental illnesses, personality disorders, creativity, and intellectual giftedness: Education in these areas should be required of all employees and supervisors, who should work to destigmatize psychiatric disabilities and illnesses. Supervisors should also learn skills that will allow them to assign tasks that suit individuals' neurological and educational strengths and to deal with the harmful effects of personality disorders in the workplace. Workers with cognitive challenges should be given the support they need rather than being chastised and humiliated. The special needs of intellectually and artistically gifted individuals should be recognized and accommodated, and their abilities should be used to benefit the organization whenever possible.

More support for workers struggling with organization and time-management issues: The titles of "professional organizer" and "coach" should be added to the list of job titles within organizations, and individuals or teams of these valuable professionals should be hired to provide support for workers struggling with the exceptional organization and time-management challenges of today's office workplaces. Their expertise could be of enormous value in streamlining organizations and helping individuals organize paper and computer files; assign workloads; and manage information, task loads, and projects.

More emphasis placed on emotional intelligence in hiring and training supervisors: Individuals should not be placed in supervisory positions purely because of task accomplishments or advanced degrees without taking their people skills into account. The manager should be considered a human-services professional and should receive training as such, not only in diversity and mental-health issues, but also in empathic listening, mediation, motivation, social resources, work-life balance, organization and time management, and other topics with which human-service professionals are typically familiar.

Less totalitarian supervisory roles: Performance-appraisal systems need rethinking to provide genuine recourse to workers who feel unfairly treated by supervisors. CEOs should not be awarded gigantic salaries purely because they're good at being "tough," and they should be held accountable if they fire someone unjustly or deprive workers of adequate salaries by inflating their own. Workers' responses to negative charges by supervisors on performance appraisals and written recommendations should automatically be attached to those documents, and workers should be able to add notes written by coworkers and secondary supervisors to help counter the effects of criticisms on future employment. Workers should be guaranteed the right to appeal negative comments to a higher authority without fear of retaliation by the supervisor. Whenever possible, 360 evaluations, which allow employees to evaluate supervisors, should be used. Hiring decisions should be based on criteria other than the opinions of past supervisors, and no worker should be denied a job because of an employer's less-than-enthusiastic reference.

Some of these changes exist only in people's imaginations, but many are already realities in more progressive workplaces. If you're interested in doing what you can to bring them into being, keep reading! Meanwhile, as you sit at your office desk, it's helpful to remember those millions of office ancestors who have gone before you, from the Egyptian hieroglyph artist to the Roman scribe to the medieval clerk to the white-gloved Katharine Gibbs graduate and the man in the gray flannel suit, as well as those men and women who will come after you in the office of the future, whatever form it takes. You are a part of them, and they are a part of you.

Blues and Battleshock Busters

1. Surf the Net until you find a picture of office workers in some past era. Print it out, frame it, and put it on your office wall. Or make a collage of scenes from old office movies. These will act as great conversation starters with coworkers.
2. Visit some antique stores and look for an item from the office past such as an inkwell, a wheel-type typewriter eraser, some type of machine, or an old-fashioned style manual. Bring it to work with you and put it on display to give yourself a permanent reminder of your profession's history and to counter feelings of disconnection.
3. Rent some old office movies and invite office worker friends to an "office film festival," with an informal discussion afterward

about how the offices in the flicks compare with your own work-places. Some good candidates include *The Fountainhead* (1949), *The Man in the Gray Flannel Suit* (1956), *Desk Set* (1957), *The Apartment* (1960), *How to Succeed in Business Without Really Trying* (1967), *Save the Tiger* (1973), and *9 to 5* (1980).

4. Watch the current TV series *Mad Men*, which is set in the office world of Madison Avenue in the 1960s and shows change as it occurs, especially for women.

5. Choose a past office era, do some research, and use it as a setting for an original short story or play. This will help to build your connection with office history and may also give you something fun to talk about and share with coworkers.

6. Visit a retirement facility and talk to some older people about their office experiences. Ask them to tell you how things have changed since their day. If they're willing to let you record them, you might want to put together an audio or video collage that you could share with others.

3

Sometimes It's About
Where You Work

In a real sense, all life is interrelated. All men are caught in an inescapable network of mutuality, tied in a single garment of destiny. Whatever affects one directly affects all indirectly. I can never be what I ought to be until you are what you ought to be, and you can never be what you ought to be until I am what I ought to be. This is the interrelated structure of reality.
— **Dr. Martin Luther King, Jr.**

To work in an office means to function interdependently with others. Thus, a huge amount depends on the quality of your interactions, not only for the health and well-being of you and your fellow workers, but for that of your organization as well. Business psychologist Jane Dutton and her colleagues at the University of Michigan Ross School of Business have extensively researched the effects of what Dutton calls corrosive connections—those that eat away at the participants' self-esteem and rapport—versus positive connections, and have found that they can make a significant difference not only in workers' wellness but also in the long-term survival and success of an organization. It is to these workplace interactions and relationships that we now turn. Our focus in this chapter is not the office world in general, as in chapter 1, but your own specific organization, work group, and office culture.

Cultures of Fear and Cultures of Love

"In the office in which I work," Bob Slocum, the main character in Joseph Heller's 1974 novel *Something Happened*, tells the reader, "there are five people of whom I am afraid. Each of these five people is afraid of four people (excluding overlaps), for a total of twenty, and each of these twenty people is afraid of six people, making a total of one hundred and twenty people who are feared by at least one person. Each of these one hundred and twenty people is afraid of the other one hundred and nineteen, and all of these one hundred and forty-five people are afraid of the twelve men at the top who helped found and build the company and now own and direct it."

Although many things have changed since the 1970s, Slocum's description is, unfortunately, still not irrelevant to many of today's office workers. A lot of organizational structures have been flattened, but many companies, operating in an age of terrifying economic uncertainty, still seem dominated by fear, poisoning the workdays of employees at all levels, from the CEO ruled by fear of scandal and bankruptcy to the middle manager afraid of being exposed as incompetent to the rank-and-file worker who fears losing his or her means of survival.

Of course, fear is always part of organizational life—it's difficult not to be afraid of those with the power to take your livelihood away, even if they treat you kindly—but in a healthy organization, even during times of crisis, fear is tempered by positive attachments between individuals and groups. The most important lesson a leader can learn, according to executive coaches Dan Baker, Cathy Greenberg, and Collins Hemingway in *What Happy Companies Know*, is that "you cannot run a successful, dynamic business on fear."

One reason so much fear plagues organizations is that in the short run, fear can serve as a great motivator. Over time, however, it becomes maladaptive, shutting down the higher centers of the brain and causing people to make shortsighted decisions. The problem, according to Baker and his coauthors, is that our brains were not designed for office life but for hunting and gathering, and haven't changed much since the days when we needed to be constantly fearful in order to survive when the year's berry crop wasn't plentiful and the tribe on the other side of the forest got most of them. When certain executives making six- or seven-figure salaries act as if they're personally in danger of starvation if their companies don't meet all their quotas; drive their workers to exhaustion; make foolish, desperate investments with company funds; or behave unethically toward customers or competitors, this is because they haven't realized that things have changed since Cro-Magnon days. They're still stuck back in the mindset of "not enough."

However, not all executives are controlled by primitive instincts, nor are all workers. When those in charge are able to talk back to their fears, listen empathically to others, and make liberal use of their higher brain centers in making decisions, they foster positive organizational cultures that make it easy for workers to do their jobs well. Successful bosses are able to appeal not just to the fear instinct, or even mostly to it, but also to the attachment instinct, which has played just as important a role as fear in enabling humans to survive. To stay healthy, employees need to feel at least somewhat attached to their places of work, their organizations, and the people they work with.

A healthy workplace culture is built not on fear but on love—or, to use a less threatening, business psychology term—positive connections. This doesn't mean that workers always agree. What it does mean is that they're able to air differences freely, without fear of reprisal. Nor are they necessarily intimate friends, but they're sensitive to one another's feelings and willing to help one another out in times of need. When things go wrong, rather than blaming others, workers are willing to take responsibility for their own mistakes. Instead of ruthlessly competing, they work together toward common goals. When relationships are positive, people walk away from encounters feeling energized and good about themselves, more confident and willing to take creative risks in their work. They're more likely to enjoy doing their jobs and experience what positive psychologist

Mihaly Csikszentmihalyi calls flow—a feeling of total engagement with work in which you forget about time. Workers who experience this state are less likely to get sick, and have a way of staying around longer. Thus, the more such relationships exist within an organization, researchers have found, the better that organization's long-term prospects.

Consider Your Own Office Culture

If you were an anthropologist studying some indigenous society in an out-of-the-way place, you'd collect data about its language and customs; then try to figure out what rules everyone tended to follow; and, finally, ask yourself what values, assumptions, and beliefs lay behind them. In other words, you'd do a cultural analysis of the place. This approach is no less applicable to the office world than to villages in Papua New Guinea.

The problem is, we get to thinking that whatever culture we spend our time in is "regular" and isn't even a culture at all. Some people may recognize that offices have a distinct culture but believe that all office cultures are the same. They're not. An office in the Pentagon is different from an office on Wall Street, which is different from an office in a small bank in Tuskegee, which is different from an office in a large university in Ann Arbor. Each office culture has its own unique set of linguistic habits, customs, rules, values, assumptions, and beliefs, which are passed down from one generation of workers to another as old employees leave and new ones are hired. And yes, there are offices in which a culture is manipulated by a tyrannical, antisocial individual into something more like a cult, a toxic culture in which rules are rigidly imposed and individuals are forced to do things that are hurtful to them, or else suffer humiliation and ostracism.

To understand your own office culture, ask yourself what most people in your workplace seem to assume about the following areas. In doing so, put a checkmark in the box next to those areas where you feel at odds with your office culture. This will give you a sense of how well your culture suits your own personality and values.

❏ How you should look.
- Is there a formal dress code?
- Do most people wear suits, sweaters and slacks/skirts, blue jeans, uniforms, or something else?
- Do some people try to display their wealth by dressing expensively?
- Are there unspoken rules about body shape?
- Are low necklines okay or not?
- What would you feel uncomfortable wearing to work? Is overdressing or underdressing more taboo in your office culture?
- Are some hairstyles, types of makeup, or facial hair forbidden or discouraged? What types are most common?

❏ How your office should look.
- Are most people's offices neat or messy? Does a messy office get its occupant in trouble?
- What kinds of furniture do the offices contain and how are these used? Are people encouraged to supplement company items with those of their own or is this forbidden?
- What kinds of things do people have on the walls? Are political or religious items openly displayed or kept out of sight? What about items with sexual innuendos?
- What kinds of personal objects do people bring to work? What items would be considered suspect?

❏ How you should communicate.
- Do most people keep their doors open or closed? If a door is closed, does that mean "Do not disturb," or is it considered okay to knock?
- Do people communicate more by e-mail, telephone, or face-to-face?
- What sort of language do employees use? Is it mostly buzzwords and acronyms or is it more original?
- What words and phrases do people use a lot?
- Are certain word combinations taboo because they're considered profane or politically incorrect?

- Are people scrupulous or careless about not using masculine pronouns for antecedents that could be either male or female?
- Do some people use a lot of long words and sentences to try to impress others or disguise their own incompetence? How do others react to this?

❏ **What you should talk about.**
- How much chitchat goes on where you work? How much gossip?
- Do people talk only about work matters, or is casual conversation common?
- Do people talk openly about feelings?
- Are the people in your office quick or slow to label anything self-expressive as "inappropriate" or "unprofessional"?
- How common is humor in your workplace? What types of jokes do people tell? What types are viewed as inappropriate?

❏ **Who should do what.**
- Would certain tasks be considered inappropriate for individuals of a particular rank to do even if they could do them correctly?
- Do some types of duties confer more status on employees than others—for example, conducting workshops as opposed to entering data?
- Are certain employees expected to make the coffee or clean out the refrigerator, or does everyone share in these duties? Who does the photocopying?

❏ **How bosses should act toward their subordinates.**
- Do bosses address subordinates as equals or as inferiors? Do they act as though they care about their employees as people?
- How do bosses give feedback to subordinates about their performances, and how frequently?
- Do bosses expect assistants to do personal tasks for them, such as buying gifts for people in their families?

- Does a particular boss have a reputation as a bully or tyrant? How do workers respond to this?
- If a boss bullies or abuses subordinates, do coworkers ignore the behavior, make excuses for the boss, sympathize with the subordinate, or encourage him or her to protest?

❏ **How subordinates should behave toward their bosses.**

- Do employees call their bosses by their first names or address them more formally?
- Is it safe for subordinates to complain to their bosses about things that bother them? Can subordinates criticize their bosses or even sometimes tell them what to do?
- Do employees sometimes go over their bosses' heads when a conflict arises?

❏ **How coworkers should act toward one another.**

- Are coworkers competitive or cooperative? Is there a sense of teamwork, or is it every worker for him- or herself?
- Do coworkers regularly share information, or keep it to themselves?
- If a conflict arises, do coworkers resolve it among themselves or appeal to a higher authority?
- Do coworkers "tattle" on one another to the boss?
- Is verbally or physically aggressive behavior among coworkers rare or commonplace?

❏ **How time should be used.**

- How conscious are workers of clock time? Are people constantly hurrying and multitasking, or are they able to do things in a more deliberate way?
- Do workers take breaks? When, and for how long?
- Do workers sometimes engage in nonwork activities while at work?
- Do most people arrive early and stay late, or vice versa?
- Do employees engage in macho competitions to see who can work the longest hours?

❏ What matters most.
- What values do people seem to agree on? Is making money all that matters, or is it considered more important to provide quality products or service?
- Do workers seem to value education? Pleasure? Relationships?
- Are change and growth welcomed or treated as threats to stability and tradition?
- How do workers and supervisors respond to conflicts of values?

❏ What happens if you break the rules.
- If you came to work dressed differently or said something most people wouldn't say, what would happen? How shocked would people be? Would they ignore this behavior, talk to you about it, talk behind your back, or complain to your boss about it? Would your job be in jeopardy?
- Do workers often challenge taboos, or is this rare? Do they talk openly about them, or is this discouraged?

Now look back to see what areas you've checked and ask yourself how good the fit is between you and your office culture. Do you feel normal and accepted at work or like a square peg in a round hole? Have you ever challenged your office culture? What might happen if you did? Do you see your office culture as one of fear, one of love, or something in between? If it's one of fear, what, if anything, could you do about it?

The World of Organizations

Office cultures exist within organizations. These are hierarchical power structures that exist for the sake of getting work done. The key word here is "power." In *Chimpanzee Politics: Power and Sex Among Apes*, Dutch psychologist and ethologist Frans B. M. de Waal writes about how adult chimps spend their days vying for status by grooming (picking at each other's coats), threatening, building coalitions, and attacking those that compete with them. Those who do best are those who are able to gain others' support when fights break out, i.e., those with power. De Waal maintains that humans are just fancy varieties of apes and that their organizational behavior is comparable to that of chimpanzees competing for power, though they also have a side that resembles their more cooperative other ape cousin, the bonobo.

Work and power are intertwined within organizations. Often a class structure is based on the types of jobs workers do. Universities, for example, are characterized by an upstairs-downstairs structure of patricians (faculty) and plebeians (support staffers) who exist in parallel universes, having little to do with one another socially. Rankism—insensitivity toward others because of where they are in the power structure—is a problem in such organizations. Although I've had many wonderful interactions with faculty, as a university support staffer, I've occasionally been annoyed by rankist behavior—a professor walking away abruptly from me in the middle of a conversation when a colleague appeared, for example. Thinking about de Waal's chimps picking at each other's coats helps when things like that happen!

Office professionals work for many different types of organizations. Some are large, some small; some operate for profit, while others do not; some have conservative cultures, while others have liberal ones; some are pyramid-shaped bureaucracies, while others have flatter structures in which power is more widely shared. Understanding how your organization compares with others can help to put your own experiences there into perspective.

Over time, organizations go through a predictable life cycle, one version of which the sociologist Max Weber described in one of his essays in 1948 (*Essays in Sociology*). Typically an organization is started by a visionary, charismatic entrepreneur, a person with a dream, who defines the culture of the new organization, though much at first is still formless, as with a lump of clay. As time goes on, however, visionary leaders give way to bureaucrats, who begin to establish routines and rules that become progressively more rigid until they become maladaptive. If the organization is able to reform its maladaptive aspects when troubles result from them, it's likely to last; if not, it's doomed to extinction.

What organizations you're attracted to says something about your personality. Organizational psychologists maintain that founders' personalities are reflected in their organizations' cultures, which tend to attract workers whose personalities fit them. Thus, if you dislike your organization, it may be because you're just not "the company type."

Get to Know Your Own Organization

If you feel that your job is meaningless, that may be because thus far you've limited your focus to your own work and the people with whom you deal each day without paying much attention to what your organization is trying to do and how you and your coworkers fit with it. What can help is a little research about the following areas:

Your Organization's Mission*
- How is the mission statement worded? Is the language abstract or concrete? Does it seem empty or meaningful?
- Is it a mission you can believe in?
- What are the real-life implications of any abstract, idealistic terms in the mission statement? If, for example, part of your company's mission statement is to provide "quality service" to customers or clients, what would this quality service look like?
- How successful has your organization been in carrying out its mission? What role have you played in its success or failure? What role could you play?

Your Organization's Structure†
- What does the organizational tree look like? How is labor divided? Are there problems because workers are required

---

* Most organizations have their mission statements posted on their Web sites.
† Go to your HR office and ask for an organizational tree if you don't already have one.

to cover too many different areas of responsibility or because workers are overspecialized and unaware of the big picture?

- How is power distributed? Are the individuals at the top of the structure all-powerful, or do individuals at lower levels also have some power? How genuine is this?

Your Organization's Key Decision Makers*

- Who are the key decision makers and what are their policies and personalities like? How long have the same key decision makers occupied their positions?
- How open to change does each key decision maker seem to be?
- Are you aware of any conflict between key decision makers? If so, how does this affect you?
- What kind of relationship does your immediate supervisor have with the key decision makers, and what influence does this have on how he or she behaves toward you?

Your Organization's History†

- How did your organization come into being? Did it start small and grow, or did it break off from a larger organization? Was a merger involved in its origins?
- Who was the founder of your organization? What was he or she like? How has this affected its present characteristics?
- How has your organization changed over the years, and what bearing does this have on your immediate situation? Has your organization grown quickly or slowly?
- Where is your organization in its life cycle? Is it a new organization or is it well established? Is it in transition to a new phase? What effect has this had on your situation?

---

* Your boss can probably tell you about these, if your relationship is such that you can ask. If not, your coworkers are your next best source of information.
† The company Web site may have something on it about this, and old-timers are also a great source.

Your Organization's Financial Circumstances*

- Is your organization a for-profit or nonprofit organization?
- How well is your organization doing financially?
- Has something recently happened that has had or might have major financial consequences? If it's a profit-making organization, for example, are profits being affected by competition from a new company? Or, if it's a government-funded nonprofit organization, has it been affected by recent budget cuts at the national, state, or local levels?
- How has your organization been affected by the recent economic downturn?

Your Organization's Plans for the Future†

- What are your organization's financial projections and what are these based on?
- Is your organization planning to develop a new product or start a new project? How will this affect you?
- Is expansion or downsizing likely to happen? Is a particular branch of the organization scheduled to be closed or a new branch opened? Are transfers from one branch to another likely?
- Is a new building in the works? When will it be finished, and how will this affect your own situation?

Good executives provide their employees with regular information about their organization's financial circumstances and future plans. If your company doesn't, you might want to talk with other coworkers and consider asking your manager to meet with you and discuss these important aspects of your workplace life. Knowing how your particular duties contribute to the whole can give your job greater meaning, which is essential if you want to feel happier at work.

---

* If your CEO made a presentation to employees about this at an annual meeting, try to get hold of the PowerPoint handout. Annual reports to stockholders or donors are also useful, though be careful to read between the lines.

† This too you may be able to learn from a CEO's annual presentation.

Rethink Your Work Group

When you see people every single day in a confined space, things can get pretty intense. Like families, some work groups are functional, working well together and enjoying one another's company; and others are dysfunctional, working at cross-purposes while making one another miserable. Over time, members of work groups, like family members, tend to adopt certain predictable roles, which may take either a positive or a negative "shadow" form, depending on whether the group is functional or dysfunctional. Some of these roles include the following:

The Leader/Tyrant: This person likes to be in charge and steps in to save the day when problems occur. The trouble is, the person *really* likes to be in charge and might do some not-very-nice things if the individual feels that his/her power is threatened.

The Wit/Clown: Others enjoy this person's sense of humor, which can be a great asset to the group—unless the jokes cause pain to others or distract them from the task at hand, at which point it becomes a liability.

The Martyr/Scapegoat: This person fails to stick up for him/herself and thus often ends up being blamed—and sometimes even punished—for everything that goes wrong. The scapegoat isn't necessarily a person with no power: Wimpy bosses make great scapegoats.

The Silent One/Ghost: This person sits in the corner and says nothing, allowing others to do all the talking and make all the decisions. Some colleagues like this, but the person's silence can make others feel uneasy and wonder if he or she is plotting a mass shooting.

The Soldier/Bully: This person enjoys going on the attack. This can be useful if the group needs defending, but if that's not the case, the warrior can end up bullying other group members, with disastrous consequences to the group. Office bullying is a serious problem that we'll talk more about in chapter 5.

The Caregiver/Codependent: This person lives to take care of others whether they want it or not. And the care never comes without a price: If you accept one of this person's cookies, you'd better be willing to listen to his or her advice about how to lose weight, raise children, reorganize your life, and more.

The Watchdog/Nitpicker: This person's purpose in life is to make sure everyone follows all the rules and no one exceeds the budget. Often this person doubles as a scapegoat who is universally hated, though the person is usually so busy counting beans that he or she fails to notice.

The Novice/Nuisance: This person is new to the group and is trying out different ways of fitting in. He or she also needs lots of help, which can be a nuisance to others when things get busy.*

Like family members, people in work groups can sometimes repeat the same dysfunctional "dances" over and over, often the same ones they engaged in when they were growing up. Triangles are particularly troublesome. For example, Justine, an assistant for two bosses, each of which tries to monopolize her time, might find herself replaying her childhood role as a pawn between two quarreling parents.

If you are involved in a dysfunctional dance at work, there are some principles to remember, which I first encountered years ago in psychologist Harriet Lerner's classic self-help book *The Dance of Anger*:

1. You can't make anyone else change his or her steps in the dance— only the person dancing can do that. Justine, for example, can't make her bosses stop competing for her time.

---

* This list was based (though substantially revised) on categories described in *The Artist's Way at Work* by Mark Bryan with Julian Cameron and Catherine Allen.

2. You *can* tell others what you would like them to do, though only those without personality disorders are likely to listen (see chapter 5). Justine might ask her bosses to get together and work out an agreement about when she is supposed to do work for each of them.

3. If one person involved in the dance changes his or her steps, everyone else will also do so. If Justine, rather than exhausting herself trying to keep up with her bosses' demands, works out a plan of her own and lets them both know what it is, this could alter the dance.

4. You don't have to be the person with the most power in the group to make the dance change. You just have to change your own steps or respectfully ask others to do so. Justine's asking for a meeting or informing her bosses of her plan could alter the dance even though she's the subordinate.

5. Most of us tend to fall into dances we learned in childhood or some other part of our past. In the workplace, bosses are often stand-ins for parents, and coworkers for siblings. Justine initially replays a childhood pattern with her employers. However, she might come to realize that she has options in her job situation that she didn't have as a child, such as talking to someone outside of the triangle or even leaving.

6. If you're involved in a dysfunctional triangle, the solution is often to bring in a fourth party. Justine might suggest that the partners hire a second assistant to work for one of them, and if they agree, the dance will come to an end.

A Word to Assistants

In the office world, some of us have independent roles, while others are tied to our bosses as assistants. Psychologically, the assistantship role carries with it both special benefits and special risks.

Serving as someone's right-hand person usually means that you get to know that person extremely well. How happy or unhappy this makes you depends on how your boss treats you and how compatible the two of you are. If you're working for someone who treats you with the respect you deserve, it can be emotionally rewarding. Human beings are hormonally designed to experience pleasure from serving others, which is why service professions such as teaching, nursing, social work, or the clergy consistently rank highest on job satisfaction scales, and the assistant who works closely with his or her boss may experience some of this biologically programmed "service effect."

In addition, if your boss is a person of status who's doing extraordinary things, you may experience some of his or her successes vicariously and feel proud to be assisting the person's efforts. Elizabeth Nels, in her memoir, *Winston Churchill by His Personal Secretary*, describes the experience of working for the prime minister on his estate, where he dictated his great speeches nightly in his bathrobe during World War II:

> On these occasions he would walk up and down the room, his forehead crinkled in thought, the cords of his dressing-gown trailing behind him. . . . Sometimes he would fling himself for a moment into a chair: sometimes he would pause to light his cigar, which with so much concentration was neglected and frequently went out. For minutes he might walk up and down trying out sentences to himself. Sometimes his voice would become thick with emotion, and occasionally a tear would run down his cheek. As inspiration came to him he would gesture with his hands, just as one knew he would be doing when he delivered his speech, and the sentences would roll out with so much feeling that one died with the soldiers, toiled with the workers, hated the enemy, strained for Victory.

From Nels's descriptions elsewhere in the book, which I highly recommend, it was clear that Churchill was not easy to work for, but many of us would still love to have had such an incredible experience. This is assistantship at its best.

However, if the boss you serve is not Winston Churchill but someone for whom you have little respect or who mistreats you, assistantship can be pure hell. The movie *The Devil Wears Prada* provides a great example. In that movie, Meryl Streep plays Miranda Priestly, a fashion-magazine editor who continually bullies her young assistant, Andy Sachs, played by Anne Hathaway. Andy rises to the challenge of meeting her boss's ridiculously unreasonable demands until she finally wins Miranda's approval, then walks away to a better life.

Even if you don't have such a boss, assistantship has its mental-health risks. The greatest risk of assistantship, as well as the greatest reward, is the attachment you may feel for the person you serve. When your whole work life revolves around serving another, it's easy to forget that your own needs—and the needs of loved ones at home—also matter. In *The Devil Wears Prada*, Andy, caught up in meeting Miranda's demands, forgets to pay attention to her relationship with her partner who, feeling neglected, breaks up with her. Bosses often exploit the attachment feeling that keeps assistants working for them when they could more profitably work their way up the ladder. This isn't always a bad thing, but if you're staying an assistant to a highly paid executive out of loyalty when you don't have enough money to pay your bills, you may need to take a more critical look at your situation.

Blues and Battleshock Busters

1. Watch an episode of *The Office*—alone or with a group of coworkers—and do a cultural analysis of Dunder Mifflin's Scranton branch. How does its culture compare with that of your own office? Things could be worse!
2. Give the cultural and organizational questions in this chapter to an office buddy and ask the other person to do his or her own analysis, then compare notes. How is your coworker's experience of your culture and organization different from your own? You can also do this with a group.
3. Has your organization ever done a climate survey? Were workers given access to the results? If so, take a look at them. What do they show about your culture and organization?

4. Do some Web surfing for information on other organizations comparable to your own. How do they compare in terms of the aspects of organizations that were discussed in this chapter?
5. Make a list of the members of your own work group. What role or roles does each of them tend to play? Are there any dysfunctional dances going on? What solutions can you think of?

4

Sometimes It's About Differences

Human beings differ from one another in a great many ways, one of which is in how we respond to our differences. Some people plow blindly through life assuming everyone is just like them until suddenly they bump, crash-bang, into a huge, glaring difference that they missed, and have to spend the next hour apologizing. Others find differences terrifying, experiencing anyone who even slightly deviates from their own bland version of normal as a hideous troll who might, if he or she comes too close, gobble them up. Still others relish the process of discovering new differences, feeling enriched by their friends' diverse characteristics.

Most of us try to get along, but differences do have a way of creating misunderstandings and conflicts even while also making others more interesting to us. In the office this sometimes gets workers defined as "difficult people"—a business term, not a psychiatric one—who simply have some unique characteristic that others have trouble understanding. Most troublesome are those differences that are least apparent, neurological quirks that might cause someone to behave differently than you do or to have trouble with different tasks, though you can't exactly put your finger on why. Many of us get into trouble by assuming that other people's brains work more like ours than they actually do. At the same time, even obvious differences such as race, gender, or age can give us trouble if we don't fully understand what challenges the difference entails for the person on the other side of the fence.

If you want to become more comfortable with the people you work with, then one skill that's a must is to be able to imagine what it's like to be someone with a characteristic you don't have, to really think about what it would be like to be Jewish or bipolar or African American or sixty years old or Harvard educated when none of these adjectives apply to you. To help you cultivate this skill, this chapter presents a catalog of differences, with special attention to their implications for the office.

While struggling to understand our differences from one another, it's important to bear in mind that we humans also have similarities. All of us were born, and all of us will die. All of us need food, water, warmth, and love. All of us were children at one time, and many of us have children, nieces, nephews, grandchildren, young friends, or pets. Most of us hate icy weather and love sunny spring days and colorful fall leaves. Most of us love music, though we may prefer different types, and hate the sound of a dentist's drill. All of us experience pain at some time or another, and most have had our hearts broken at least a few times. All of us fear losing our livelihoods and want to feel that the work we do matters. And most of us are glad when Friday rolls around. If you keep these and many other human similarities in mind and use them to build bridges, you'll find that the differences become less important, and that there are far fewer "difficult people" in the office than you originally thought.

In his Philadelphia speech on race, President (then Senator) Barack Obama said, "I believe deeply that we cannot solve the challenges of our time unless we solve them together—unless we perfect our union by understanding that we may have different stories, but we hold common hopes." This is no less true in the office than it is anywhere else.

A Catalog of Differences

Physical Strength, Flexibility, and Coordination

Some of us are natural-born athletes and some of us aren't. While typing at a computer all day, which is what most office workers do, doesn't take a lot of strength, it does take coordination, especially hand-eye coordination. If you have the coordination needed to type fast in response to what you see, you're always going to get things done more quickly than others do. If, on the other hand, you lack this kind of coordination, you may find it difficult to keep up with the workload and need to have especially good time-management skills.

Energy Level

Contrary to popular opinion, this is mostly a matter of biology, not morality. Some people—often labeled workaholics—are naturally driven, while others—typically described as lazy—are naturally laid-back. In addition, some people have a nice, even flow of energy while others cycle through "high" periods of extreme productivity and "low" periods when they can barely drag themselves to work. The office world tends to reward the people with the even flow. Energy cyclers do best in jobs where they can throw themselves into big projects like writing an article or helping a boss get a grant proposal out, then coast until the next big project. Biologically this is complex, involving thyroid hormones, adrenaline, testosterone, estrogen, serotonin, dopamine, and other neurotransmitters and hormones as well as one's overall state of health. Most of the time, however, bosses and coworkers, frustrated by someone's lack of productivity, are unaware of these factors, to which even the underproducer him- or herself may be oblivious. This ignorance can have serious consequences.

Mood Cycles

Most of us have our emotional ups and downs, which often go hand in hand with energy cycles. Some days we feel terrific, others terrible, and still others somewhere in between. For most people, these moods (another word for them is "affect") could be graphed as sine waves, gradually rising and falling either above or below the x-axis, the point where they feel nothing at all. Some people's moods, however, deviate from this pattern. They may be continually above the line (hypomanic) or continually below it (depressed), cycle way above and way below (bipolar), or stay perpetually close to the line (flat affect). The lengths, frequencies, and intensities of moods also vary. People with flat affect tend to talk in monotones and aren't likely to be sympathetic if you try to tell them your troubles. People with more intense moods can be hard to be around because their moods can affect yours, but they can also be more exciting and empathic than even-tempered people. Moods can, of course, be affected by what happens in the workplace, becoming more positive when people's relationship needs are met. Both positive and negative moods can be contagious: When those around you feel good, you feel good too; when they feel bad, so do you.

Anxiety Level

Some people are born worriers whose systems are continually being flooded with adrenaline, while others are able to let things go. Anxiety levels are both biological and environmental, as most physically anxious people grew up among other physically anxious people, and anxiety tends to be contagious—both at home and in the office, though people deal with their anxieties in many different ways. Anxiety in the workplace is often combined with its close companion, guilt. Thus, people who are highly conscientious, staying late to add and readd columns that already balance out, are typically also anxious.

Coping Style

People have different ways of responding to their anxious and depressed feelings. Some people simply give in to their fears, their sadness, or their lack of energy, which may make them difficult to be around, while others work to counter these feelings by talking back to negative automatic thoughts, getting support from others, or using any number of other coping skills, some of which you'll learn about in chapter 9. In the workplace, all of these can be effective. For those who are good at coping, it can be frustrating to watch other people not cope, replying "Yes, but . . ." when given strategies that have proven to be successful. The trouble is, not everyone has the brain chemistry or psychological history needed to accept help.

Attentiveness

For some people, paying attention is much easier than it is for others, who may be distracted by either their surroundings or the thoughts in their heads. Attention is not a simple thing. All of us pay attention more easily to something that really interests us—for example, a gripping novel or a movie—than something that bores us. It can also be more difficult to be attentive if you're feeling anxious because someone's looking over your shoulder. While managers generally consider daydreaming at work a bad thing, their most creative workers are likely to also be the least attentive.

While some workers do have brain-based attention problems (popularly known as ADD for "attention deficit disorder" or, officially, ADHD), for many of us concentration problems are merely the result of an overloaded working memory, which is the ability to hold information in your mind for a few seconds while you're doing a task. When workers are forced to multitask too much, they become easily distracted and don't perform individual tasks as well. ADD specialist Edward Hallowell calls this F-state, the "F" standing for words such as "frantic," "frenzied," "forgetful," "flummoxed," "frustrated," and "fragmented," and believes that it's epidemic in the modern "crazy-busy" workplace and world.

Memory Differences

Few of us have perfect memories, and memory is multidimensional and not necessarily consistent across the board. You may have an excellent memory for memorizing poetry or music and yet be unable to remember to send a fax before it's due. You may be great at remembering numbers but not so great at remembering words. You may be able to remember everything that happened to you in your childhood but be unable to remember the instructions your boss just gave you. Or your memory may be either strong or weak across the board.

In the office world, you rarely have to memorize dates, but you do have to remember to do things, a type of memory known as pro- spective memory. If yours is poor, it's going to be hard for you to do jobs such as event planning, where you have to remember to do a great many little tasks—though you can usually get by if you keep your to-do list up-to-date, absolutely essential if you have prospec- tive memory problems.

Memory sometimes becomes an issue in the office for middle-aged and older workers. While memory loss is normal from middle age on and doesn't necessarily mean you're doomed to wind up with Alz- heimer's, the excessive demands on the memory posed by today's information-overloaded workplace are an extra source of stress for many senior workers, who struggle to hide memory weaknesses and may be terrified of being "found out" and fired or forced to retire before they can afford to do so.

Big-Picture Versus Detail Thinking

In any meeting, pay attention to who wants to spend the whole meeting talking about the price of pencils and who keeps demanding that the group stop and reconsider its goals. Chances are, brain scans of these two types of people would reveal significant neurological differences. Some brains are wired to take in every twig of every tree but not the whole forest, while others are wired to focus on the for- est but miss the individual trees. Those in the first group tend to work step-by-step, while those in the second tend to work on every- thing at once. In the office, big-picture people often think detail people are petty for counting every last Post-it tablet in the supply cabinet, and detail people think big-picture people are lazy for not doing this.

Creativity

Some of us are wired to think and act creatively, while others natu- rally conform to patterns established by others and may feel fright- ened any time anyone steps outside the lines. For whatever reason, office workers who aren't creative often seem to dislike those who are, sometimes intensely, and can at first be critical of original ideas that they may later come to accept. This causes pain to the creatives, who often also have sensitive egos. Hence all those novels, plays, movies, and TV shows about sensitive, creative souls being tormented and misunderstood by uncreative bosses and coworkers.

Cognitive Strengths and Weaknesses

One fallacy that psychologically naive bosses often fall into is the "just plain smart" fallacy, the belief that if a worker is smart, he or she should be good at everything. This is rarely the case. All of us have brains wired to do some tasks easily and find others difficult, and even developmentally disabled individuals may be good at certain things. The smart manager is able to spot each worker's talents and weaknesses and adjust task assignments accordingly. Doing this can make an enormous difference in the employee's productivity and job satisfaction.

Sensory Thresholds

Each of us is wired to function best at a different level of sensory stimulation. Some of us are "sensation avoiders" who thrive in a sensory deprivation chamber. Others are "sensation seekers" who crave color, noise, and excitement. When these two types of workers have to share an office, trouble is bound to result. The sensation seeker will inevitably drive the sensation avoider crazy with unwanted noise, motion, and emotional intensity until the sensation avoider begs to be moved somewhere else.

Sensory Style

Each of us takes in the world through a different combination of sensory channels. Some of us are most sensitive to sounds, others to visual patterns, and still others to how things physically feel. This can have a big effect on how we learn. If you're an auditory learner and someone says, "Let me show you," expecting you to mimic actions, you may find this difficult until your teacher explains what you need to do in words. If, on the other hand, you're visual or kinesthetic, a purely oral explanation may sound like a foreign language to you. If you have to do oral presentations, it's important to keep people's variable learning styles in mind and make sure you include something for everybody.

Gender

The office world was created by and for men, and thus it's not surprising that many aspects of that world seem to suit most men better than they do most women. Not only are women in the office more likely to feel conflicted between work and family responsibilities, they may also feel a stronger need for connection than men—who started out as saber-toothed tiger hunters—are likely to consciously feel. While sterile, distant offices in which men can boldly go where no man has gone before may suit them just fine, women may feel emotionally deprived without a warm work nest and frequent e-mails to loved ones. These differences, however, are by no means universal. Men in today's world are often more involved in child rearing and relationships than was once the case, while women may have become more career-driven and competitive. Thus, the primary gap these days may be less between men and women than between connectors and disconnectors of both sexes.

Sexual Orientation

The office world was originally created by heterosexual, often homophobic males. It is thus a world in which "Don't ask, don't tell" is still the dominant attitude in most arenas where sexuality is concerned. By disclosing their sexual preferences to others in the workplace, homosexual, bisexual, or transsexual workers—especially in more conservative organizations and industries—risk not only being the victims of bigotry but also being accused of inappropriateness for revealing personal information in an environment in which workers, whatever their sexual orientation, are expected to keep their private lives private. Having to stay in the closet at work every day rather than being themselves may thus contribute to these workers' sense of isolation and loneliness.

Race/Ethnicity

The office world was created by European Americans, who denied all other groups admission until the civil rights movement got going in the 1960s. When minority citizens began to filter into the lower echelons, they had to act as "white" as possible to have any chance of advancement. Many groups are still seriously underrepresented and thus feel pressure to park their ethnicity at the office door. Since "acting white" generally means keeping your hands to yourself rather than connecting through touching; keeping your feelings inside rather than expressing yourself openly; behaving competitively rather than cooperatively; and using colorless office-speak rather than your own beautiful dialect, this is a daily loss for many workers, especially those from more affiliative cultures, where close connection is a way of life. As racial and ethnic groups continue to mix and merge and minority workers to advance, however, the influence of affiliative cultures in the office may be expected to grow.

Religion
The office workplace in Europe and America was originally created by Christians and Jews. However, because religion is such an emotionally charged subject, in my experience it has become almost as taboo as sexuality in most office workplaces, except in those industries dominated by a particular religion. Yet even in pluralistic organizations religion is still there, just below the surface, influencing people's daily behaviors and peeking out from time to time in the form of a prayer on someone's bulletin board, a necklace with a religious symbol, or a head covering.

Age
The relative ages of workers are important in the office workplace for two reasons. One is that different generations of workers seem to have different values, attitudes, and beliefs that affect how they do their jobs. This may be partly a matter of acculturation, but I believe it's mostly a matter of where they are in their life spans. Members of each age group have different issues they're struggling with, some of which may put them at cross-purposes. Twentysomethings may find it difficult to break into the office world and may be starting out in temporary or internship positions, while the rest of us may find their superior electronic skills terrifying. Those who recently graduated from college may miss the days when they had more control over their schedules and find office work a drab sequel to their more spontaneous school days. They may also be wrestling with identity

issues, and browse graduate school sites on the Internet while waiting in a low-status job for their real careers to begin.

Those in their thirties and forties may still be waiting for life to start, or they may have decided to become career office workers. Often this is a result of having families they need to support, for which they may have had to defer dreams of more exciting careers, though they may turn back to those dreams as their children become more independent. Flexible scheduling is more important to them than to workers whose children are grown.

Office workers in their fifties and sixties are beginning to realize that life doesn't go on forever—and neither do their career options. In the office world, if they've worked their way up to positions of high status, they may feel proud of their accomplishments; but they may also feel overstressed by the responsibilities that go with the glory, especially if they're struggling to pay for college educations, take care of elderly parents, or help raise grandchildren.

Those older workers who haven't wound up in high-status positions may feel trapped and invisible, especially if they're not in jobs where promotions are likely. Age discrimination is extremely common, forcing some older workers to take menial jobs and even to do without health insurance at a time when they're most likely to need it. Nor, in an era of dwindling 401(k)s, can they look forward to carefree retirements. While high-status workers with good salaries may still be able to spend their golden years on the beach, those who had lower-status positions may end up working as grocery store cashiers.

Older workers may also be affected by declining health and memory issues—they may struggle to drag themselves into work when they don't feel well, struggle to keep learning that next computer program, struggle to make it to the finish line. However, while these challenges might put their younger coworkers over the edge, older workers' superior coping skills may equip them to better handle such obstacles. Having already survived a great many troubles, they have the advantage of knowing that they can fall apart and still put themselves back together.

Class

Office workers' class backgrounds can be anything from underclass to upper crust. This can be a source of tension, with upper-middle-class employees regarding working-class coworkers as vulgar for drinking Pepsi instead of mineral water, while working-class folks view their middle-class counterparts as snooty. Those with manufacturing roots may wonder why office workers never unionized and why their coworkers don't stick up for their rights more. They may also be annoyed by the tendency of middle-class types to talk about unpleasant things only indirectly, while they themselves are more likely to "tell it like it is." At the same time, they may feel self-conscious about using less standard English than their middle-class colleagues, who may be put off by the way they speak.

Education

When you're going to college, you may think that once you get out and get an office job you'll be able to use what you've learned, and that people will be impressed if you got a degree from a prestigious school. This is often not the case. In hiring you for an administrative office job, for example, your employer may mostly care about how skilled you are at using Excel. Once you've got a job, even if you got a degree in business, you'll find that half of what you learned is irrelevant; and as for a liberal arts degree—forget it! Some rank-and-file office workers may have a lot more education than others, but when you want someone to explain to you how the new online payroll system works, it makes no difference whether that person got an A in Romantic Poetry. When deciding whom you'd like to invite out for lunch, though, it might be a different story.

Job Title and Rank

Your official title can affect how much you like your job as well as how you're perceived by others. For this reason, management has a way of replacing titles with low-status connotations with titles that make the same job sound more prestigious. After a while, however, the fancier title begins to sound as unimpressive as the original one. This is what has happened with "administrative assistant," a title that once meant being a supervisor or dealing with complex finances and now means pretty much what "secretary" used to mean, such that there are even greeting cards for bosses to give their employees on Administrative Assistants Day. Meanwhile, as long as people have jobs of different ranks, there will probably always be some people who treat those of lower rank like chairs and drinking fountains, not human beings.

Health and Disability Status

How workers feel and what they're able to do can have a huge effect on their performances in the office and what types of help they need. Employers are required by the Americans with Disabilities Act to provide appropriate accommodations for those who disclose disabilities, which vary depending on the type of disability. While prospective employers may admire the strength of those candidates who have overcome a physical disability to be qualified for the job, if you disclose a mental disability, you're not likely to get hired. For that reason, many people with mental disabilities choose not to disclose them and then, after they've gotten the job, struggle without the accommodations they need for their disability.

Hobbies and Interests

Although rank-and-file office employees may often seem like clones in the workplace, this is just a disguise. After hours, the clone disguise comes off as the worker dons a scuba-diving outfit, picks up a paintbrush, or reports for duty at the volunteer fire department. If you want to enjoy life more at the office, make it your business to find out what people do when they're not at work, and look for people whose interests match your own. Think of each person as a treasure chest with a musty old cover—all you have to do is lift the lid and there's gold inside!

Communication Style

As a result of both brain wiring and education, some of us are naturally more adept than others at putting our thoughts into words or making sense out of the words we take in. Also, different cultures—including, according to Deborah Tannen in *You Just Don't Understand*, the cultures boys and girls grow up in—make different assumptions about whether one should be brief when speaking or give more details, keep feelings hidden or express them, aim to impress or strive to connect, use clichés or create new language, and many other communication characteristics. Thus, any time you're dealing with someone from a culture different from your own in the office, it's important to find out what his or her linguistic assumptions are.

Need to Conform

Some people are comfortable only when dressing, speaking, and acting like those around them, while others feel a strong need to distinguish themselves. As psychologist Solomon Asch showed in a famous social psychology experiment, some are so afraid of being different that they'll even fool themselves into believing that lines of different lengths are really the same, just because everyone else says they are, even though they can see perfectly well that they aren't. In the workplace, if their bosses think the latest management fad is wonderful, they'll think so too even if it's obviously useless and adds stress to their lives. Those who prefer to conform are likely to be more comfortable in the office world than those who don't, though nonconformists, by getting a great idea and doing something exceptional that catches the attention of the boss's boss, may suddenly leap to the top of the career ladder, to the disgust of their hardworking but less imaginative coworkers.

Need for Personal Space

This is both neurological and cultural. Some of us are wired to be hypersensitive to intrusiveness, while others don't mind people barging in on them. Some of us come from "contact cultures," in which touching is part of an individual's communication style, while others come from cultures where not only touching but even making eye contact is regarded as immoral.

Need for Status

Some office workers like feeling ordinary, while others crave notoriety. This may have to do with how your caregivers responded to your attempts to distinguish yourself when you were growing up.

Those with little need to be "somebody" are ideally suited to be assistants. Those with a need to stand out are likely to be unhappy in such roles but may thrive in more independent roles that allow them to visibly excel.

Need for Autonomy

Some workers don't mind having someone looking over their shoulders all day long, while others long to be their own bosses. If private health insurance were cheap enough, they would work for themselves, but it's not, so here they are in the office, chafing under someone else's oppressive regime. For them, hell is a place where others micromanage everything they do. Those with little need for autonomy may regard those who need a lot of it as whiners for complaining about being oversupervised.

Values

A major source of conflict in the office is the erroneous belief that what is important to you is—or should be—important to someone else. To some of us, for example, morality is about working hard, saving money, and following all the rules. To others, it's about being compassionate and flexible and doing what they feel deep down is right, regardless of what the rules say. To some, money, promotions, praise, personal time, relationships, freedom, or a clear conscience mean more than they do to others. All of us are continually making decisions about which of these rewards to favor, and we need to respect others' right to decide differently.

Openness to New Experiences

Given the opportunity to try something new, some people greet it with open arms and others react cautiously. The world needs both types of people, but it's good to know which type you are and which type your boss and coworkers are. If your boss doesn't jump up and down with enthusiasm when you propose that he or she purchase a new type of equipment, for example, it could be that your boss is just not very open to change. Neuropsychologists describe some people as having a "novelty gene" that makes them crave new experiences. These people find repetitive work unpleasant, though the craving for novelty may motivate them to climb the success ladder in order to keep doing new and different things. The challenge for them is to stick with any job long enough to get good at it.

Deal with the Differences

The differences we've gone through in this chapter are only a few of the variations that can affect how we experience our jobs, our co-workers, and our workplace lives. Once you've recognized that you and someone else are different in a particular way, it can sometimes be enormously beneficial simply to acknowledge that difference in words and talk about how it affects your relationships. It's important to always do this respectfully, without implying that you're better than the other person. If, for example, you're often at loggerheads with a person whose thinking style is different from your own, you might say something like "I've noticed you seem to focus more on details, whereas I'm more of a big-picture person. Does it seem that way to you?" Along with this, you can point out ways that you're similar: "I feel like both of us are really conscientious," for example. This approach will often break down walls, but if you still find some people difficult even after you've tried it, don't worry—it doesn't work with everyone, and we'll talk about the exceptions in chapter 5.

Blues and Battleshock Busters

1. Do a difference profile of yourself. Go through all the differences just described and write a few paragraphs describing yourself in terms of them, or describe yourself to a trusted friend or counselor. Which differences are most important to you? Which have made you feel most misunderstood? How could you help others to understand them better? Now look back at what you've written and ask yourself how well your unique set of characteristics suits you for your particular job situation. Are some tasks hard for you because of differences? What could you do about this? Are you and your job a good match? Although you may not

be in a position to leave right now, it's useful to know in order to plan for your future.

2. Ask an office friend out for lunch, and share this chapter with the person. Ask your friend to do a difference profile for you, and see how this compares with what you found. Then do the same for your friend if he or she is willing. How have your differences affected your relationship? What similarities do you have that have enabled you to bridge them and still be friends?

3. Do a difference profile for someone with whom you have difficulties. Write down everything you know about what makes this person different from you. Also write down those things you have in common. Now use this information to rethink your approach to dealing with the person.

5

Sometimes It's About Crazymakers

If you're having problems with someone at work, defining differences and searching for common ground are often all you need to do to improve the situation. Most of us, however, have had the experience of trying this approach with someone and getting nowhere. If this happens repeatedly with the same person, you may be dealing with what clinicians call a personality disorder. People with personality disorders have a life history of causing misery to others while believing that they're just fine themselves. They rarely seek therapy, unlike their victims, who form a large proportion of those in treatment for depression and anxiety. I call these people crazymakers* because of the harmful effects they have on the mental health of those who don't take steps to protect themselves from their mind games.

While it might seem uncompassionate to label human beings with such a pejorative term, I believe that calling people with personality disorders crazymakers is justified if it helps you to remember how

---

* For the term "crazymaker," I'm indebted to Mark Bryan, Julia Cameron, and Catherine A. Allen, who use it in their book *The Artist's Way at Work.*

dangerous they can be. This can be difficult, as people with personality disorders often join forces with our self-delusions so as to get what they want from us before dumping us in the ditch. Just because you don't allow crazymakers to poison your life doesn't mean you can't feel compassion for them—it takes either the wrong brain chemistry or the wrong upbringing or both to make a crazymaker, and these folks chose neither—but you also need to show compassion toward their potential victims by not encouraging crazymakers' misbehavior.

Like ice cream, crazymakers come in different flavors—narcissistic, obsessive-compulsive, dependent, antisocial, histrionic, passive-aggressive histrionic, and paranoid, to name a few—but they are all similar in behaving hurtfully to others. Encounters with them can leave you feeling bruised, battered, or enraged. Psychologist Albert J. Bernstein, in *Emotional Vampires*, associates them with Dracula because of their tendency to make you feel drained, as though all your blood had been sucked out. If you suffer from a serious case of office blues, there's a fair chance there's at least one crazymaker in your workplace life.

You can never solve problems with crazymakers, because they will always treat *you* as the problem and engage in all sorts of manipulative games to get their way. Business gurus agree that bosses need to refrain from hiring or promoting them, but because they can be extremely clever in marketing themselves and may even seem to have leadership qualities, they often get jobs and promotions anyway, sometimes even to the top of the pyramid. Thus, most of us have to deal with them in the workplace sooner or later.

Anyone who interacts frequently with a crazymaker needs to use special strategies to stay sane. As is well documented by clinicians, these people's thoughts, feelings, and behaviors are qualitatively different from those of other people, and dealing with them successfully requires a whole different set of skills than you need to build relationships with non-crazymakers.

How to Recognize a Crazymaker

Learning to recognize a crazymaker is one of the most important skills you can develop to stay healthy at work. This isn't easy, because crazymakers are experts at fooling people into thinking they're like everybody else. Few people, even mental-health professionals, are able to recognize folks with personality disorders the first time they meet them, as they can be extremely charming—until they don't get what they want. If an initially charming crazymaker turns on you, don't beat yourself up for having been taken in. Crazymakers are geniuses at manipulation.

The best way to tell if you're dealing with a crazymaker is to take stock of your own feelings during and after an encounter. If you frequently leave conversations with a particular person feeling furious, terrified, tearful, bewildered, or in doubt of your own sanity, you may be dealing with a crazymaker. If you feel that you have to watch your every move or the person will do something unpleasant, you may be dealing with a crazymaker. If you feel pressured to do things that you know are wrong, you may be dealing with a crazymaker. If you waste hours rehearsing speeches that you're never able to make when the person is actually there, you may be dealing with a crazymaker. If people in your office tiptoe around in someone's presence, compare notes about the person's outrageous behaviors, label the person "jerk," "jackass," "scoundrel," "schmuck," "asshole," "bastard," "bitch," etc., or split into factions arguing about how to deal with the person, you're almost certainly dealing with a crazymaker.

In Yann Martel's *Life of Pi*, the son of a zookeeper, while on a voyage in which his father's zoo is being transported from India to Canada, experiences a shipwreck and winds up in a lifeboat with a Bengal tiger. Pi survives by catching fish and feeding them to the tiger, gradually gaining power over it as it becomes more dependent on him. If someone in your office makes you feel as though you're trapped in a lifeboat with a tiger, that person may be a crazymaker. Like tigers, crazymakers cause pain to others not because they're bad, but because they lack the ability to reflect on their own actions and think in moral terms, or take the needs of others into account.

Unfortunately, because they're unable to look at themselves when problems occur and instead regard others as the problem, crazymakers rarely seek treatment, and unless they do long-term work with a specialist in personality disorders, they're unlikely to get better. Meanwhile, well-meaning attempts by friends, bosses, and coworkers to "fix" the crazymaker by being kind and understanding are generally unsuccessful, and often result in the would-be fixer being hurt and the crazymaker becoming worse. This happens often in the workplace.

While it's important to learn to recognize a crazymaker, it's equally important to take your time before concluding that this is what you're seeing. Therapists rarely diagnose people with personality disorders before working with them for an extended period of time. And it's easy to mistake some of the differences we talked about in chapter 4 for signs of a personality disorder. For this reason, it's always best to begin by being compassionate and understanding, listening and empathizing and making allowances. But when someone causes distress to others over and over and fails to take responsibility for his or her hurtful actions, there comes a time when you have to recognize that the usual rules for good relationships don't apply to this person. At that point you need to shift gears and adopt another set of rules that will protect you and others from the dangers of dealing with a crazymaker.

Rules for Non-crazymakers Versus Rules for Crazymakers

Non-crazymaker Rule #1: *Work to build a relationship.*
Crazymaker Rule #1: *Work to build your power.*

As you get to know someone over time, relationships normally become closer and more rewarding, and power is shared. This will not happen with a crazymaker. Accept the fact that with a crazymaker you can never have a real relationship, only power games. If you crave closeness, this can be difficult, but it will be easier if you can cultivate friendships elsewhere. The only thing you can build with a crazymaker is the power to protect yourself and others from the person's toxic behaviors, the way Pi builds his power over the tiger and thus manages to survive.

Non-crazymaker Rule #2: *Be generous.*
Crazymaker Rule #2: *Decide how much you'll give the person and give only that.*

Crazymakers are black holes of greed who can never get enough of anything. Where non-crazymakers may feel an obligation to give back to those who give to them, crazymakers view others' generosity as evidence that they can take advantage of them, which they inevitably will. It's okay to give to a crazymaker, but give him or her only what you've planned to, and be prepared to deal with protests when you stop.

Non-crazymaker Rule #3: *Be genuine.*
Crazymaker Rule #3: *Playact.*

To deal effectively with a crazymaker, you must pretend to buy into the person's view of him- or herself and the world. Thus, it's okay to flatter a narcissistic crazymaker even if you think he or she is a loser, pretend that petty details are as important to you as they are to an obsessive-compulsive crazymaker, or agree that evil is everywhere to humor a paranoid crazymaker. By feeding the person's worldview this way, you gain power, as Pi gained power over the tiger by feeding it fish, and the only way you can deal effectively with a crazymaker is from a position of power.

Non-crazymaker Rule #4: *Share thoughts and feelings.*
Crazymaker Rule #4: *Keep your thoughts and feelings to yourself.*

Crazymakers are constitutionally unable to empathize and will view anything you share with them about your inner life as ammunition they can use against you in order to get what they want. If a crazymaker does something that upsets you, never let the person know. Maintain an external appearance of calm no matter what storms are going on inside. The crazymaker, lacking the ability to empathize, will not be able to see through this.

Non-crazymaker Rule #5. *Be flexible.*
Crazymaker Rule #5. *Be rigid.*

With regular folks, it's healthy to bend the rules sometimes. With crazymakers, you need to be absolutely rigid in enforcing them as quickly as possible after a violation, though it's important to be clear about what they are. This means if you're the boss of a crazymaker, fire the person the next time he or she breaks the rules, not the third or fourth time.

Non-crazymaker Rule #6. *Never say negative things about someone behind the person's back.*
Crazymaker Rule #6. *Compare notes with others struggling to deal with the crazymaker.*

We're talking survival here. With a crazymaker in your midst, you need all the support you can get and so do others. In discussing the crazymaker, be aware that these folks are often sources of conflict about how to deal with them. One party favors toughness while the other favors compassion. A good way of resolving such a conflict is to point out that sometimes the kindest thing you can do with someone is to be tough. Like children, crazymakers need people to set the limits with them that they can't set with themselves, and by setting these limits you'll be contributing to the buildup of life lessons that might, if they accumulate enough, eventually overwhelm the person's defenses and cause them to shift.

If you're like most people, you've been taught to approach your fellow human beings with kindness and empathy and to try to understand and forgive when you feel hurt. With four out of five people you meet, these are wonderful ways to interact. But with the fifth person, the crazymaker, the kindest, most compassionate way you can act is to make yourself into a brick wall. Remember, when you give in to the manipulations of a crazymaker, you're encouraging the person not only to hurt you some more but to hurt others as well. If you can't be compassionate to yourself, try being compassionate to the people who may be next in line.

The Office from Hell: A Gallery of Crazymakers

When you first took this job at CM Enterprises, you thought every-one in your office was charming. For a while everything was fine. Then, one by one, you began to discover that the people you thought were so nice were, in fact, a lot of impossible crazymakers. Each, however, is slightly different from the others, afflicted with a differ-ent type of personality disorder. (Note that not all the official person-ality disorders are represented in this section, just those you're most likely to encounter in the office world.)

The first person to disillusion you is Bart, your boss. You and your significant other are planning a romantic getaway that you've both been looking forward to for weeks. Several months ago, you asked Bart if you could have Friday off, and on Monday you re-minded him of your plans. Both times he said it was fine. You're packing up to leave on Thursday night when he sticks his head in the door. "Don't forget to give me a report on the Stevens project tomor-row," he says. You remind him that you won't be here.

"Oh, but that's impossible," he says. "I have to have that report before I meet with Jeremy tomorrow afternoon. And I'll want you to come with me to explain things if Jeremy has a question."

You remind him that he said you could have tomorrow off and show him an e-mail to prove it. "I don't care what I said," he tells you. "I need you here tomorrow to take care of that report."

Furious, instead of going on your trip, you go home and update your résumé, then report to work the next day. After the meeting, Bart comes in and praises you for the wonderful job you did on the report and your helpfulness with Jeremy. "I knew I could rely on you," he says, patting you on the shoulder. Flattered, you forget about your job search, but a few weeks later, the same thing happens again.

Bart is a **narcissistic** crazymaker. He believes other people exist purely to meet his needs and is completely incapable of putting him-self in their shoes. Narcissists take their name from the legendary Greek god Narcissus, who became so enamored with his own reflec-tion in a pool of water that he fell into it and drowned. They are obsessively concerned with maintaining their own images, for which no sacrifice—theirs or yours—is too great. They may be genuine superstars, or they may be people who see themselves as brilliant but misunderstood. Either way, they'll ignore your needs unless you force them to do otherwise.

Narcissists are most problematic if you work for them, and if you work for a superstar, that person is probably a narcissist. To survive working for a narcissistic boss, the best strategy is to shamelessly kiss up to the person while cultivating some type of skill you can offer that will enable him or her to look good. If you can help him or her write an autobiography, create a personal Web site, or launch a media campaign, he or she will think you walk on water. To increase your power even more, you should also encourage the narcissist to tell you about him or herself. Once you've increased your power, you can use it to demand more reasonable treatment from the narcissist.

Meanwhile, back at CM, you next find out what Cheryl, with whom you share an office, is really like. At first, you're impressed with what a hard worker Cheryl is. She's always there when you get to work in the morning and is still there when you leave at night. She never takes a coffee or lunch break, nor does she take the time to chat with coworkers, surf the Net, look out the window, or do anything else that takes her away from her desk. You've never even seen her take a bathroom break. Over time, this begins to make you more and more uncomfortable. Is your boss going to expect you to work as hard as Cheryl works? you wonder. The mere thought makes you feel exhausted. You decide to try to get to know her so as to find out why she's such a grind. You wonder if she's afraid of being fired. Maybe she's on probation or under pressure at home to move up the ladder and make more money.

You invite her out to lunch. At first she says she's too busy, but you repeat your invitation several times, and finally she succumbs. But rather than telling you anything about herself, she spends the whole lunch hour complaining about the sloppiness of coworkers who don't meet her standards of perfection. "*I* was brought up to think you have to *earn* your paycheck," she says, "unlike *some* people." You wonder if in her mind you're part of the "some people." Meanwhile, you make a mental note not to subject yourself to another lunch with Cheryl.

Cheryl is an **obsessive-compulsive** crazymaker.* What people of this type want is to feel virtuous, even if it means they have no friends. Virtue to them means following rules to the letter, not being kind or compassionate, and they can be harshly judgmental toward those who bend or break them. Natural-born bureaucrats, they have minds that overfocus on petty details but tend to miss the big picture. They make some of the world's worst bosses, micromanaging their employees until they quit, yet their superconscientiousness often gets them promoted.

If you work with an obsessive-compulsive crazymaker like Cheryl, it's important to control any competitive tendencies you may have and recognize that people can be good at their jobs in different ways. Try to admire the person for his or her conscientiousness and express your admiration without telling the person what you don't admire. The world needs some Cheryls, but it also needs people who are able to see the big picture and to empathize with others. Don't worry about whether or not the person sees you as a bum—he or she probably does, but that doesn't mean that's what you are. Only you have the right to decide what you're worth.

You've just begun to figure out how to deal with Cheryl when you start having problems with Jena, who works for you. Her tasks are routine and shouldn't require a lot of supervision, but Jena continually interrupts your own work with unnecessary questions, which she asks in an unpleasant, whiny voice. If you ask her to stuff envelopes, she wants to know how you want the letters folded, whether to lick the envelopes or use a sponge, and whether to put ten or twelve in a bundle. She seems incapable of deciding anything for herself. When you finally confront her about this, she bursts into tears and wails, "I knew I'd be a failure!" Feeling like a heartless tyrant, you take her out for tea and spend the next two hours listening to a litany of her personal problems. Every time you try to get up and go back to work, she begs you not to desert her. Finally, you make your escape, but somehow you still feel like a bad, uncaring person.

---

* Obsessive-compulsive personality disorder is entirely different from obsessive-compulsive disorder, a neurologically based illness defined by obsessive thoughts and compulsive behaviors.

Jenna is a **dependent** crazymaker. People with dependent personality disorders can never get enough nurturing and can be highly manipulative in their efforts to make others give it to them. Don't be fooled by their apparent weakness: Beneath the surface they're tough as leather, and if you refuse to nurture them, they'll quickly find someone else to bleed. Anything but take care of themselves.

The worst way to deal with a dependent crazymaker is to cut the person off too suddenly. This may result in the crazymaker turning into a stalker who will show up bleeding on your doorstep. Instead, you need to wean dependent crazymakers gradually by hooking them up with other people who can help meet their dependency needs. Give them a list of names they can call if they run into trouble. Then tell them you won't be available for the next one, two—later three; still later, four—hours.

Not long after that, you find out about Brian, Bart's partner. When you first met Brian, you thought he was delightful. He had a great sense of humor, and you even had fantasies that he might ask you on a date. Then one afternoon, you hear shouts coming from Brian's office. "You f——— idiot!" you hear. "How many times have I told you to . . ." A little while later, Freddy, Brian's young assistant, emerges from the office looking pale and exhausted. Later Freddy tells you that Brian had blasted him over a slip of paper he forgot to file, a totally trivial matter. It's not the first time, he says, and he's had about enough. Freddy gives notice a few days later, having found a less lucrative but also less toxic job elsewhere. He's the fourth assistant to work for Brian in the past six months. Much to everyone's delight, not long after that, Brian himself is fired and arrested after it comes out that he has been charging personal expenses and making fraudulent ATM withdrawals on his company credit card.

Brian is an **antisocial** crazymaker. Psychiatrists sometimes call antisocial crazymakers psychopaths. They are people without consciences, and they crave emotional intensity and sensation. Some are bullies who take pleasure in physically or mentally torturing their victims, while others live on the edge by engaging in high-risk, illegal activities. They're the opposite of obsessive-compulsive crazymakers in that instead of rigidly following rules, they consider themselves to be above them. They can be highly manipulative and may use their skills to get others to do things that could get them into serious trouble. Then, when the police show up, they're nowhere to be found, while the other person takes the rap. Whatever havoc they wreak in other people's lives, you can be sure of one thing: They won't feel the least bit guilty about it.

In *Snakes in Suits: When Psychopaths Go to Work*, psychologists Paul Babiak and Robert D. Hare suggest that psychopaths may be uniquely designed to make their way up the corporate ladder to top positions in today's office world for several reasons:

1. They can be extremely charming.
2. They're good at dominating others and thus may come across as "leaders."
3. Many businesses have needed to make radical changes in recent years in order to survive and thus have tended to hire executives who "shake the trees, rattle cages, and get things done."
4. In today's marketplace, corporations are often fast-paced, high-risk, and high-profit, with few ethical or legal constraints, which is likely to appeal to sensation-seeking psychopaths.

If you're so unfortunate as to work for an antisocial bully as Freddy does, you need to act fast, before you become seriously depressed. First, sit down and write out everything you can remember of the abusive incidents you've experienced, and continue to document any further episodes. Ask supportive witnesses to do the same. Then take this information to a higher authority in your organization or, if the authority isn't supportive, a lawyer. If your organization allows the bullying to continue, quit, whether you have another job to go to or not, and take legal action if you can.

After Brian leaves, your company hires Natasha to take his place. All the men in the office think Natasha is wonderful, and all the women despise her on sight. Tall and built like a fashion model, she also dresses and walks like one, pirouetting seductively in the common area, swirling her crimson designer cape, before unlocking her office door. She has a soft, alluring voice that becomes even more sensual when she asks someone for a favor.

One day during a meeting, everyone is quietly listening to Bob, one of the marketing people, do a presentation when suddenly Natasha's hand flies into the air, bloodred nails and all. "I just have to ask something," she says breathily, as all eyes turn toward her. "Do you really believe this product is worth buying? Do you really believe that in your heart of hearts? I mean really . . ." Bob gapes at her, thrown totally off balance, as Natasha moves to the front of the room and takes over the show.

Several weeks later, you hear shouts and sobs coming from Bart's office. "You told me I could have the Simpson account!" Natasha howls. "You told me! I can't believe anything you say anymore. I'm going to file a grievance and then you'll be sorry." Then come sounds of pleading, and then silence except for muffled sobs into someone's shoulder. In their half cubicles in the common area, the assistants roll their eyes in disgust.

Natasha is a **histrionic** crazymaker. Histrionics are natural-born drama kings or queens. They'll do anything for attention, including using their sexuality and whatever artistic flair they may possess. They can't stand to have people's eyes focused on anyone but themselves, and they throw world-class tantrums any time they feel their needs have been ignored.

The best way to deal with a histrionic crazymaker's tantrums is to ignore them, just as you would the tantrums of a two-year-old. Better yet, act bored, allowing your eyes to wander toward the nearest computer screen. Never reward a tantrum by giving in to it—just let it play itself out.

Natasha's assistant, Beverly, is a sad-looking overweight woman in her midfifties. Beverly is also the office receptionist. You think you ought to like Beverly, because she's always doing nice things for people, but you don't. Beverly brings chocolate chip cookies to work, regularly cleans out the department refrigerator, and is always willing to do others' work when they're overloaded. It makes you feel terrible to dislike somebody who does all these nice things, but you can't help it.

From twelve to one every day, another worker relieves Beverly while she sits in the lounge and eats her sandwich from a brown paper bag. One day, you sit down next to her with some leftovers you just warmed up in the microwave. "I sure wish they'd turn the air-conditioning on," you say. "It's getting hotter by the minute. Do you mind if I open the window?"

"No, that's fine, I don't mind," Beverly answers meekly, drawing her sweater around her as soon as you've propped the window open.

"Oh, I'm sorry—is that too cold for you?" you ask.

"No, no, I'm all right." She sighs and rubs her hands together as though they're in danger of being frostbitten. You know you should just get up and close the window again, but you're too annoyed with Beverly, who reminds you of your mother, for guilt-tripping you instead of saying what she wants.

She coughs, not very realistically. "I have an awful sore throat," she says with a pained look. "I think I'm coming down with something." She pauses, but you still don't close the window, feeling like a monster but unable to move.

Tension builds in the room until suddenly Beverly picks up her half-eaten sandwich and rushes out the door, sniffling and blowing her nose, just as Morris, another coworker, comes in with his salad and gives you a puzzled look. You spend the rest of the day hating yourself and hating Beverly even more for making you hate yourself.

Beverly, like Natasha, is a histrionic crazymaker, but of the **passive-aggressive** variety. Passive-aggressive crazymakers push you away by refusing to acknowledge negative feelings or tell you what they want. Often they're people of low status who lack the energy or problem-solving ability to improve their lots in life. They have a million subtle ways of expressing anger. These include bad-mouthing you behind your back, sabotaging your work, sniffing, snorting, sighing, rolling eyes, choosing words or phrases that imply criticism, or giving you the silent treatment. Many of their tactics are designed to make a conscientious person feel guilty. While they never shout and throw things as histrionics do, it's helpful to treat all of these more subtle behaviors as disguised tantrums. Trying to get a passive-aggressive to make a decision is enough to make you want to stuff yourself with chocolate bars. They leave the decision up to you, but you'd better guess right, because if you don't, they'll say something that makes you feel as though you should never have been born.

To survive encounters with passive-aggressives, you need to accept the fact that they're simply unable to verbalize their own needs, and do it for them. Tell them what their actions tell you and act accordingly. In the case of Beverly, for example, tell her that you can see by the way she's rubbing her hands that she wants you to close the window, then do so. If she protests and begs you to open it again, stick to your guns. Don't get tied up in knots trying to figure out if you're a terrible person or not; either take some type of action or walk away.

After you get back from lunch, Jason, another coworker, stomps into your office and sits down in the chair opposite your desk, clenching his fist. "I have a question for you," he says. His voice has a nasty, suspicious quality, that of a batterer questioning his wife about infidelity, and you feel your gut tighten as he leans toward you. "Why didn't you give me Bart's message about the deadline for the Foster contract being moved up? Bart told me he told you to tell me."

Frantically, you search your memory of your last meeting with Bart and draw a blank. "I'm sorry," you say, "I just don't remember. There was so much going on at the time . . ."

Jason pounds your desk with his fist. "Don't try to make excuses," he growls. "You think I don't know what you're up to. You thought if you didn't tell me I'd miss the deadline and you'd get the associate job instead of me, didn't you? Oh, I know how you people think—you're all against me. Well, you'd better just hope I get that job, because you're going to pay for it if I don't, pay for it big-time! You're all going to pay!"

Jason not only gets no promotion, he gets fired after several other employees file complaints against him for harassment. He leaves making threats against everyone and is later apprehended by a security guard trying to enter the building with a loaded gun.

Jason is a **paranoid** crazymaker. Of all types of personality disorders, this is the most dangerous. Most domestic abusers are paranoid crazymakers, as are virtually all those who commit mass public shootings and emotionally kidnap people into cults, though only a few act out their paranoia in such extreme ways. Paranoids can't stand ambiguity. Life is filled with random events, but to them nothing is random. Everything has to mean something, and their minds work overtime trying to force all the details into a coherent whole, which generally amounts to some type of conspiracy. Paranoid crazymakers are masters of mistrust who view themselves as victims and others as relentless, united persecutors upon whom they frequently try to take revenge.

If you run into a paranoid crazymaker, be careful. Never try to tell a paranoid that he or she is imagining things, which will only make the person see you as part of the conspiracy. Nor should you try to convince a paranoid that you are trustworthy. You can't. Don't try to be a hero—it's both futile and dangerous. Have as little to do with the paranoid as you can, and if you have to deal with the person, keep your wits about you. These people can be great at hypnotizing others into believing their craziness. Don't allow them to isolate you from others. Talk to someone outside of the workplace about the paranoid crazymaker and start looking for an escape route. This is not a safe place to be.

The crazymakers just described are only some of the types found in books on personality disorders, but I believe they're the ones you're most likely to run into at work. Knowing something about them may save your sanity and perhaps even your life. I will talk more in part 3 about how to deal with some of the specific ways crazymakers can behave.

Blues and Battleshock Busters

1. Avoid crazymakers as much as possible. "Of the thirty-six alternatives," says a Chinese proverb, "running away is the best."
2. Don't waste precious energy trying to change a crazymaker. Only life experiences or years of the right kind of therapy can do that, and even then, the odds aren't great.
3. Address problems with crazymakers immediately and decisively, especially broken agreements. Don't get caught up in endless lose-lose conflicts with yourself over how to deal with them. Don't waste time and energy rehearsing speeches you'll never make.
4. Ask yourself if a crazymaker reminds you of anyone in your past and how your current situation differs. Consider what, if any-

thing, you might be avoiding by keeping the crazymaker in your life. What are your fears?

5. Don't allow crazymakers to hypnotize you. Make sure you retain the capacity for logical, critical thinking, and try to think before you act.

6. Maintain an appearance of strength even if you feel weak and scared inside.

7. Don't accept a role in a melodrama with a crazymaker. If you find yourself acting out emotions, behaving in ways that aren't "you," or wondering if you're crazy yourself, that's probably what's happening. Ask yourself if you're playing the role of victim, persecutor, or rescuer in the drama. According to personality-disorder specialist Greg Lester—upon whose training seminar much of this chapter was based—dramas with crazymakers typically involve these three roles, and they're great at switching roles when you least expect it, forcing you into a different one. For example, a dependent crazymaker might play the victim by begging you for help with a project, casting you in the role of rescuer, then turn persecutor by demanding that you give up more and more of your time, making you the victim. If this happens, rather than play the new role, walk away.

8. Watch an episode of *The Office* or *Mad Men* or read through a book of *Dilbert* cartoons. Which characters, if any, do you see as crazymakers? What types of personality disorders do they have? How do the non-crazymakers deal with them? Try to identify dramas involving persecutors, rescuers, and victims. Who plays which role? Does any character switch roles, and if so, how does this affect the others?

6

Sometimes It's About You

As challenging as office life may be, none of us arrives on the scene empty-handed. Each of us comes laden with baggage—attitudes and past experiences—that can have a huge effect on how we respond to the people and events in our daily work lives. If you want to get past the blues and battleshock and start feeling really good at work, at some point you have to start opening up your bags and taking a look at what's inside them.

First, you need to get yourself a journal, if you don't have one already; and, if possible, take some time off to retreat and reflect. A weekend at a lake cabin is ideal, but an evening in your own attic will do. If you're not into writing, another option is to go with someone else—preferably not someone from your own office—who needs to retreat and reflect too, or to go with a group, and spend your time talking as well as writing about how your personal experiences relate to your office life. As you open up these six "bags"—i.e., topics to think, write, or talk about—don't be surprised if a few unsavory things fly out. That's what's supposed to happen. Facing previously unacknowledged facts about yourself or your loved ones can be painful, but it can also be enormously liberating. So let's get started.

Bag #1: The Meaning of Work

To John, an only son who grew up in a small Nebraska town, work means pride, male identity, and independence. To Betty, the child of a single mother in a poor neighborhood in Detroit, work is a means to a better life for oneself and others. To Yang, who grew up in mainland China under communism, work means sacrificing oneself for the greater good.

Each of us grows up receiving different messages from those around us about the meaning of work, some positive, some negative. In the book of Genesis, work is presented as a punishment for original sin—though the New Testament presents a more positive view of work as a means of serving God by serving others—and the "Protestant ethic," a phrase used by sociologist Max Weber for a phenomenon that is still very much a part of Western culture, treats work as a form of discipline by means of which one purifies one's soul. Other cultures regard work very differently. In Zen Buddhism, work is considered a form of meditation, and "right livelihood" means finding work that is socially just. Work can be experienced as a burden, a punishment, a purifier, a battle, a means of salvation, a form of tyranny, an addiction, an annoyance, an identity, a pastime, a source of pride, a means of connecting, a path to enlightenment, or a joy to be savored for its own sake.

The messages we receive from others about work have a powerful influence on how we come to see it ourselves. Take a few minutes to consider what your own caregivers, community, culture, or past work experiences have taught you so far about the nature of work. What types of work did your parents and grandparents do? What do you remember them saying about work? Did they talk about it in positive or in negative terms? Did you ever feel neglected by them because of their work? What chores did they expect you to do, and how did you feel about them? Did they work with you, or expect you to do things on your own? Did they encourage you to earn or save money as a child or adolescent? Were they supportive of your schoolwork and your career ambitions? What did your teachers, counselors, and peers communicate to you about work?

If your caregivers neglected you because of their work, allowed themselves to be exploited, or failed to earn a living or support your own career efforts, you may feel sad or angry. Don't try to fight these feelings, but explore them.

After reminiscing for a while, move on to considering how the attitudes about work you grew up with have affected how you feel toward your present job. Are you resentful that you have to work at all because you were taught that a woman is supposed to stay home, or that work is a man's burden? Do you feel you have to overwork or sacrifice your own career interests for those of others, or sacrifice your present happiness for the sake of the future? Were you taught that you could succeed at work or that you were doomed to fail?

The benefit of looking at the past is not to relive it but to think about what you might be habitually doing that was adaptive *only* to the past, not to the present. If you are the middle child in a large family, for example, it might have been adaptive to knock yourself out to get all As so as to get Mom and Dad's attention, but over-achieving might not be so adaptive now that you're grown up and need to spend time nurturing relationships with family and friends.

Bag #2: The Meaning of Office Work

I graduated from Oberlin College in 1970. Oberlin is a school that has both an excellent conservatory—the initial reason I went there, starting out as a violin major—and a liberal arts college that has a long, distinguished tradition of political activism. Founded in the 1830s, it was the first U.S. college to admit both men and women and one of the first predominantly white colleges to admit African Americans. It played an active role in civil rights, from the Underground Railroad to the twentieth-century civil rights movement. My freshman year at Oberlin was 1966, when U.S. involvement in the Vietnam War was just ramping up. The years that followed were not only marked by constant political protest at Oberlin and elsewhere but by questioning and challenging of authority on every level.

Although I was never one to jump on the bandwagon politically, my personal life was nevertheless affected by Oberlin's and my generation's cultures of protest and social consciousness. At places like Oberlin, the attitude that one should not simply buy into whatever the authorities came up with but take a good hard look at it first had a big influence on how we baby boomers looked at our prospective careers. A certain mythology arose in which all of the larger institutions in society—business, government, schools, the military—were lumped together in a single allegorical entity known as the Establishment. People were divided into two categories: "Straights" and "Freaks." Straights were conformists who did what they were told and whose only goal was to make money by pleasing the Establishment. Freaks were those who might play along temporarily in order to survive but had nobler ambitions than to wind up with a house in the suburbs. They were the good, creative people who were interested in doing something that was "socially relevant," i.e., would make the world better in some way, unlike the inferior Straights, who were blind to the sufferings of the oppressed and cared only about being good cogs in the Establishment wheel.

No one at Oberlin in the sixties had plans to go to business school, which would have been unthinkable. If you planned to spend your life selling real estate, you kept this to yourself. Acceptable career options were to go to medical school; to get a law degree and become a public defender like Ralph Nader; to go teach in Appalachia; to join the peace corps; to join a commune in Colorado; to become a social worker, a nurse, or a writer; to sing or play in a rock group; or to go to graduate school in one of the liberal arts. That was about it. While it was recognized that you might have to compromise your principles by temporarily taking a job for the Establishment in order to realize your higher ambitions, such jobs—office, factory, or service—were referred to as (excuse my French) "shit jobs" that you endured only as long as you had to.

Needless to say, these idealistic but snobby views had an effect on my attitude and work ethic when, after graduating, I discovered that the world was not beating down my door as I'd been led to expect, and my first job was that of a clerk-typist. While I told myself that there were no real shit jobs except those that required you to hurt someone, and that all jobs at organizations that did something worthwhile were worthy of respect, it was hard to shake off the feeling that my routine office work was anything but throwaway time.

By the eighties and nineties, attitudes toward office work even among Oberlin grads had changed as countless hippies reinvented themselves into yuppies, but while I no longer thought of my job in such simplistic terms, the rebel, the questioner of authority that my college years helped to shape, is still very much a part of who I am. This has been both a blessing and a curse. Because I haven't always settled for being a good wheel cog, life has taken me some interesting places, but during times when I've been forced to do routine work just to survive, my attitude has resulted in restlessness and office blues.

That's my story; what's yours? What forces shaped your own attitude toward office work? Did you grow up seeing it as glamorous but out of reach to your own social class, or menial and spelling failure? Was it what Mommy or Daddy did, or was it what other people's mommies and daddies did? Which books, TV shows, movies, and cartoons helped to shape your attitude toward the office world? How did gender, race, class, personal attractiveness, and other characteristics shape the roles people played in the office world? What was going on when your particular generation came of age, and how has this affected your attitude toward office work? Your answer may be very different depending on your age group. Do some writing about what office work means to you in light of your history.

Bag #3: Why You Took This Job

When I was in training as a social worker, my first internship was in a clinic where we did couples therapy. One question I learned to ask couples was what attracted them to each other in the first place. Often I'd find that as they'd struggled to cope with the stresses of daily life, they'd forgotten why they decided to get married, and going back to square one would help them to reconnect. I suggest you take the same approach in order to reconnect to your job. Think back to the time when your job was just an idea at the back of your mind. Now ask yourself three questions:

1. Why did you look for a job at all—any job?
2. Why did you apply for an office job?
3. Why did you apply for and accept *this* office job?

The following are some possibilities that may help you get started. Check the responses that seem to apply to you.

1. Why did you look for a job at all—any job?
    - ❏ I didn't want to starve.
    - ❏ I had a family to support.
    - ❏ I needed health insurance.
    - ❏ I needed to put the kids through college.
    - ❏ I needed to save for retirement.
    - ❏ I wanted to buy or help buy a home.
    - ❏ I wanted to save some money so I could go back to school.
    - ❏ I wanted to save some money to start my own business.
    - ❏ I wanted to get out of debt.
    - ❏ I was raised to think work was just what a man did.
    - ❏ I got tired of asking my husband for money.
    - ❏ I lost my business.
    - ❏ I didn't want to be a burden to _____.
    - ❏ My parents kicked me out of the house.
    - ❏ My spouse nagged me.
    - ❏ I was bored at home.
    - ❏ I thought I'd be happier if I worked.
    - ❏ I'm happier working than not working.
    - ❏ I wanted to get off welfare.
    - ❏ I thought it would help my self-esteem.
    - ❏ Add your own: _____.

2. Why did you apply for an office job?
    - ❏ It was the only kind of work I was qualified for.
    - ❏ The salary and benefits were good.
    - ❏ I thought it would be fun.
    - ❏ I thought I'd be good at it.
    - ❏ I wanted to work my way up to president of the company.
    - ❏ It had more status than working on an assembly line.

❏ I hated being a waiter/housecleaner/factory worker/ _____
_____.

❏ My back gave out.

❏ I wanted regular hours.

❏ I wanted to have my nonwork time to myself.

❏ I was raised to believe that offices were just where you worked.

❏ It's what I did in the military.

❏ It's what my parents did.

❏ I didn't get to do _____.

❏ I couldn't do _____ anymore.

❏ Add your own: _____.

3. Why did you apply for and accept *this* office job?

❏ It was all there was.

❏ They recruited me.

❏ I got promoted to it.

❏ I got demoted to it.

❏ I saw an ad.

❏ It was posted on a Web site.

❏ Someone sent me an e-mail.

❏ A friend of mine already worked here.

❏ I worked here before and came back.

❏ I heard it was a great place to work.

❏ The salary was good.

❏ The benefits were good.

❏ The people seemed nice.

❏ I was impressed with my boss.

❏ I liked the location.

❏ It was close to where I live.

❏ I liked the building.

❏ I got to have my own office.

❏ The work seemed interesting.

❏ It was really high-tech.

❏ I thought I could learn something.

❏ I wanted to get into the organization.

❏ I saw it as a stepping-stone on the way to _____.

❏ I wanted to get some office experience.
❏ The type of business interested me.
❏ I believed in what the organization did.
❏ I felt safe here.
❏ I thought it was a job I could be good at.
❏ They provided child care.
❏ The hours were flexible.
❏ I could work part-time.
❏ I liked the atmosphere.
❏ I felt like they needed me.
❏ I thought I'd be happy here.
❏ I was tired of waiting for something to come along.
❏ I was desperate.
❏ The boss thought it would be a better fit for me.
❏ I must be a masochist.
❏ Add your own: _____.

After you've checked off the applicable responses to each of these questions and/or added your own, look back over them. Which factors weighed most heavily with you? How many of the factors you checked off have to do with someone else, and how many have to do with you? How many have to do with the mere fact of the job being open and offered to you, how many have to do with the quality of the job itself, and how many have to do with where the job might get you in the future? Ask yourself how your job decision relates to the way you made other decisions, such as your choice of college, home, or mate. Do you tend to make decisions rationally, with a cost-benefit analysis, or to just "do what feels right"? Did you discuss your decision with anyone? What sort of advice did you receive? How did you feel when you got the job offer?

Now look back over your list and compare your actual job with what you hoped and expected it would be. Are there ways in which you've been disappointed? Have there been some good surprises? Do you feel that your prospective employers presented you with a true picture of how things would be? If not, how do you feel about this?

Bag #4: The Career You Left Behind

When your parents' friends asked you what you wanted to be when you grew up, did you say you wanted to be a database manager or an administrative assistant? Probably not. You most likely said you wanted to be a ballerina or a baseball pitcher, or maybe a doctor or a teacher. Maybe you took the first steps toward fulfilling those fantasies when you got into your high school and college years, or maybe your fantasies changed when you took a course with an inspiring teacher or discovered a talent you hadn't known you had. Maybe you worked hard to try to make your dreams come true and maybe you even managed to do what you loved part-time or on a piecemeal basis, but were unable to find a way to make a decent living at it, because either you weren't good enough or others weren't fair enough, or because the opportunities simply weren't there. Or maybe you did manage to make a living doing what you loved for a while, but then the stock market plummeted, your world caved in, and now here you are, longing for yesterday. Maybe as you sit at your office desk your heart is aching over unrealized career dreams, as in Langston Hughes's poem "Harlem":

> *What happens to a dream deferred?*
> *Does it dry up*
> *like a raisin in the sun?*
> *Or fester like a sore—*
> *And then run?*
> *Does it stink like rotten meat?*
> *Or crust and sugar over—*
> *like a syrupy sweet?*
> *Maybe it just sags*
> *like a heavy load.*

> Or does it explode?

When Al was in elementary school, he began playing the clarinet, and as he grew older and his talent blossomed, he came to love classical music and dreamed of becoming a clarinetist in the New York Philharmonic. Al played well enough to get into a conservatory, and although he'd come to realize that the NYP was unlikely to hire him, he knew that there were other, less prestigious symphonies for which he might audition. When Al graduated, however, he was dismayed to discover that there were only four openings in the whole country for full-time symphony clarinetists. Year after year, he tried out for these few jobs while struggling to make a living teaching and playing in part-time professional groups, but he was never offered a full-time position. Then Al fell in love and got married, and he and his wife began to talk about having children. It was time to get real, he decided. Al was good at math, and after taking a few business courses, he wound up with a job as a financial assistant. Although he received several promotions in his job, Al still felt like a failure. Nobody at Al's office had any idea, as he sat at his desk daydreaming in the late afternoons, that he was hearing the beautiful clarinet solo from the opening of George Gershwin's "Rhapsody in Blue" in his mind and was filled with an almost unbearable sadness.

Because society needs so many more secretaries, financial assistants, computer programmers, and proofreaders than it does clarinetists, ballerinas, professional basketball players, or even doctors, college professors, and psychotherapists, offices are populated by large numbers of people who would rather be doing something else, many of whom have a history of failing to realize their dreams. Their suffering is made worse by "American Dream" movies that make us believe that if we want something enough and work hard enough for it, we can get it, which may cause them to blame themselves. Unfortunately, in real life it doesn't always work the way it does in the movies. In real life, having the wrong brain chemistry, the wrong height, the wrong fingers, or even just the wrong luck, as Malcolm Gladwell demonstrates in *Outliers*, often *can* keep your dreams from coming true, temporarily or permanently, no matter how hard you try. In real life too, love often trumps career fulfillment, as in

Al's story, though the unfulfilled career still remains inside you, yearning to be realized as you go about your daily office duties.

Now consider your career dreams, assuming you had any that haven't been realized. (If you didn't, you can skip the rest of this section.) What were your childhood dreams? How did they change as you grew older? Did you begin laying the groundwork for fulfilling them? What happened? What caused you to let go of your dreams? Would they now be impossible to realize, as in the case of a would-be Olympic figure skater who becomes too old, or could you still bring them at least partially into being? If they're not impossible, what steps could you take now toward actualizing them? Are there ways in which your job might contribute to your doing so, either by providing income or by providing you with some type of experience you could use?

Do some talking or writing in response to these questions, then take a break and go for a swim, listen to soothing music, or do something else that gives you comfort. Thinking about your lost career can be painful, especially if you believe the gates to be irrevocably closed. If you haven't allowed yourself to begin grieving your lost career, you can expect to spend some time over the coming weeks on an emotional roller coaster, but sooner or later you must go through this, not around it, if you want to start making the most of what life has given you. Grief is not something you need to be ashamed or afraid of, but a journey that ultimately leads to a clearer sense of your own purpose in life and to greater compassion toward others. As you begin to grow in your job and reach out to your coworkers, you'll probably find that you're not the only one in your office grieving a lost career dream. Sharing your sadness with others can be a powerful way of connecting, and connection is what needs to happen for you to pull out of the blues.

Bag #5: Your Life Outside of Work

What's happening in your life when you're not at work can have a big impact on how you feel at work, and vice versa. How does your extra-work life affect your office days? Do you go to work exhausted from battles with family members or roommates? Do you spend too much time partying and go to work with a headache? Are you sitting up late studying for courses or doing night shifts as a crisis counselor? Do you have a second job and, if so, are you doing the same thing you do at your regular job or something different? Do you spend time sitting at a computer at home after sitting at a computer all day at work? Do you spend your evenings in front of the TV? How much satisfaction does this bring you? Do you travel a lot? How does this affect your work life? Are you able to live within your means or are you up to your ears in debt? What effect has your financial situation had on your employment options?

Now look at how your work life affects your extra-work life. Does your work schedule enable you to spend time with family and friends? If not, what effect is this having on your relationships? Does your schedule allow you to give your children, pets, or dependent relatives adequate care and, if not, how are you dealing with this? Do you have interests that your schedule won't allow you to pursue? How do you squeeze in errands, home maintenance, and medical appointments? Do you have an extracurricular passion you'd like more time to pursue? Is cutting back your hours to part-time a realistic option? Is your passion something you could do part-time and get paid for?

As you consider these questions, you'll begin to realize that work and "life" aren't two separate spheres, but are continually interwoven, so that the way to improve one is often to make changes in the other. We'll talk about what extra-work changes you might make to improve your office life in chapter 10.

Bag #6: Self-defeating Habits

Finally, whatever baggage you might bring to the workplace and however challenging your situation, there comes a time when you have to ask yourself if you've developed any habits that could be contributing to your own office blues and battleshock. This can be difficult. It's so much easier to see yourself as an innocent victim of circumstances than to look in the mirror. Some people engage in incredible mental acrobatics in order to avoid confronting themselves.

On April 22, 1979, an article in the *San Francisco Sunday Examiner* described a driver's account of an accident:

> As I approached an intersection, a sign suddenly appeared in a place where a stop sign had never appeared before. I was unable to stop in time to avoid an accident. The telephone pole was approaching. I was attempting to swerve out of its way when it struck my front end.

This is what we don't want to do, and yet all of us fall into it at times, telling ourselves that the mean old world just has it out for poor little us instead of asking ourselves what *we* might have done differently. When we do muster up the strength to look at ourselves, we may discover that some of our habits are just plain self-defeating. If and when you come to such a realization, you should be glad, for if you're the one who's causing your own misery—which may or may not be the case—then that's a lot easier to fix than if it's someone or something else.

What kinds of behaviors might office workers engage in that might worsen or even bring on blues and battleshock? Here are some possibilities:

Setting yourself up to feel guilty: Do you regularly do things you know might get you into trouble and then worry about what might happen? For example, do you spend half your work time surfing the Internet, all the while fearful that your boss will begin to notice what you're doing? It's hard to be happy when your conscience is troubling you.

Clutter and chaos: Is your desk covered with an ocean of papers? Is your hard drive in chaos? Is there trash on the floor of your office? Living in a mess is blues-creating for most of us.

Dysfunctional dances: Do you and someone else at work have the same conversation over and over that always leaves you feeling lousy? Think about changing your lines and there's a good chance the other person will change his or hers.

Self-neglect: Do you stay up too late at night and consequently arrive at work exhausted and perhaps also late? Do you try to make up for your lack of energy by overeating? Do you use coffee, cigarettes, or other substances to try to create an artificial sense of well-being? If you change these habits, you'll be surprised at how much kinder the office world will become.

Negative self-talk: Do you repeat the same negative statements over and over to yourself? How do these make you feel? If you're saying, "This is hopeless," over and over, is it any wonder that you *feel* hopeless?

Knee-jerk blaming and shaming: When something goes wrong, even if it's a hurricane or a forest fire, do you routinely look for someone else to blame? Or do you immediately assume that it's your fault even when it's not? Stop blaming and shaming and start problem solving.

Poor hygiene: Do you go to work without bathing or wear clothes or a hairstyle you know will put off others in your workplace, then feel sorry for yourself because you're lonely? Take a look at yourself and rethink your habits!

Noisemaking: Do you whistle, hum, rattle papers, or talk loudly when others are trying to concentrate? Do the windowpanes rattle when you speak? Then don't be surprised if you get lots of complaints from others.

Inviting hurt: Do you compulsively try to talk to your boss as if he or she is your best friend, then feel hurt when the boss sets professional boundaries? Do you keep trying to change someone who's a crazymaker? Take better care of yourself.

These are just some of the ways we can dig our own office graves. It's mostly a matter of doing something that has negative consequences and then acting as though the consequences came out of nowhere when we ourselves created them. As the twentieth-century cartoon character Pogo used to say, "We have met the enemy, and he is us!"

Blues and Battleshock Busters

1. Go back through old photo albums and look for pictures of yourself doing work, either at home or at a place of employment. What do you remember feeling at the time?
2. Talk to your parents or other older relatives about what work means to them. How does it compare with what it means to you?
3. If one of your parents worked in an office, revisit it and see how it compares with the way you remember it.
4. Get a group of workers from different cultural backgrounds together to talk about what work, office work, and their own jobs mean to them, inviting them to share relevant experiences.
5. Sit down with your significant other or a close friend and talk about how your jobs and personal lives fit together.

PART II

Starting Fresh in the Office:
The First Big Steps

7

Make a Work Companion

Psychotherapist or not, I thought I was going to lose my mind. Six months into my job as an administrative assistant, I continually felt overwhelmed, distraught, miserable, and enraged. Then one Monday morning, after a brief vacation when I'd had a chance to reflect on things, I had an inspiration. I went to the supply cabinet and took out a brand-new spiral notebook with blue pages. On the outside, I wrote the words, "Cindy's Friend." That marked the beginning of my recovery from a major case of office blues and battle-shock.

From then on, I kept the blue spiral notebook next to my computer, clinging to it as though to a life raft in a flood. At first, I used the notebook only to jot down all the incidents that upset me, the "snags" in my day, and to spout off about them. As time went on, I began categorizing different types of snags as I recorded them. After I'd done that for a few weeks, I found I could think more clearly. It occurred to me that it might help me focus if I wrote down the tasks I was trying to do when the snags occurred, placing a checkbox next to them where I could mark when I'd finished the task. When I'd been doing this for several months, I realized that thus far I'd only been noting the bad things that had happened. Maybe if I wrote down the pleasant events as well, I'd become more aware of them and feel better. I called these events boosts, bursts, and flashes, and drew little icons to represent them. Over time, I developed a few more names and pictures. I called this sanity-saving notebook my Work Companion. I'm now about to start filling up my sixth blue spiral notebook, and they remain an important part of my daily work life.

You might think I spent so much time writing in my Work Companion that I got nothing done. Not so. I found that by noting down tasks and snags, I was able to find better ways to deal with them and to work much more efficiently, which more than made up for the writing time. And by allowing myself to vent for a few lines now and then, I saved myself far greater amounts of time obsessing about upsetting incidents and getting nothing done as a result.

As I continued to use my Work Companion over a period of several years, my work life gradually became less tumultuous and more pleasant until I hardly needed it anymore. But I can truly say that when I was completely desperate it saved my sanity and probably my health as well. Thus, if you only do one thing I suggest in this book, I hope you'll at least try making and using a Work Companion. This will require discipline, as you may sometimes have to let an urgent task sit while you scribble something down, but believe me, it's worth it!

In my organizing work, I've sometimes helped women clean out jewelry boxes in which multiple chains were entangled with each other. Teasing these separate chains apart little by little takes a lot of patience, and there's no way you can pull one out of the clump without it affecting all the others, as they're interconnected. The same can be said about the mess of intertwined tasks, events, feelings, and thoughts at the office. The Work Companion can help you to disentangle all these phenomena a little at a time, tugging now at this strand, now at that until eventually everything—both internal and external—is in a new place that works better for you. Note that this doesn't mean separating thoughts from feelings, because feeling and thinking, as neuroscientist Antonio Damasio shows in *Descartes' Error*, are parts of the same process. The Work Companion, then, is not about getting feelings out of the way so you can think but rather learning how to use your feelings to think more clearly.

Although you'll use the data you collect in your Work Companion to figure out what changes you need to make, you'll find that the process of making entries itself is as important as the information. This process helps you to slow down and separate yourself from feelings of anger, frustration, jealousy, or fear in responding to whatever challenges you encounter in the course of your day. Your thoughts become clearer, and your actions more decisive. Instead of floundering in a sea of troubles, you'll be able to take the best next step, dealing with even the most challenging tasks and events one by one instead of trying to do everything at once.

Don't think of your Work Companion as merely a book in which you write a significant amount once a day, as you might in a diary, but as a friend who sits next to you and witnesses everything that happens and with whom you carry on a constant conversation, the way sportscasters converse about a game as it progresses. From now on, no matter what happens at work, you'll no longer have to deal with problems alone.

How to Make Your Work Companion

Your physical Work Companion should feel good to you. I like stenographic spiral notebooks, as they're easy to grab and to open, and the pages are big enough to write a fair amount on. I use a steno pad with blue paper because I find blue soothing. Another good choice is a bound composition book, the kind with the black marbled cover. Bound cloth-covered journals are not as good since they're harder to keep open and may attract attention by looking personal rather than professional.

Some people might prefer to keep their Work Companions in their computers. I don't recommend this, as I believe the act of handwriting will help to ground you emotionally, slowing you down and taking you out of the electronic bubble for a brief spell. A tangible book gives your eyes a badly needed break from the computer screen and feels good in your hands. In addition, a computer Companion may be problematic where privacy is concerned, as anyone who walks into the room might inadvertently read what's on the screen.

The writing implement you use for your Companion should also feel good to you. I use a #2 yellow Paper Mate Sharpwriter automatic pencil because pencils feel more natural to me than pens (wooden pencils would feel even more so, but they require constant sharpening not to become smudgy), and I like being able to erase, but you may prefer something else. If you choose to write in pen, you might want to get a special pen that you use only for your Work Companion, a classy one that weighs heavier in your hand than the cheap, throwaway pens with which offices are typically stocked.

If at all possible, keep your Work Companion next to your computer throughout your workday, with your favorite writing implement handy. If, for security reasons, you don't feel safe doing this, try to keep it in your pocket (you'll need a mini-size Companion for that), in your purse, or in a drawer that's easily accessible. The easier it is for you to get to, though, the more you'll form the habit of using it.

Work Companion Fears

Fear is the enemy of change. Some of your fears about using a Work Companion may be about bad things that could really happen, while other fears may be completely irrational defense mechanisms that will tend to evaporate once you realize that they're counterproductive. Even when fears are reality based, however, you don't have to automatically give in to them. In such cases, you'll need to decide how much you're willing to risk for the sake of your future happiness. You can also strategize about how to minimize genuine dangers. Here are some common Work Companion fears.

Fear #1: Someone Might See What I'm Writing

This is a legitimate fear. The wrong person seeing what you wrote, depending on what that is, could cost you your job. Is anyone at your office likely to look at your Work Companion? To get the maximum benefit from it, you need to feel that it's a safe place where you can record your real feelings, the things you can't say to anyone around you. There are two ways the security of your Companion might be violated. One way is by accident. Someone may be looking for information and start leafing through your notebook, not realizing that it's private. To counter this possibility, I write PRIVATE—KEEP OUT! on the cover of each new Work Companion, draw a skull and crossbones on the outside, and keep a rubber band around it when I'm not in the office in order to get the attention of hard-core daydreamers who might not even notice this warning. This works for me because I have my own office and feel confident that I can trust the people I work with to respect my privacy, but alas, not all office workers are so fortunate.

The other type of Work Companion security violation is deliberate. If this seems likely, you'll need to work extra hard to keep your Work Companion secure. One strategy that you should use no matter how much you trust your boss and coworkers is to always shred or erase passages in which you vent angry feelings toward anyone in your workplace.

Fear #2: I'll Spend Too Much Time Writing to Get Any Work Done

In any job you do have to work, after all, and it's conceivable that some particularly introspective office worker could spend whole days doing nothing but writing in his or her Work Companion. If you find this happening to you, you'll need to set some limits with yourself. You don't have to write everything that happens in your Companion, but the more you use it, the more it will help you. Some days you'll write a lot, and others hardly at all. Think of your Companion as containing a *sample* of your workplace experiences, not a complete record. If you average more than half an hour a day of writing, you're probably doing too much.

Fear #3: My Boss Will See Me as Wasting Time Even If I'm Not

Some bosses may look at things this way, but I believe most will not if they understand what you're doing. Thus, unless you're working for a tyrant, you may want to tell your boss about your Work Companion.

In describing your new tool, emphasize its benefits to your boss's agenda, which is typically to get as much work out of you as possible. Assume that your boss doesn't care if you suffer from the office blues or not, so long as you get the work done. You might say that you're trying an experiment in which you're going to be documenting your work-flow throughout the day. Explain that your purpose is to record snags in the flow so that you can better problem-solve about how to deal with them and work more efficiently. If your boss asks to see what you've written, you can choose a noncompromising page to show him or her.

Fear #4: I Wouldn't Be "Me" If I Did This

This one's totally irrational, as "me" is a construct of your imagination and you have the power to create a new "me" anytime you choose. In all my years as a psychotherapist, I've found that one particular fear more than any other seems to prevent people from finding happiness: the fear of losing their identities if they do something they're not used to doing. Trust me, if you start writing in a Work Companion, you'll still be "you"—just you writing in a Work Companion.

Fear #5: I Won't Keep It Up and Then I'll Feel Like I Failed

Also irrational. This assumes that you have no control over your own behavior, but you do. Only you can decide whether you keep writing in your Work Companion. Furthermore, depending on how natural writing is to you, you may find that doing so feels good, and people are always motivated to do what feels good.

How to Write in Your Work Companion

How you write in your Work Companion is as important as what you write. If your workdays tend to be stressful, each encounter with your Work Companion should constitute a minibreak from that stress. Grabbing it and scribbling a mile a minute is the wrong way to write in it.

The right way is slowly and deliberately, making it easy to read.

Every time you pick up your pen or pencil to write in your Work Companion, slow your breathing and relax any tense muscles. Then take your time as you begin forming words on the page. Notice how the way you do this affects how you feel. I like to print rather than write in cursive, in good-size, first-grade-style letters, because printing gives me a feeling of clarity. I try never to hurry, no matter how many unfinished tasks are screaming to be done. I remind myself that gathering this data will save me time that will more than compensate for the time I'm spending to do it.

Although the process of writing is what matters most, you'll also be looking back through your Companion for patterns, which is another good reason to print rather than write in cursive. Each morning, write out the date, spelling out the month name. This both makes each day's entries easier to find later and helps you to slow down and relax.

For clarity, I use simple symbols to indicate different types of entries—a box to make a check in next to a task, a sun for a burst of pleasure, an arrow for what feels like a poisonous dart, a face with a smile or a frown for a reflection. Using signs and labels helps me to detach myself from emotions that might otherwise overwhelm me. If a task seems overwhelming, writing down the first step as a "task" with a little box next to it makes it feel less so. If a coworker says something that makes me feel attacked, the act of making a little arrow helps me begin processing the emotion before I've even written down what I feel, putting it more at a distance. If I'm worried about something, drawing a cloud before describing it somehow reduces the oppressiveness.

What to Write in Your Work Companion

In almost any job—some more than others—you have to keep a lot of thoughts to yourself. This is especially true if you deal with the public, but even interactions with your boss and coworkers can leave you with all sorts of unspoken, pent-up words yearning to be released, like children on the last day of school. Your Work Companion is your place to put these words. In an office culture where people are often tied up in knots for fear of saying something "inappropriate," everything is appropriate to say to your Work Companion.

However, your Work Companion is not just a place to express feelings. It's also a place to gather data so that you can figure out what problems you need to solve in your workplace life and brainstorm for solutions to them. Rather than simply recording things as they happen, it's helpful to break down the material using labels to help you make sense of what's happening both internally and externally as you write. You may have fun creating your own labels and icons. Eventually, you may end up using only icons, but I recommend that in the beginning you use labels along with them. My own labels include REFLECTIONS, TASKS, SNAGS, DARTS, BOMBS, CLOUDS, FLASHES, BOOSTS, BURSTS, and STARS, defined as follows:

1. **Reflections:** These are simply thoughts and feelings about what's going on. I use plain old smiley and sad faces for reflections, but you may prefer something more creative.

    ☺ *Reflection: Lovely walk to work in the springtime air, a beautiful morning. Am feeling energized and ready to go!*

    ☹ *Reflection: C. is getting on my nerves. I can't stand the way she constantly preaches her "no excuses" philosophy at me, uses a stopwatch to measure the time we spend at lunch, and brown-noses the boss. What's her problem? Question is, can I talk to her about this or do I just have to grin and bear it? I might be able to talk to her, but the time has to be right.*

2. **Tasks:** I write each task down as I begin to work on it, and put a checkbox next to it. That doesn't mean this is my to-do list. It isn't—I make my to-do list, which is much more complex, in Outlook. The purpose of writing tasks in my Work Companion is just to help me focus on the job at hand. If you have a task where you're constantly being interrupted or if you have a brain that's distractible, this can be difficult. Writing down what you're doing right before you do it and checking it off when you're finished can help you stay on track. It also enables you to later connect snags with the particular task that was interrupted.

☐ *Task: Proofread sales report.*
☐ *Task: Call Financial Operations and ask about voucher.*

3. **Snags:** As you begin work on a task, sooner or later you may encounter some sort of a stumbling block, a problem that you have to solve before you can continue with the task, a snag in the flow. At first, you may just wish to confine yourself to the term "snag" with an arrow or other symbol, but as you continue you'll see that snags fall into different categories that can be labeled accordingly. Here are some of the snag types I've used—you may come up with others, depending on what type of work you do:

   Tech snag: A computer, printer, or other machine or online system isn't behaving the way it's supposed to, preventing you from completing your task.

   > *Tech snag: Fax machine didn't receive fax Clara tried to send me.*

   Interrupt snag: Somebody or something interrupts you, diverting your attention from the task at hand.

   > *Interrupt snag: Bob came in, panicking, couldn't find Sampson report and I had to stop and help him look.*

   Communication snag: You misunderstood someone else or the other person misunderstood you.

   > *Communication snag: Susan thought I meant I sent the copy to the printer when I only sent it to the copy editor.*

   Missing-person snag: You try to contact someone who proves to be unavailable.

   > *Missing-person snag: Got a message that Gerald's on vacation so I couldn't get the voucher signed.*

   Missing-paper snag: You need a paper or papers you can't find.

   > *Missing-paper snag: Couldn't find my notes about Lee's changes to detergent ad.*

   Missing-info snag: You need some type of information to complete the task that you don't have.

   > *Missing-info snag: Don't know how to fill out wire transfer forms.*

   Conflict snag: A disagreement prevents you from completing the task.

> *Conflict snag: Allison said I should use a Form F but Judith said to use a Form Y.*

Thought snag: An upsetting thought occurs to you that distracts you from your work.

> *Thought snag: I wrote the date and remembered that this was the day my mother died.*

Error snag: You discover that you've made a mistake.

> *Error snag: I sent the request to the wrong reviewer.*

Brick wall snag: You try to explain something to someone who either doesn't get it or doesn't want to hear what you're saying, and you end up feeling as if you're talking to a wall.

> *Brick wall snag: I couldn't seem to make the woman in Payroll understand that this was an urgent situation.*

Body snag: Something bothers you physically and interferes with your work.

> *Body snag: I'm getting a sore throat.*

These are just a few possibilities. You'll probably think of other snag categories of your own as you begin using your Work Companion, depending on your own particular work situation.

4. **Bombs:** Hopefully you won't experience too many of these. Bombs are much bigger and more upsetting events than snags. They do more than just briefly interrupt your work-flow. They're the kinds of events that blow a hole in your day, maybe in several days. After a bomb goes off, you may need to cry, go for a walk, spend an hour writing, or talk to a friend or a counselor. You may even need to go home or take a mental-health day.

💣 *Bomb! Boss told me he's putting me on probation.*

💣 *Bomb! Sandy told me that Judith has terminal cancer.*

💣 *Bomb! My confidante, Ruth, told the boss everything I said to her about him.*

5. **Darts:** These are smaller events than bombs, but they hurt. People with office battleshock often feel like human targets filled with arrows, which is why I use an arrow to represent a dart. Each time

you feel attacked, unless it's a bomb-size attack, note it down as a dart. Doing this will help you to realize that what feels like a malicious attack often isn't. All of us have sensitivities that others may stir up unintentionally, and most of the time, they're just trying to get their needs met, not destroy our sanity. Or a dart may result from someone else's frustrated response to an error you made—as we all do—that you need to take responsibility for. Though this response can be an overresponse, you need to remember that if you hadn't goofed, there wouldn't have been any dart. Some people become perfectionists trying to avoid ever getting hit with darts, but this is self-defeating, as the constant anxiety the perfectionist feels is almost as unhealthy as being attacked by darts. Remember this: A dart is just a dart is just a dart.

→ *Dart: Boss spent fifteen minutes lecturing me after I messed up his hotel reservation.*

→ *Dart: Brenda made a snide remark in the meeting about "people who always turn in their expense reports late" and was looking right at me.*

6. **Clouds:** These aren't things that happen to you, like snags, but worries about things that *could* happen or vague feelings of uneasiness about an uncompleted task. They tend to take the form of "what if."

    ○ *Cloud: What if Jack's reimbursement still hasn't gone through?*

    ○ *Cloud: What if the boss finds out I forgot to lock up last night?*

7. **Flashes:** These are moments of blazing insight when all becomes clear, ah-has, great ideas. Flashes can be about tasks, about other people, or about yourself.

    ✳ *Flash! I just realized that if I move the Brookings files into my office and put the Smithson files out in the common area, I can save a huge amount of time.*

    ✳ *Flash! I just realized that I've been reacting to Barbara as if she's my mother.*

8. **Boosts:** These are favors others do for you. They include both help with a troublesome task and boosts to your ego in the form of praise. My symbol for them is a hand, as in a helping hand.

    Boost: Boss came in and said I did a great job on the Williamson manuscript.

    Boost: Anita helped me find the form online that I need to hire a consultant.

9. **Bursts:** These are small or large "sunbursts" of pleasure. Recording these is particularly important, as it will help you be more aware of the things that feel good in the course of your workday and to create more of them.

    Burst: Looked out the window and saw a great sunset.

    Burst: Cinnamon coffee cake Janice brought tasted great.

10. **Stars:** These are the equivalent of gold stars that music teachers used to give their pupils. In this case, you give yourself stars for doing things you'd like to do more often, such as self-care activities.

    ★ *Star: Did 5 yoga stretches.*

    ★ *Star: Drank 16 ounces of water.*

What Else to Write in Your Work Companion

So far, except in the case of reflections and tasks, the examples I've given simply consist of noting different kinds of experiences as they occur. This is fine for tasks, flashes, boosts, and bursts, but with the unpleasant events—snags, bombs, darts, and clouds—you may need to do more than that. Along with noting the event, you'll also record how you feel—in most cases in just one or two words—how you responded, and how you might respond differently the next time a similar event occurs. In other words, you'll move in the direction of converting feelings to problem solving.

In writing about negative feelings, try to be honest but brief, and resist the temptation to inflate. Acknowledge your feelings, but don't give them more attention than they merit. Try to look at feelings as data, information about what's going on. The point here isn't to waste precious time and energy wallowing in misery but to take note of the feeling, consider what unsolved problems it signals, and move on to solving those problems. If at all possible, label the feeling with one or two words such as "sad," "angry," "confused," or "scared." If the words that first occur to you are very intense, deflate them to less intense words—change "furious" to "angry," "terrified" to "scared," for example. This will help to detoxify the negative feeling.

The exception to this is when a bomb happens, when the technique of *flooding*—deliberately making your feelings more intense to try to move through them—can be helpful. Just pull out all the stops and try to think like a two-year-old having a tantrum—the crazier the better—until you find yourself getting bored and writing about things in more neutral terms, however long that takes. If it's a big bomb, you may need to do a lot more writing, talking, crying, and big-time processing of feelings over days, weeks, or months to get to this point, perhaps with professional help.

In the case of mere snags, however, once you've labeled your feelings, it's time to proceed to the next step, which is to consider your response to the snag. If you already responded, what were the consequences of your response? Did you just spin your wheels out of frustration or did you do something productive? What else could you have done? What would you do differently next time? If you didn't respond yet, what possible courses of action are open to you and, which is best? (In part 3 of this book, we'll look at some types of snags and provide some suggestions about how to deal with them.) For example:

> *Tech snag: Fax machine didn't receive fax Clara tried to send me. Felt frustrated and aggravated with Roberta for not letting me get the new machine I asked for last week. Gave Clara fax number for machine downstairs. Need to call service line to see what can be done and let Roberta know the outcome of her decision.*

> *Interrupt snag: Bob came in, panicking, couldn't find Sampson report and I had to stop and help him look, which left me feeling irritated and exploited. Actually I didn't have to.*

I could have told him I was tied up with something urgent myself, which I was. Next time I won't fall for it.

In writing about your responses to snags, you may also experience flashes of insight. This will happen more and more as you continue using your Work Companion on a daily basis, and over time, patterns will begin to emerge. When you realize that you're writing for the fifth time that your computer crashed when you performed a certain operation, you may decide it's time to call in a computer expert. When you find yourself writing the same complaint about a coworker over and over, you may decide to have a talk with the person. Human nature is such that we often seem to have to go around in the same circle a certain number of times before we realize that we need to do something different. Getting to this point of realization is what chapter 8 is about.

8

Make a Job Transformation Plan

"Most creative persons," psychologist Mihaly Cziksentmihalyi writes, "don't follow a career laid out for them, but invent their job as they go along." While you've been using your Work Companion to get through each day, you've also been doing something else: gathering valuable data about your work life. Now you can use this information to figure out what issues you're dealing with as well as what to do about them. Your task in this chapter is to convert your Work Companion data into a Job Transformation Plan, a roadmap for changing blues and battleshock into peace and quality of life in the office.

Spend an Evening with Your Work Companion

When you've been writing in your Work Companion for two or three months, take it home with you for just one evening. On your way home, stop at an office supply store and pick up a box of different-colored highlighters and a second spiral notebook. Then, after dinner, put some quiet music on and settle back in your favorite

chair with a cup of tea and your Work Companion. On the outside
of your new notebook, write the words JOB TRANSFORMATION PLAN-
NER. Open the first page and write the date, just as you would in
your Work Companion. Then open your Work Companion. Your job
tonight is to look for patterns in what you've written over the last
months, noting them down and exploring them in writing. I suggest
doing this work at home or somewhere else away from work, as
physical distance from your workplace may help you to think more
objectively about what goes on there.

"But my time belongs to me!" you may want to shout. "I go
home to get *away* from work. I don't want to waste any of my precious personal time thinking about what I'd rather forget." Of course
you don't want to, but do it anyway.

Do a Quantitative Analysis

When social scientists gather data about human beings, they have
different ways of analyzing it. One way is to do a *quantitative* analysis, which means using numbers, and another is to do a *qualitative*
analysis, which involves words. Your analysis of your Work Companion data should be both quantitative and qualitative. Let's start
with the numbers. Here's what to do.

Step 1: Tally Up
After today's date, write QUANTITATIVE ANALYSIS and underline it,
then list each possible type of Work Companion entry (see chapter 7
for a list). Then go back and tally up the number of each type in your
Work Companion and record the numbers. For example:

Reflections: 20   Communication snags: 5
Tasks: 80   Missing-person snags: 3
Snags: 122   Missing-paper snags: 20
Tech snags: 15   Missing-info snags: 22
Interrupt snags: 30   Thought snags: 5

Error snags: 17   Flashes: 18
Brick wall snags: 5   Boosts: 2
Bombs: 1   Bursts: 3
Darts: 25   Stars: 30
Clouds: 17

Step 2: Identify the Issues

Now look back at the numbers. What is the story they tell? What problems do they reveal? This will vary from category to category. Here are some rough guidelines for interpreting the numbers in each category, assuming that you're looking at one month's regular, frequent entries in your Work Companion:

Snag types, darts, and clouds: 0–5=not a big problem; 5–10= could be a problem; 10–15=you need to look at this; over 15=a major problem.

Bombs: 1–2=you need to look at this; 3–5=a major problem; over 5=you're working in a disaster area—why?

Flashes: 0–5=you're not an idea person—be sure to keep an open mind toward those who are; 5–10=you have some ideas, but not so many you're likely to get off track; over 10=you may have more ideas than you're able to put into effect easily.

Boosts: 0–5=either you're not getting much support from others or you're not aware of it when you do; 5–10=you're getting some support but could do with more; 10–15=you're getting plenty of support; over 15=you're getting so much support you may begin to feel smothered.

Bursts: 0–10=you experience little pleasure at work; 10–30=you experience occasional moments of pleasure that help you get through the day; 30–60=you have some fun at work, but you still get things done; over 60=your workplace is a country club.

Stars: 0–10 = you need to take better care of yourself at work; 10–30 = you're doing a fair job at self-care; 30–50 = you're doing a good job at self-care; over 50 = you're doing a great job at self-care.

These numbers are only rough estimates, and you'll need to factor in how much you write in your Work Companion and what categories matter the most to you. If your numbers are like those listed in the tallies in Step 1, and you've made regular, frequent entries over the course of a month, you might draw the following conclusions, among others:

Snags: 122

> **Tech snags:** = 15 Things could be better in the tech department. You need to look at specifics and see if equipment needs repairing or replacing or if you need to let someone know that an online system is repeatedly malfunctioning.
>
> **Interrupt snags:** = 30 Interruptions are a major problem for you. You need to figure out who the primary interrupters are and perhaps ask for some quiet time when you can close your door and work undisturbed.
>
> **Missing-paper snags:** = 20 Your paper management skills need work.
>
> **Missing-info snags:** = 22 You may need to reorganize your information, acquire more training, or hook up with better resources in some areas.
>
> **Error snags:** = 17 You need to do some troubleshooting to identify problem areas and try to reduce the number of mistakes you make, which both cost you time when you have to redo things and provoke negative feedback from others that can affect your mood.

Darts: 25 = you frequently feel attacked in your workplace. In other words, you experience pain on a daily basis. You need to figure out what this is about and do something about it *now*, before you become clinically depressed or physically ill. You don't deserve to be hurt!

Clouds: 17=you worry a lot, perhaps because you so often feel attacked.

Flashes: 18=you're a highly insightful person. This means you're almost sure to think your way to a more rewarding work life, though you may need to work to keep from getting distracted by your many great ideas.

Boosts: 2=either you get little support from your boss or coworkers and need to find ways to get more, or you're not tuning in to the kindness of others as much as you could. Work to build more positive connections and offer help to others.

Bursts: 3=you experience few moments of pleasure in your job and may not take note of them when you do. Doing something about this may help you pull out of the office blues.

Stars: 30=you're doing a good job of taking care of yourself at work.

Step 3: Troubleshoot and Problem-Solve
Now revisit each issue, with the goal of pinpointing the exact problems you're dealing with and figuring out what to do about them. The key word here is "specific." Often you may find that problems are smaller and more easily solved than you think. Look at one type of entry at a time, beginning with the snags. Don't worry if solutions don't immediately pop into your head for all the problems you identify. What's important at this point is just to get the process started.

Here are some things to keep in mind for each type of entry.

Snags
Go back to your Work Companion and highlight those types of snags you experienced most frequently. They're your most significant problem areas. Use different colors for different snag types, which will make them easy to see. Then look at all the occurrences of one of these snag types, such as missing-paper snags; let's say you've

highlighted these blue. What do all the blue entries have in common? Are most of the papers you can't find of one particular type, say, sales reports? What change could you make to solve the problem and reduce the frustration you experience from all those frantic paper hunts? Could you move the sales reports into a particular file where they'll be easier to find?

Each time you recognize a new pattern, list it in your Job Transformation Planner, then explore it in writing. For example:

> *Tech snags: My mouse keeps freezing up. Must have a loose connection. Maybe I should try a wireless mouse. Will talk to the computer people about this.*

> *Interruption snags: Many of the interruptions are from people in the marketing department asking questions I could answer collectively. I need to schedule a meeting with them.*

> *Missing-information snags: I keep having to leaf through the big manual that has a zillion pages explaining how to use the various financial systems. I need to make myself a cheat sheet so I can get to the most important information more easily.*

Darts

The big question with darts is always this: Is it me, is it them, or is it both? When the pain from a dart was still smarting, you might not have been able to make an honest assessment of this, but after some time has gone by and you're in a more analytical frame of mind, you may be able to see things more clearly. Here are some questions to ask yourself as you look back through all your darts:

1. Who were the dart throwers who repeatedly made you feel attacked?

2. How many darts were in response to an error that you made? Do you think now that the person's response was out of proportion to the error? Do you always feel pain when you're corrected even when the correcting is done kindly? What is this about?

3. How many darts were in response to errors that someone thought you made that you didn't? In other words, were you being blamed unjustly?

4. How many darts were merely results of miscommunication? Of these, who failed to understand whom? Do you find it painful when someone doesn't understand you, or when you don't understand someone else? What is this about?

5. How many darts were related to your own memory or concentration failures? Do you seem to have more memory or concentration problems than others do?

6. Was the dart thrower frustrated by your inability to meet some sort of need that he or she had? If so, what was the need? Was it your responsibility to fill it or could you have directed the person elsewhere?

7. Was the dart thrower mostly talking about *you* or simply about something you *did*? The former is more likely to be bullying— which has to do with the dart thrower, not with you—than the latter. If the dart thrower attacked you and not just your work, what weapons did he or she use? Nasty names? One-liners? Threats? Talking behind your back? Group attacks?

8. What automatic thoughts went through your mind when you felt attacked? What patterns do you see in these thoughts? (I'll present some possibilities later in this chapter.)

9. What was the dart thrower's situation? Was he or she under a lot of stress? Do you know anything about the person's past that might account for the dart-throwing behavior?

10. Did you try to talk with the dart thrower about the attacks? With anyone else? Do you think you still should?

For example,

→ *I often feel attacked when Mary corrects my mistakes even though she tries to be nice. Something in her tone of voice makes me feel like she's adding up the numbers in her mind and is thinking about whether to fire me or not. Is this my imagination or is that really what's going on? Maybe I need to just ask her how she thinks I'm doing.*

→ *Ricardo gets annoyed when I ask him a question about
something he thinks he told me before. I don't think this is
fair. Do I really have to have a perfect memory? A human
being isn't a perfect tape recorder. I do write things down,
but sometimes he goes so fast it's impossible to catch everything, and sometimes details slip through the cracks. I've
said this to him, but it doesn't seem to sink in. Maybe he
feels insecure about his ability to communicate effectively in
English, which is his second language. Reassuring him that
he's not a bad communicator seems to help.*

Bombs
These may require more in-depth exploration than snags or darts.
Think back to the time when the bomb went off. What happened?
How did you feel? How long did it take you to recover and what was
this process like for you? Were you bothered by repetitive thoughts or
feelings of anxiety afterward? Did these affect your appetite, your
sleep, your ability to experience pleasure, or your relations with others? Did you talk with anyone about the bomb, and if so, how did he
or she respond? Did you get counseling help? How do you feel about
the event now? For example:

💣 *The day I got the e-mail announcing that Bob would be
getting the promotion I thought I was getting, I felt like
I'd been socked in the stomach. I didn't want anyone to
know I was upset, so I managed to stay at my desk, but I
got almost nothing done. All I could think about was what
mistakes I might have made that cost me a promotion that
I felt I deserved more than Bob did. Then I began to wonder if my own qualifications even had anything to do with
it. Was age a factor? Was I a victim of gender discrimination? Should I talk to the boss? Should I talk to a lawyer?
All that night, I lay awake thinking. The next day I woke
up feeling terrible but I didn't feel like I could take a
mental-health day because this would just prove that they
were right to promote Bob and not me. Even taking an
hour off to go to a counselor might prove this, but on the
other hand it might be worth it if it saves my sanity. I'm*

feeling a little better now, but my disappointment still hangs over me like a black cloud, so I think maybe I'll give my therapist a call. I probably should start looking for another job, but I don't feel like I'll be successful if I don't get past this first.

Clouds

Look back through all your clouds. How many of them are unfinished tasks and how many of them are upcoming events that you dread? Do certain unfinished tasks hang over you for days like gray clouds in a stationary front? What do these tasks have in common? Here are some possibilities:

1. They're tasks you particularly dislike, in which case, you're probably procrastinating, always putting them at the bottom of your to-do list. The question is, why do you dislike them? Are they tasks that require skills you haven't yet developed, information you don't know where to find, or talents you don't feel you possess? Are they tasks that involve a lot of repetition or frustration? Do they require you to interact with someone you dislike?

   ☁ *I often seem to put off doing reimbursement vouchers. This is because I so often run into brick walls with them. They have to be approved by various people, any of whom may send them back saying I did something wrong and have to do the whole thing over. When they're just run-of-the-mill reimbursements it's okay, but most of the time they're not. Either they require a wire transfer or the person wants the money sent to a different address or some other monkey wrench gets caught in the wheels so it ends up taking forever, and meanwhile, I know the person is waiting for the money. This makes me feel like I'm caught in a vise.*

2. They're simply tasks that take a long time, longer-term projects that you keep planning to do every day but that get shelved while you respond to a zillion e-mails and interruptions.

○ *Every morning I come in determined to reconcile this month's accounts, but by the time I finish my e-mails a couple of hours have gone by, and when I finally get going, someone always comes in and interrupts me with a fire to put out. I feel caught between my conscience nagging me about the accounts and all the competing demands pulling me away from doing them. It's torture, like in the Middle Ages, when they used to stretch people until they came apart.*

3. They're tasks that aren't important, but it still bothers you that you haven't done them. In this case, you may need to work at letting go of your empty in-box fantasies, which in most present-day offices are unlikely to be realized.

Not all clouds are procrastination-related. Do you dread certain events as they approach? What do these have in common? Are they situations where you expect to get negative feedback, as in performance appraisals or meetings with a bullying supervisor? Do they involve facing up to something painful that you'd rather not think about? Or are they situations where you expect to have to say something difficult or exert your authority in some way?

○ *I dread having to give negative feedback to the people who work for me. I try to be tactful, and most of the time they just listen and say "Okay," but I'm always afraid they'll get mad and go complain to my boss. I was the youngest child in my family, and I'm not very comfortable with authority, I guess. I hate having my success depend on what I can get others to do.*

Flashes, Boosts, Bursts, and Stars
With the more positive types of entries, look for deficits and ask yourself what's going on. Do you seem to have relatively few flashes of insight? If so, what's blocking your creative thinking? When you encounter a problem, does your mind go blank from anxiety? Relaxation techniques, which I'll discuss in chapter 9, may help you to think more clearly.

Do you hardly ever get a boost from anyone in your workplace? If so, you should ask yourself how often you do favors for others. If you scratch someone else's back, he or she may feel more like scratching yours. Do people in your workplace know that you need to hear about the good things you do as well as the bad ones? How would you feel about reminding them?

Are you low in the burst-of-pleasure department? If so, how is your pleasure equipment working? Does food taste good to you? Do you feel anything when you look at a sunset, listen to music, experience moments of intimacy with others, receive a compliment, or complete a task that you've done well? Are you rushing around too much to ever be able to experience anything pleasurable? What would happen if you slowed down once in a while and let yourself enjoy the moment?

☼ *I realized there's nothing pretty to look at in my office. I'm so tired of looking at nothing but off-white walls. I need to find some good pictures to hang up and also get some plants. Maybe I'll ask the boss if I can hang up a bulletin board where I can put posters and poems and things that I particularly like.*

☼ *I'm rushing around so much, I never get a chance to enjoy anything. I know this isn't healthy, but I'm afraid if I stop working for even a moment, I'll get fired. I do feel pleasure when I finish a task, but I don't often pause to enjoy the feeling. I just hurry on to the next task. I need to take a moment or two first.*

Is your Work Companion characterized by a dearth of stars for doing things to take care of yourself? Is this because you never do anything of this sort or because you forget to give yourself credit for it?

★ *I have hardly any stars in my Work Companion even though I've been following the Weight Watchers eating plan and losing weight. Maybe I should give myself a star each time I make it to the next meal eating only foods on the plan. I tend to forget to give myself pats on the back.*

Do a Qualitative Analysis

Now that you've figured out what the numbers can tell you, it's time to look beyond the numbers and do a qualitative analysis. You can start your analysis by reading back through what you've written over the last months from beginning to end, noting down any thoughts that occur to you in your Job Transformation Planner.

As you do this, ask yourself one question in particular: When something upsets you, what automatic thoughts go through your mind? Cognitive therapists such as Aaron Beck, Albert Ellis, David Burns, and others help people to feel better by suggesting ways to change their thoughts. This works because thinking and feeling are interconnected. To feel better, you need to reexamine the thoughts that automatically pop into your mind. This technique is an essential part of countering office blues and battleshock. Jot down any negative thoughts that you repeatedly come across or that occur to you as you read back through your Work Companion, preceding each thought with the initials "AT," for "Automatic Thought." For example:

> AT: *This job is a total waste of my time.*
> AT: *My boss thinks I'm an idiot.*
> AT: *I just know I'm going to be laid off.*
> AT: *I'm a complete failure.*
> AT: *If it weren't for Susan, I'd be happy in this job.*
> AT: *I should be able to pay better attention to instructions.*
> AT: *Bart is much smarter than I am.*
> AT: *My interview was horrible.*

Now go back through the ATs you wrote down, and next to each, write the type of thought it is and at least one reality-based counter-thought. Below are some types of thoughts cognitive therapists have identified, most of which are common lingo for people working in mental health fields. For a more complete typology, see David Burns's *The Feeling Good Handbook.*

All-or-Nothing Thinking

"Because it isn't all one way, it's all the other way." This is rarely the way life is. Most of reality comes in shades of gray. Example:

AT: *This job is a total waste of my time.*

Counterthought: *There are things I can learn from any job if I'm willing to think creatively.*

Mind-reading

You think you know what other people are thinking, but you don't. Example:

AT: *My boss thinks I'm an idiot.*

Counterthought: *I don't know what my boss thinks of me but I can ask for feedback on my performance.*

Fortune-telling

You think you can predict the future but you can't. Example:

AT: *I just know I'm going to be laid off.*

Counterthought: *I might be laid off or I might not, but either way, I can deal with it.*

Labeling

Otherwise known as name-calling, which is also a form of all-or-nothing thinking. People are too complicated to be summed up in one word or phrase, and doing this, whether to yourself or to someone else, is both distorting and disrespectful. Example:

AT: *I'm a complete failure.*

Counterthought: *I've succeeded at some things and not at others, but I've always tried hard and deserve respect for my efforts.*

Blaming

You hold others responsible for your own problems. Example:

AT: *If it weren't for Susan, I'd be happy in this job.*

Counterthought: *Susan does some things I don't like, but I'm in charge of my own happiness.*

"Should" Statements

When someone "shoulds" you, he or she is playing God, demanding that you meet some sort of ideal standard that may not fit who you are. Don't do this to yourself. Example:

AT: *I should be able to pay better attention to instructions.*

Counterthought: *I sometimes find it hard to focus on instructions, but I can find ways of compensating.*

Negative Comparisons

Comparing yourself negatively with others is counterproductive. Example:

AT: *Bart is much smarter than I am.*

Counterthought: *Bart is good at some things, but I have talents too.*

Horriblizing

Inflating a negative reality into something much more catastrophic than it is. Finding out that your spouse has six months to live is horrible; doing badly in an interview isn't even close. Example:

AT: *My interview was horrible.*

Counterthought: *I made some mistakes in my interview, but I choose to look at it as a learning experience.*

Make an Office Wish List

After doing both a quantitative and a qualitative analysis of your Work Companion data, you should have a pretty clear picture of what issues you need to address in order to feel happier during your office workdays. All that remains now is to summarize these issues in the form of an Office Wish List and add any other wishes that occur to you. Imagine that a fairy godmother showed up with a magic wand and could change everything you don't like about your job, but that she required you to specify what changes you want. What would be on your list? Don't worry about whether your wishes are large or small, realistic or unrealistic, but do make them as specific as possible. "A new boss," for example, is too general. Instead, write "A boss who gives clearer instructions" or "A boss who doesn't call me nasty names" or something else specific.

When your list is finished, it might look something like this, though probably a bit longer:

1. A mouse that works!
2. A good time-management system
3. A cheat sheet of information I need on the online financial systems
4. At least three hours a day of uninterrupted work time
5. Someone at work that I can talk to as a friend

However long your list is, don't despair. Some things on it you can probably never have without quitting your job and giving up all its advantages, but that's okay. Remember, to overcome blues and battleshock and feel happier, all you have to do is start taking constructive actions to improve *some* aspects of your workday, not every single thing. What matters is that you begin responding actively to your situation, as action is the best antidote there is to both anxiety and depression.

Make Your Job Transformation Plan

Look back at your Office Wish List. Which wishes, if granted, would make the most difference in how you feel about going to work? Not how successful you'd be, but how you'd *feel*. Which ones would be easiest for you to make come true and which would be most difficult? Which could come true quickly and which would take awhile? Which wishes could you take care of on your own and which would require someone else's help? Does fulfillment of some wishes seem like a prerequisite for others? Considering all of these factors, choose five wishes and list them from easiest to most difficult.

Now take a look at part 3 of this book, which offers lots of suggestions for dealing with specific types of problems. Skim through the chapters, checking off those issues that are relevant to your wishes, and look at the suggestions for dealing with them. Then, after each wish, list the first three steps you could take to make the wish come true, with a checkbox next to each. For example:

1. A mouse that works:
    ☐ Step 1: Talk to a tech person and choose mouse type
    ☐ Step 2: Get boss's approval
    ☐ Step 3: Ask tech to order mouse

2. A good time-management system:
    ☐ Step 1: Set up categories in Outlook
    ☐ Step 2: Load tasks to be done into Outlook
    ☐ Step 3: Print out first day's task list

3. A cheat sheet of information I need on the online financial systems:
    ☐ Step 1: List all financial systems in Word and identify most problematic ones
    ☐ Step 2: Go through manual and find information
    ☐ Step 3: Enter information in Word file for most problematic systems

4. At least three hours a day of uninterrupted work time:
    ☐ Step 1: Read article on workplace quiet times and productivity
    ☐ Step 2: Discuss interruption problem with boss
    ☐ Step 3: Bring up interruption problem in meeting

5. Someone at work that I can talk to as a friend:
    ☐ Step 1: Attend book group
    ☐ Step 2: Attend yoga group
    ☐ Step 3: Invite one person out for lunch

Don't overwhelm yourself with a giant master plan to change anything and everything at once, or even with laying out every last step for making each wish come true. The idea here is just to get started. A few months from now, you'll repeat this process and make a new Job Transformation Plan that will focus on some of your remaining wishes.

Transform Your Job

With your Work Companion and Job Transformation Plan in hand, go back to work and try to do at least one step for one wish each day, starting with the easiest step. Put the steps in your Outlook (or other) to-do list and make them a priority. Do them in any order. You may wish to do all the steps for one wish, or move around from one to another. Don't worry if it seems as though you can't make all five wishes come true in a month. No bell is going to ring and count you out if you don't. Just keep taking one step each day toward making one wish come true. Notice how this makes you feel and write about it in your Work Companion. And congratulate yourself. You're now well on your way out of blues and battleshock and heading down the yellow brick road toward a peaceful, happier, and healthier workplace life!

9

Optimize Your Energy

In *The Power of Full Engagement*, psychologist Jim Loehr and media genius Tony Schwartz maintain that managing energy rather than time is the key to optimal work performance, health, and happiness. Many cases of office blues and battleshock may disappear when workers begin making energy-building changes in their personal lifestyles. If you dread coming to work in the morning, try changing a few habits relating to sleep, food, water, substances, exercise, relaxation, and relationships and you may actually begin to enjoy it. This chapter will help you rethink your lifestyle so as to optimize your energy at work.

Roll Back Your Sleep Schedule

I put this one first for a reason. I believe getting enough sleep is the most important thing you can do to increase your energy at the office, not only because it's been shown to have all sorts of good effects on your health, but because it makes you more likely to engage in other energizing activities. Many energy boosters are best done in the morning before you go to work, and when you don't go to bed early, you don't get up early. When you don't get up early, you don't have time to exercise, meditate, eat a healthy breakfast, cut up the vegetables for your lunch, kiss your loved ones, or do anything but stumble into your clothes and out the door. Once you get to work—assuming you don't fall asleep at the wheel, a real danger—you yawn your way through the day, your head filled with fog, too exhausted to resist the temptation to bolster your waning energy with short-term fixes like junk food and caffeine.

Sleep experts tell us that it's not enough to get the requisite eight hours of sleep; it needs to be eight hours of *good, deep* sleep. Some people suffer from sleep apnea, a dangerous condition that requires medical treatment. If you snore a lot, wake up a lot during the night, and are constantly tired, talk to your doctor about having a sleep study done. Others have trouble with insomnia, which is often stress related. Thus, it helps to do things at bedtime that will relax you, such as drinking warm liquids, taking baths, or reading—preferably something a little boring—and not to do things that rev you up, such as watching a grisly local newscast.

Benjamin Franklin said it best in *Poor Richard's Almanack*: "Early to bed and early to rise makes a man healthy, wealthy, and wise."

Get Organized at Home

You're up early, with time to spare for everything you need to do to have a great day. That is, until you waste nearly an hour looking for the important paper you need to take to work with you. By the time you shut the door on the chaos you call home, your head is in a complete tizzy. If you're good at compartmentalizing, you may be able to leave your clutter behind, but many people carry it with them in the form of a chaotic mindset and depressed mood. Thus, if you want to feel better at work, it can help to get your household under control. This can be difficult if you're working full-time, especially if you have children, but it's worth the extra effort.

Household organizing comes easier to some people than to

others, and some folks can't do it without professional help. If that's you, contact the National Association of Professional Organizers (www.napo.net) for a referral to an organizer in your area. You might also want to take a look at my two previous books, *Making Peace with the Things in Your Life* and *One Thing at a Time*, which will help you to figure out what's going on and why the clutter keeps coming back.

Since your goal is to feel better at work, I suggest you start by making those changes in your home and personal property that are likely to have the biggest effect on your work life. Clean out your purse, briefcase, and car. Create homes near the door for your keys, glasses, watch, wallet, purse, briefcase, lunch bag, and other items that you take to work with you every day so you'll always be able to find them when you're ready to go. Finally, establish a routine of packing your lunch and laying out your clothes before you go to bed at night.

Walk to Work Rain or Shine

I used to get up every morning and jump on the treadmill, which never felt like the greatest way to start the day. Walking faster and faster while getting nowhere on an ugly, noisy machine reminded me a little too much of life on my more dismal days, though I managed to make it more pleasant by watching movies or listening to books on tape. Then something happened. An addition to our office building was finished, some folks moved in from another facility, and suddenly the structure where I'd always parked easily was packed with cars. Since my schedule involved coming to work later than most folks, I now faced daily parking battles. Finally, after having to park several times in a public lot where I had to pay despite having a university sticker I had already paid for, I had an idea. Instead of exercising on the treadmill, I could park in the big main parking lot near the stadium and walk up to campus every day, which took about twenty minutes each way.

It was the middle of January when I parked my car in the lot for the first time. The snow was powdery and the air cold and crisp.

Dressed in mittens, a scarf, boots, and a warm hooded coat, I crunched my way along the sidewalk, across the railroad tracks, past the athletic building, and down a little elbow street past an old house I'd lived in when I was a student. Passing the food and drug store where we used to get milk, a tiny café, and rows of dormitories while breathing in the cold air, I felt more alive than I'd felt in months. By the time I got to work, I was energized but also ready to go inside. The place I'd always seen as a prison now felt like a warm sanctuary from the elements.

From then on, I continued to walk to work each morning, varying my route from one day to the next and watching the seasons change. Each day there was something different to see: a train passing in front of me on the tracks, two students moving boxes up a flight of stairs, a squirrel sitting on top of a fence with an Oreo cookie in its mouth. In the spring I threw Frisbees back to young people in the park when they whizzed out of line, and checked the lilac bushes in front of a certain house each day to see how the blossoms were doing. In the fall I shuffled through maple leaves and paused to watch the university marching band go through its maneuvers. For several months I monitored the progress of an old shop being transformed into a dance studio and was delighted when I could finally make out the silhouettes of figures whirling behind the drawn shades. Thus, I began to feel reconnected both to nature and to the lovely community that driving had isolated me from. In the summer, not wanting to arrive at work in a sweat, I began instead going for a walk in my own neighborhood before taking a shower in the morning. As a result, I also got to know our neighbors better.

My own experiences have left me feeling that walking to work, or at least walking somewhere, is probably the biggest single change you can make to get the blues out of your workday and out of your life. The ideal blues-shaking program includes a twenty-minute walk or bike ride outdoors before and after work in all kinds of weather, except in conditions that might be life-threatening, such as high winds, thunder and lightning, floods, ice, hail, excessive smog, or extreme heat or cold. Note that if you don't feel safe in the neighborhood, it's best to walk somewhere else or travel with a group.

Treadmills are for times when being outside could be dangerous.

It's better to use a treadmill than to get no exercise at all before you get to work, but bear in mind that the treadmill has a number of serious drawbacks relative to walking outside:

1. You don't get any sunlight, which you need to ward off seasonal affective disorder (SAD).
2. You don't get any fresh air, which feels good in your lungs and helps to wake you up.
3. You don't get to connect with the outdoors and your community by experiencing changes in the seasons and the human world.
4. You're walking on a machine that goes nowhere, which may set you up for a certain hopeless, mechanical way of seeing life that can carry over into other realms.

If at all possible, do at least part of your walking in the morning, as this will help to wake up your brain. I once heard a renowned psychiatrist say that aerobic exercise is like taking a little bit of Ritalin and a little bit of Prozac. In other words, a brisk walk in the morning is better than coffee. Note that you don't have to walk all the way to work to walk for twenty minutes before you get to work. You can park at a distance, as I do, and walk the rest of the way, or you can take a walk in your own neighborhood before you leave, or you can park near your workplace and take a walk around it.

However you decide to do your walking—or bicycling, if you prefer, which works just as well—be sure to observe traffic signals and safety rules. Headphones with music can be great at work or on the treadmill, but I don't recommend that you use them on the street, as you need your ears as part of your safety equipment. Also, shut off your cell phone when you walk so that you can focus totally on the sights and sounds you encounter. Instead of blabbing away at someone you can't see, practice the lost art of *looking around*. Open your eyes, ears, nose, and skin and notice a sign being painted, the tinkle of an ice cream truck, the scent of coffee or bacon or flowers, or the feel of a breeze on your face. These sensations tie you to the earth and to the human race, and taking a rich mixture of them into your office with you will help you to stay grounded for the rest of the day.

Rethink Your Commuting Habits

Although walking is the ideal way to get to work, doing so from portal to portal can be impossible in a world in which business and residential areas are often far away from one another. If you can arrange to live near where you work, by all means, please do, and enjoy walking to work. If, on the other hand, you're forced to spend hours of your life stuck in a car, bus, or train, don't let that be time that you spend fussing and fuming because you're not getting there as fast as you think you should or, worse yet, spend it working. Instead, use it to relax or do something you enjoy.

If you commute by car, audiobooks can nourish your mind and calm your nerves. And, of course, there's always the radio for news or music. If you want to save money and protect the environment, how about carpooling? If you like the people you travel with, it can add companionship and fun to your day.

Commuting by train or bus can be much more relaxing than doing so by car. Freed from the stress of driving, you can relax, listen to the clickety-clack of wheels on rails, read, or watch the scenery go by—assuming you can get a seat. Trouble is, during rush hour you often can't. Relaxing while stretching to hang on to a strap above your head and straining to keep your balance can be difficult. During these times, focus on your breathing, write letters or poems in your head, or chat with the person whose elbow is sticking you in the ribs. Although you're on your way somewhere, practice staying in the now until you get there.

Eat and Drink Healthier

Ever wonder why so many office workers are overweight? This is not just because of the sedentary nature of our work. It's also because office buildings everywhere are filled with fattening food traps to tempt compulsive overeaters into their iron jaws. You walk to the elevator and pass the candy machine—snap! You go to a meeting and sit drooling at the plates of doughnuts in the center of the table—snap! You clean up from your boss's catered lunch and your boss tells you to help yourself to the gourmet leftovers—snap! You pay a visit to the business office and are greeted by a box of chocolates on the counter—snap! A coworker takes you to lunch at a place that has no entrées with fewer than a thousand calories on the menu—snap! What's the use? you think. If you don't give in this time, you'll give in next time, so you might as well go for it now. When you start thinking that way, you can be sure that the higher centers of your brain have fallen sound asleep and your reptilian brain—the lowest, least human part of your brain—is now firmly in charge. You can also be sure that your energy will suffer.

Because office life can be isolating, the only way that many of us have of joining with one another and reminding ourselves that the world is real is to stuff something sweet and/or oily into our mouths. Connecting with coworkers and with the real world by means of food can be fun, but it has its price. Indulged too often, the snacking instinct leads not only to being overweight—a major health risk for office folks—but also to sluggishness, sleepiness, and guilt, all of which may serve to undermine anything else you're doing to try to feel better.

The best antidote to overeating in the workplace is some type of human connection that isn't around food. Spend a little time each day schmoozing, check in with a loved one by phone or e-mail, or go for a walk with someone during lunch. Some office workers have formed weight-loss or exercise groups and have even brought Weight Watchers or other weight-loss programs into the workplace. Make a list of food traps and give yourself a star in your Work Companion every time you pass by one of them without getting snagged. Plan routes in your building that allow you to avoid predictable food traps. And if you're planning an event, make sure fruits, veggies, and other healthy snacks are available for the nutritionally conscious—stick up for your rights!

Bear in mind that for optimum energy it's as important to eat enough of the things that are good for you as it is not to eat the things that are bad. Weight Watchers recommends at least five servings of fruits or vegetables per day, two glasses of skim milk, two teaspoons of omega-3 oils (olive and canola are two of the most commonly used—these have been shown to help stabilize mood), a daily vitamin, protein at every meal, and whole grains. All this stuff feeds your brain as well as your body. If you work an eight-hour day, it's especially important to be sure you have some protein at lunch so your blood sugar will be less likely to take a dive at three in the afternoon. For a steady flow of energy, eat five to six low-calorie, highly nutritious meals each day.

Food, however, isn't the only substance that can mess with your mind and your mood. What you drink also matters. Alcohol is likely to be an issue at the office only if you're a hard-core, using alcoholic (in which case, you probably won't keep your job for long—get to an AA meeting now!). What's more likely to be a problem are the after-effects of drinking. More than a glass of wine with dinner or a single bottle of beer to relax after work is too much if you want to feel good at work the next day. Do yourself a favor and confine your partying to the weekends.

Many office workers swear by caffeine. Drinking lots of coffee may help you to stay alert, but too much caffeine comes with a price tag, namely, jitters, irritability, and acid reflux. The other problem with using caffeine is that it enables you to keep going when your body is telling you to rest, which is bound to take its toll over the long run. Getting plenty of sleep and exercise will do the same thing caffeine does without the nasty side effects.

While the occasional soda won't kill you, making it a daily habit is also unhealthy. Nondiet soda adds calories, and most types are filled with chemicals that do heaven only knows what. While soda is bad for you, water is quite the opposite. You should have six to eight glasses per day, which may be inconvenient at the office, as you'll have to spend more time in the bathroom, but it's worth it for the extra energy it will give you.

Noncaffeinated tea can be a good way of getting extra water at work. Different kinds of teas affect people in different ways, some making you more alert, others making you more relaxed. Buy a variety pack of teas to keep in your office and choose the type according to what you feel you need at any given moment. The boxes will also add a colorful, homey touch to your space. You should also bring a pretty cup and saucer or mug to work. You don't have to perform a full-blown Japanese tea ceremony to make tea drinking a pleasant ritual at a particular time of day, preferably in the company of others. In one place where I worked, we had a scheduled tea time at three o'clock every afternoon. Needless to say, job turnover there was unusually low.

Break the Nonstop Habit

When did it become uncool to take a lunch break? Where did coffee breaks go? What about midafternoon chats? In recent decades, a new law seems to have been passed by certain office workers: Thou shalt remain at thy work station with thine eyes glued to the screen throughout the entire workday, no matter what. If you're following this unwritten rule, stop! It's not good for you, nor, in the long run, will it be good for your employer, who will have to find someone to take your place when you collapse onto your keyboard from exhaustion.

If you're a confirmed nonstopper, you may need to change this habit gradually. Start by taking a half-hour lunch break somewhere other than your office (preferably outside of the building), then increase this to an hour, assuming that's what you're allowed. If you eat in a restaurant, this may take the whole hour, but if you bring your lunch, it usually takes no more than half an hour, which will leave you another half hour to do something fun and energizing. Some workers like to nibble a sandwich while still working and save the whole lunch break for other pursuits, such as visiting a museum, jogging, or taking a nap.

Once taking a lunch break has become habitual, you need to add some other, shorter breaks to your day. These include five-minute minibreaks at the end of each hour you spend at the computer, in order to do eye exercises and neck stretches, drink some water, or go to the bathroom; and ten-to-fifteen-minute morning and/or afternoon chat breaks. These are for building relationships with coworkers, which will enable you to work together better and thus benefit your employer. Plan them regularly into your schedule, setting a time limit for yourself and sticking to it scrupulously. Is your workplace a fascist ministate where even a ten-minute chat break once a day is likely to get you fired? Then try to plan an errand that takes you to another department once a day and make friends with people there.

Some people have the mistaken idea that doing anything at work besides work is theft. You are, after all, being paid for your time, so you should work every minute you're there, they say. Problem is, when you work nonstop day after day, you tend to burn out, which isn't going to do your employer a lot of good. Loehr and Schwartz, in *The Power of Full Engagement*, write that energy tends to diminish both when we overuse and when we underuse it. Thus, what's required is balance between energy expenditure and energy renewal. The authors compare this "work-rest" ratio to the way elite athletes are trained. "We call this rhythmic wave oscillation, and it represents the fundamental pulse of life. . . . We are oscillatory beings in an oscillatory universe. Rhythmicity is our inheritance." In other words, work needs to be mixed with a little play now and then for people to do their best work.

Slow Down!

In today's office world, the pressure to do everything fast is often unremitting. If you want to hang on to your health and well-being, you need to resist this pressure and consciously choose the speed at which you work, varying your speed from slow to fast with the circumstances. In his book *In Praise of Slowness: Challenging the Cult of Speed*, Carl Honoré writes that our obsession with doing more things faster has become an addiction and that speed isn't all it's cracked up to be. "Evolution works on the principle of survival of the fittest, not the fastest," he writes. "Remember who won the race between the tortoise and the hare."

Just as most of us habitually check our odometers from time to time while driving on the highway, it's helpful to do regular "speed checks" while working. If you realize you're moving superfast, ask yourself why. If your boss is breathing down your neck and something absolutely has to be done, you may choose to work quickly, albeit with full knowledge that this may increase your error rate. If not, slow down and breathe.

Also, don't allow the need to rush at work to set your pace after you leave. If you drive home, use the slow lane and allow others to pass you while you enjoy listening to music or an audiobook. If you walk, enjoy a nice relaxed stroll. At home, practice doing chores such as dishes slowly and see how it makes you feel. Take time to cook something from scratch occasionally even if it takes up half your evening. When a relative calls whom you haven't heard from in a while, relax and reconnect. Slow down and live.

Make Relaxation Habitual

There are countless ancient and modern ways to cultivate a "relaxation response." To cope with the stresses of office life, you need to find one that works for you and make it part of your daily routine. You don't have to become a Zen monk to make relaxation habitual. You may be able to get to the same place through music, golf, or walks in the woods. What's important is that whatever techniques you use cover all the bases. These include:

- Slowing and deepening your breathing
- Relaxing your muscles
- Focusing your attention
- Tuning in to feelings
- Letting go of worries
- Becoming spiritually centered

Meditation is perhaps the most efficient way of covering all six of these bases, but there are lots of other things you can do to cover at least some of them, and any combination of activities that addresses all six will work just as well. What you do matters less than how you do it.

Slow and Deepen Your Breathing

When you get tense, you're likely to hold your breath a lot, and when you do breathe it's shallow and from the chest rather than the diaphragm. The result is insufficient oxygen to the brain for feeling good and thinking clearly. If you spend even a few minutes each day deliberately breathing slowly and deeply, then when something stressful happens, you'll find yourself automatically countering its toxic effects with slow, deep breaths, blowing out all the poison with oxygen. Try breathing in to the count of three and out to the count of sixteen while sitting quietly or walking slowly. Do this three times before you switch on your computer each morning, three times after lunch, three times after your afternoon break, and three times any time something particularly stressful happens.

Relax Your Muscles

The most direct way of doing this is progressive muscle relaxation, focusing on one muscle group at a time, from the top of your head to the soles of your feet. You might want to use a recording to guide you through the sequence. Try deliberately tensing and then relaxing each set of muscles as you come to it. Stretches can also help to relax muscles. These can be anything from formal yoga positions to rolling your head in a circle at your desk a few times a day. Another route to muscle relaxation is massage, by either a professional or someone you trust. As with breathing, you need to become conscious enough of your muscles that you'll automatically counter tension whenever it arises in the course of your workday.

Focus Your Attention

Concentration, for most of us, can be trained. This requires patience, because our brains—some people's more than others—are wired for thoughts to wander. In Zen Buddhism, they call this monkey mind. Daydreaming is, after all, a rich source of creativity, and how much monkey mind is good for you depends upon the type of work that you do. If you're a writer or an artist, you may need to actually cultivate *more* of it, though this may result in mismatched socks and kettles boiling over. Most routine office jobs, on the other hand, require high levels of concentration so as not to mix up someone's reservations or forget to attach a file to an e-mail.

If you want to train greater concentration in order to meet the demands of office work more effectively, you may be able to do so by simply sitting in a chair focusing on your breathing or counting to five over and over. If your mind wanders off, don't beat yourself up. As Jon Kabat-Zinn—whose meditation books and recordings I highly recommend—says on one of his recordings: "If your thoughts wander off a thousand times, just bring them back a thousand times." Note that if you suffer from ADD, you may find that you need some sort of external stimulation to concentrate. In this case, guided meditation using a recording or walking meditation may work better for you than trying to stay focused while sitting.

Tune In to Feelings

To start feeling happier from eight to five, it's essential that you develop the "What do I feel?" habit. If you practice meditation, try to notice each feeling as soon as you become aware of it, and immediately give it a one-word name. Think of feelings as clouds passing across the sky in endlessly changing patterns. Don't get stuck in the feeling, just name it and let it go. Likewise, when you're at your desk, do a feeling check at least once per hour and note down the results in your Work Companion. If you feel something unpleasant, write your feelings away.

Let Go of Worries

As you meditate, make a point of considering each thing that's worrying you and letting it go, perhaps with a prayer. Ask yourself what constructive actions you could take to eliminate each worry. Bear in mind that thinking about possible disasters does serve a purpose, in that it gets you thinking about what you need to do to prevent them. On the other hand, thinking about them over and over after you've already decided on preventive actions—assuming any are possible— serves no purpose at all. If you believe in God or a higher power, turning your worry over to something greater than yourself can be a great source of relief.

Become Spiritually Centered

Most religious and many secular psychological practices go beyond just training concentration and processing feelings. The more you cultivate the art of conscious relaxation, the more you may begin to feel that you're in touch with God, your creative unconscious, or whatever you want to call it. You may begin to feel as though a plumb line has been dropped down through you so that no matter what external darts and bombs attack you, nothing can throw you off balance. This is the experience some people call being centered.

Find an Outlet

At one time, in my current job, I was plagued with the feeling that I had no voice. For whatever reason, I'm a person with a strong need to express myself, a need that I had to totally suppress when I was at work, where I spent much of my time alone and where my boss and coworkers were all much too busy to listen to my great ideas and emotional outpourings. Then, after I joined a local church, I decided I'd like to sing in the choir. In order to sound better, I thought I'd take a few voice lessons, and my choir director referred me to a fabulous teacher named Wendy. After making some special arrangements with my boss, every Friday I'd leave the office at 11:30 and drive out of town to Wendy's lovely lakeside home. For the next hour, I'd stand next to her piano soaking up sunlight and positive energy while she coached me through scales and exercises, arias, and Broadway songs. Each week, my soprano voice grew stronger, which felt wonderful, and I'd sing in the car all the way back into town. On days when I felt particularly daring, I'd even blast out a few phrases of song in the stairwell of the parking structure, pausing to savor the sound of my voice, ten times its normal volume, echoing down the flights of stairs as though I were in a huge concert hall. By the time I got back to work, I felt thoroughly cleansed, content to keep my mouth shut for the rest of the afternoon.

For me, singing has provided a wonderful outlet, as well as a way to connect with others. But what's yours? If you work in an office and don't already have one, you'll need to get a new hobby, especially if you have a strong need to express yourself. Music is ideal, the more nakedly emotional the better—I especially recommend Italian opera and African American blues—but other arts can also be beneficial. For some arts, such as creative writing, cartoons, videos, or stand-up comedy, you may even be able to use your office experiences as material. Creative arts and crafts such as knitting, weaving, or sewing not only allow you to make a statement and receive praise but also feed your office-starved senses with colors and textures. Dance and other movement arts will help counter feelings of physical restlessness.

Sports can provide healthy outlets, especially for anger. Tennis, racquetball, softball, squash, volleyball, golf, and many other sports all provide the same benefit: a small, round object that you can imagine is your boss, your snooty coworker, or your irritating subordinate, and wop to kingdom come. While most sports are about winning, group sports are also about connecting, so being part of a sports team can help to compensate for workplace loneliness.

Take the Time Off You Deserve

American workers get less paid vacation time than workers in almost any developed society, yet strangely enough, many workers don't even take off all the days they're entitled to. In a few cases this might be because people love their jobs, but I believe it's more often because of fear. Fear of getting fired if they take more vacation days than their coworkers do, fear of getting so behind that they'll never catch up, fear that someone else will step forward to fill the gap while they're gone and make them look bad, fear of the boss realizing that they're not indispensable. Workers need to band together to counteract this fear. We need to support each other in taking vacation breaks—as well as lunch breaks, coffee breaks, and all other kinds of breaks—to which we're entitled, rather than seeing other people's vacations as opportunities to defeat them.

Meanwhile, if you haven't been taking all your vacation time, you need to ask yourself why, face your fears, and take those vacation days! Research shows that not taking enough vacation time increases all sorts of medical risks. One study showed that men who took no annual vacation were three times as likely to suffer heart attacks as those who went away, and another showed that women's risk of dying of heart disease was doubled by foregoing a vacation. In other words, not taking a vacation is just as bad for your heart as smoking, drinking, or eating high-cholesterol foods. Think about it.

Speaking of illness, many workers also go to work sick, worsening their own illnesses and spreading their germs to their coworkers. The trouble is, it's not always easy to tell if you're sick enough to stay home. Is waking up with a sore throat and runny nose sick enough, or do you have to have a fever? Is a tummy ache enough of a reason, or do you have to have vomiting or diarrhea too? You lie there and debate with yourself, then call your boss and do your best to sound as if you're on the verge of death. Then, instead of resting all day, you spend the time worrying about whether your boss was convinced or not.

To avoid such dilemmas, it helps to develop an illness policy, which you may want to discuss with your boss, doctor, or HR department. Find out what they consider sick enough to stay home, decide what your criteria will be, and let your boss know. My own policy is that I don't go to work with a fever, vomiting or diarrhea, or extreme pain; in the early stages of a cold, when it's most likely to be contagious; or any time a physician advises me not to. If you have to go to work with a cold or other contagious illness, be sure to cover your mouth when you cough and wash your hands frequently. To avoid catching others' germs during epidemics, walk up and down stairs rather than using elevators, as being in an enclosed space with someone who's sick is one of the easiest ways to expose yourself to dangerous germs.

Finally, whether or not your workplace officially allows this, give yourself permission to take a mental-health day now and then, though only when you really need it. This is not something you should schedule, but regard as an option when you've been hit by a bomb—either inside or outside the workplace—or are experiencing some of the following symptoms accompanied by the persistent feeling that you need a break:

- Weeping
- Uncontrolled displays of anger
- Difficulty sleeping
- Nausea or changes in appetite

- Obsessive thoughts that interfere with your work performance
- Confusion or memory loss
- Anxiety

Taking a day off may help to alleviate these symptoms, or it may not. If it doesn't, you should seek professional help through your doctor, therapist, or employee-assistance program.

If you do take a mental-health day, spend it doing whatever your inner voice tells you will help your mood the most. Your only job on a mental-health day is to find a way to feel better. Ask yourself the question "What do I need?" and listen to the answer. If what will make the most difference is for you to balance your checkbook and pay your bills so you won't have to worry about that part of your life, do it. If you feel starved for pleasure, rent a bunch of videos and watch them. If you feel sleep-deprived, spend the day in bed. When you get back to work, take a few minutes to write in your Work Companion about what you did during your mental-health day and how it made you feel.

One issue many office workers wrestle with is how to inform their employers that they'll be taking a day off for purely psychological reasons. Of course, it's best to be honest, but alas, some supervisors still haven't heard that depression and anxiety are biological illnesses and should be treated accordingly. If you're working for such an ignoramus, you have my permission to say you "don't feel well." If you're having acute mental symptoms and don't give yourself a break, there's a good chance you'll soon become physically ill anyway.

Find an Outside Confidant

In the 1950s, when life was simple, many men in the office world had wives—and sometimes also secretaries—whose whole purpose was to support their emotional well-being and careers. This was great for the men but not so great for the women, who often harbored resentment toward husbands or bosses who took far more than they gave. As more women began to seek fulfillment for themselves in the

1970s, many men grieved the loss of support they'd once received and were forced to learn new skills in order to fill the gap. In the twenty-first century, few of us—male or female—would choose to have the kinds of relationships people had in the fifties. Yet all of us need support, someone to supply at least some of what 1950s wives supplied to their husbands. Anyone who deals with daily workplace stresses needs a supportive confidant—someone on the outside who can help to provide perspective—to stay healthy.

Your confidant doesn't have to be a spouse or significant other, though this is fine if you happen to have one. Your confidant can be a close friend or a group of friends who get together to grumble about their jobs and give one another advice. Other possibilities are a therapist, a support group, a clergyperson, a congregation, a neighborhood, a political group, or some combination of any or all of the above.

Encounters with the right confidant should leave you feeling energized. He or she asks you how your day or week went and really wants to know. Your confidant empathizes with your feelings but doesn't overindulge you by letting you go on and on about what you're unwilling to change. Your confidant celebrates success with you and comforts you when you fail. Your confidant says things that make you feel good about yourself as well as things you need to hear to be better. Your confidant encourages you to set boundaries with those who abuse you and tells you it's okay to stay home when you're sick or to take a mental-health day. None of this is to say that the relationship has to be a one-way dependency—it's perfectly all right to also be your confidant's confidant.

PART III

From Blues and Battles to Peace:
One Change at a Time

Note to the Reader: In writing part 3, I did not assume that every reader will want to read this section straight through from beginning to end. If you're not a cover-to-cover type of reader, you may prefer just to use it as a resource, especially for making Job Transformation Plans. Every person, every office job, and every organization is different, and you may find that some sections and suggestions are more relevant to you and your circumstances than others. Skim through the various sections of each chapter and make checkmarks next to those that seem to apply to you, then go back, read the material, and look at the "Blues and Battleshock Busters." Take what works for you and ignore the rest.

10

Peace with the Place

Although this book is mostly about the psychological side of office life, the psychological cannot be separated from the physical. The degree of confinement or inactivity to which you're restricted during your workdays; the manner in which buildings and rooms are constructed, furnished, and decorated; levels of sound, temperature, and lighting; and the types of equipment you use—all these physical arrangements can affect your mind as well as your body, and many of them also carry messages from your employer about your relative importance. Too often, these messages are negative, the subtext being, "You don't matter."

The most frequently denigrated office space invention—if *Dilbert* is anything to go by—is, of course, the infamous cubicle. The original idea behind the cubicle was to give workers who would otherwise have been annoying each other in one big room at least some semblance of privacy. Somehow, however, it didn't work out quite as planned. The cubicle gives workers some privacy and ownership, but it can also make them feel isolated and humiliated. Perhaps this was why the creator of the snap-on cubicle, Robert Propst, eventually repented, calling his invention "monolithic insanity." The cubicle provides a perfect example of an emotionally not-very-intelligent management decision.

Although some avant-garde employers are making changes to improve the physical environments of office workers—I'm told that at Google, for example, they have beanbag chairs, paper lanterns, lava lamps, and other comfort items as well as massage stations where workers are free to take laptops—many still fail to think outside the cubicle about the boxes we call offices, or to consider the physical and psychological effects of their decisions, which are mainly about cost-cutting. For your organization's sake as well as your own, then, it's important that you let your employer know how physical arrangements affect you, and that you work with your boss and coworkers to address problems. You can't, however, expect others to do all the work—you'll also need to make some changes yourself, both external and internal. This chapter will help you to better understand the physical challenges of office life and to figure out what to do—and what to ask others to do—about them.

❒ "I feel like I'm in jail": Confinement

In the winter, you may never see the sun. You may spend half or more of your waking hours in one room, perhaps even in one chair. As the hours, days, and weeks drag on, you may begin to suffer from "office fever," the counterpart of "cabin fever," the stir-crazy feeling that afflicts people cooped up in their houses for too long during blizzards or heat waves.

Confinement is one of the biggest challenges of traditional office life, which has often been compared to serving time in prison. And the space into which workers are confined is becoming smaller all the time. Facility Performance Group, Inc., an organization that tracks office trends at seventy large corporations, reports that work spaces have diminished 25–50 percent over the past ten years for most office workers.

The situation of being confined to a single building, room, or cubicle seems to bother some people more than it bothers others. This is a matter of brain-wiring plus conditioning plus cognition. Those with claustrophobic neurochemistry may find it most aversive. Are you the kind of person who always wants the blinds or drapes, if not the windows, open instead of closed? Does the mere thought of having an MRI make you break out in a cold sweat? Do you love the feeling of roaming across an open field? If so, working all day in a single office may be particularly hard for you.

But confinement means more than being indoors; it also means *not* being outdoors, which for all of us has its physical and mental-health drawbacks, especially during winter months, when a deficiency of sunlight can put you at risk for seasonal affective disorder. Even if you don't suffer from SAD, you may feel justifiably sad about being disconnected from the natural world, with its infinite variety of plants, animals, humans, and scenery. To some workers, nostalgia for the days when the human race still roamed largely free—or for their own childhoods, when they had the run of the neighborhood—can be painful.

Blues and Battleshock Busters

1. Remember that an enclosed space can be viewed two ways—as a prison or as a sanctuary. If you've ever had an outdoor job, you know what it's like to envy those fortunate souls who don't have to endure extremes of weather but instead can work someplace safe and warm and dry. If you haven't, next time you pass a construction crew plugging away under the blazing sun or in the freezing cold, think about what this must feel like to the workers.
2. Walk outdoors as much as possible—see chapter 9 for suggestions on outdoor walking.
3. Walk inside your building as much as possible. Volunteer for errands. Hand-carry a package down to the mailroom. Go talk face-to-face with someone in another department instead of phoning. During breaks, explore your building, check out the office library, or go down to the front desk for a chat. These walks will not only energize you but also enable you to form connections or gain knowledge that may prove unexpectedly useful in your work. You may want to keep track of your steps with a pedometer.

4. Look out of a window from time to time. If your office doesn't have a window, go find one. Every time you look out, try to see something new.

5. Engage in plenty of outdoor activities when you're not at work. Camping is especially good for office workers as it will make you appreciate the comforts of civilization when you get back.

6. To protect yourself from SAD during the winter months, you can purchase a special light box from places like Northern Light Technologies (www.northernlighttechnologies.com) to use during the early morning hours that will give you what you don't get from the sun. If you believe you suffer from SAD, you may also want to talk to a therapist or read books/Web sites on the subject.

7. Put up framed landscapes, calendars, postcards, and other visuals on your office walls that connect you with the outdoors.

8. Use a slide show of outdoor scenery as your screen saver.

9. Play recordings of natural sounds—birds, waterfalls, etc.—using headphones as you work.

10. Depending on your circumstances, you may want to talk with your employer about possibly doing all or part of your work at home or somewhere else besides your own office. Many workplaces are experimenting with telecommuting and other alternative arrangements. It may be that total confinement to a single location is unnecessary given the type of work that you do. If you're able to work outside the office on a laptop, a little Web surfing reveals all sorts of fancy equipment that will allow you to work anywhere from your car to your kitchen to an inflatable office tent that comes stored in a bucket. Bear in mind that working somewhere else besides your office may subject you to higher levels of distraction and temptation, however. If you require absolute silence to do your best work, you'll need to choose your surroundings with that in mind.

☐ "All I do is sit": Inactivity

Inactivity in office jobs is problematic for two reasons. The most obvious of these is that if you're inactive all day, you may not be getting enough exercise to keep from gaining weight and to keep your heart, lungs, and brain functioning as well as they need to for optimum physical and mental health. Recent studies have even found that office workers are more at risk for developing blood clots than passengers on long-haul flights. A less obvious reason is that some people's brains are wired to produce feelings of restlessness, which in childhood may or may not be expressed as whole-body hyperactivity but in most adults is apparent only, if at all, as small muscle fidgetiness. These are the people who sit drumming on the desk with their fingers, fiddle with their pens, or rock back in their chairs during meetings. Even folks who appear sluggish on the outside may be plagued by internal restlessness, which can make it hard for them to focus.

It's a known fact that aerobic exercise is an absolutely wonderful treatment not only for restlessness and inattention but also for depression and anxiety. When you're sitting in front of a computer for hours on end, the only thing you're exercising aerobically is your fingers, which isn't likely to result in the increased production of dopamine, serotonin, or endorphins that can significantly benefit mental health. Thus, probably the biggest step you can take to counter the office blues is to increase the amount you move around in space, both within and outside of your workday. Some of these movements need to be large ones, but small ones count too, and hand, arm, or head/neck exercises may be beneficial both in loosening up tense muscles and in giving restless feelings an outlet.

Increasing your activity level isn't the only thing you can do, however, to deal with inactivity. You can also do some mental work.

Blues and Battleshock Busters

1. Talk to someone who's performed backbreaking labor such as hauling boxes or scrubbing floors and imagine what it would be like to work eight hours a day in such a job. From the physical laborer's standpoint, the idea of being able to "just sit" might seem like the height of luxury.
2. Remember this: Buddhist monks spend hours and hours "just sitting" and view this as the most spiritual thing they can do, a

prerequisite for finding peace and enlightenment within themselves.

3. Pay attention to how you sit. Are both of your feet flat on the floor? Are you slumping forward in your chair? Sit with dignity, in a way that's relaxed but alert.

4. If you suffer from feelings of restlessness, give yourself permission to engage in small, repetitive movements such as finger drumming so as to concentrate better, reminding yourself that this is just how your brain is wired. If you share space, though, you'll need to discuss how this affects others and do some problem solving if it bothers them.

5. Any time you go to another floor in your building, take the stairs instead of the elevator.

6. If your work organization has a motivational fitness program you can report hours of exercise to, sign up.

7. Start a noontime exercise group with interested coworkers or take a class together. If your organization provides fitness facilities, take advantage of these.

8. At least once every couple of hours, get out of your chair and either walk somewhere, run in place for a few minutes, or do a few aerobic dance steps or yoga stretches to get your blood flowing again.

9. On the weekends, spend at least an hour a day doing aerobic exercise. Choose a type of exercise that you know you'll enjoy.

10. Devices such as the "Walk at Work" tripod, developed by Dr. James Levine of Mayo Clinic (see www.gizmag.com/go/7298) attach a workstation to a treadmill and allow you to work and exercise at the same time. If you think your employer might be willing to foot the bill, check these out.

❏ "I'm sick of beige, white, and gray": Sensory Deprivation

In one of my favorite cartoons, Dilbert refers to his cubicle as "my sensory deprivation chamber." For workers who are office allergic, that about sums it up. As discussed in chapter 4, human brains are wired to crave different levels of sensory input through different sensory channels, i.e., sight, hearing, smell, taste, and touch. Some of us are sensation seekers who just can't get enough sensory input and others are sensation avoiders, minimalists who may feel oppressed by even moderate intensities of stimulation. A third group might be described as "sensation ignorers," people who appear oblivious to their surroundings, which they experience in purely functional—or fiscal—terms.

One obvious way that office workers may vary sensationwise is in their responses to color. Some may be just fine with beige/gray/white; others would prefer pastels but nothing brighter; still others may feel an intense craving for color. These variations may stem not only from brain-wiring differences but also from cultural backgrounds, as ethnic groups differ in the prevalence and intensity of colors that clothing and household items are decorated with. Those who come from homes filled with turquoise, magenta, and royal blue may experience a sense of loss every time they come to work in Beigeville. Thus, color and office décor can be diversity issues, and one suspects that thus far, the tastes of certain groups—especially women and people of color—have been largely ignored by those who make decisions about them. The most common excuse for the lack of color in offices is that people's tastes vary; hence, out of fear of offending some people, decision makers have created anonymous, lunar, fluorescent-lighted environments that offer warmth and comfort to no one, perhaps out of the misbelief that people will work harder in a state of chromatic starvation.

In addition, some people seem to have a greater need than others for organic sensations, craving the sight of wooden furniture and floors, the feel of natural fabrics, the sounds of birds, the warmth of natural lighting, and the scents of living plants while spending their work hours in a bubble of electronic beeps and glass, metal, and plastic where the only smells are those of overheating CPUs.

Most contemporary offices seem to have been decorated by sensation ignorers with little need for either organic sensations or color, people who appear "tone deaf" to the aesthetic—and emotional—reverberations of their highly functional decisions about the colors of walls, carpets, and filing cabinets; the coldness of unnatural lighting;

and the materials that doors, floors, and furniture are made of (i.e., anything but good-quality, nicely finished wood).

The majority of office workers seem to assume that sterile is just the way offices are, but this was not always the case. If movies are anything to go by, offices before the mid-twentieth century were much more like rooms in people's homes than they are now. Wood was far more plentiful, and walls were often painted with color, though not necessarily always the most appealing ones (a common choice was institutional green, about which color-sensitive commentators often complained).

Sensory deprivation in the office is not simply a visual matter. Along with suffering from a lack of visual stimulation, workers may crave different sounds than the usual murmur of conversation punctuated by an occasional electronic buzz or beep. And who knows how many psychiatric leaves would have proved unnecessary had blankies and stuffed animals, optimal sources of tactile comfort, not been verboten by the guardians of office conformity.

Blues and Battleshock Busters

1. Be brave. Don't let anyone deprive you of the types of sensations you need to feel healthy and to do your best work at the office. If your boss is a minimalist and you want that promotion, you might have to do this discreetly for the sake of "impression management," but do it. Among your coworkers, be a trendsetter, not a clone. Push the limits of your office culture and make things a little better for everyone. However, if you share space with someone whose tastes differ from yours, be considerate and willing to compromise.

2. Put visuals on your office or cubicle walls that make you feel good. Buy some framed prints or tack favorite posters, postcards, photos, poems, prayers, or cartoons to your office bulletin board (if you don't have one, ask if you can get one). Choose visuals that make you feel good to look at or that relate to your own hobbies and interests, bearing in mind that anyone who comes into your office will be seeing them too. In

addition to making you feel good, they may act as great conversation starters.

3. If you don't feel safe putting up visuals, instead bring a small art book or photo album and take a visual break each day to feast your eyes, or spend a few minutes now and then browsing your favorite museum Web site.

4. Bring a few objects from home that you find comforting, things that connect you with nature, the past, or your life outside work. Don't limit yourself to the standard golf trophies and family photos. If looking at your favorite Hummel figurine makes you feel good, challenge the culture a little and bring it. Be careful, however, not to bring so much stuff that you become known as a hoarder, which won't do your self-esteem a lot of good.

5. Buy a plant and bring it in, making sure it's likely to do well under artificial lighting if you don't have an office window.

6. Bring in a few warm fuzzies to address your unmet tactile needs. If maintaining a professional image is important to you, keep your fuzzies locked in a drawer and use them only when your door is closed. In my own office, I have a blanket, a small stuffed dog, and a warm shawl, all of which I use liberally when the temperature drops—physically or emotionally. If you don't feel comfortable doing this, wear a furry coat or sweater to work and keep it draped over the back of your chair for extra warmth.

7. For extra tactile sensations, get a massage during your lunch break, or exchange neck rubs with a buddy.

8. If you crave sound, bring in headphones, plug them into your computer, find your favorite radio station's Web site, and listen to music while you work. If your work is understimulating, you may find that music actually helps you concentrate better. Music, which is about emotions, also helps to counter the emotional flatness of office life, and it has the additional advantage of blocking out distracting noises. For those with ADD, headphones with music can be a medical necessity—if your boss complains, get a note from your doctor.

9. For aromatherapy, keep some nice scented hand lotion in your drawer or, if you have your own office, use an organic scented air spray.

10. Don't neglect taste, depending on your diet. Bring healthy but tasty snacks and enjoy your favorite teas and coffees while at work.

❏ "I'm working in Grand Central Station": Sensory Overload

While some people crave more sensation in their office workplaces, others, especially those working in large rooms with no more than half cubicles separating them from other workers, may feel overwhelmed by too much noise and confusion. Bright fluorescent lights, the drilling sounds and smells of nearby construction, constant electronic whirs and beeps, and chatter on all sides can make concentration difficult, especially for those who are naturally distractible. Sensory overload can also result in fatigue, headaches, irritability, and dissociated feelings of fishbowl unreality.

Blues and Battleshock Busters

1. Resist the temptation to think of irritating sensations as attacks. Even though it might feel like it, that jackhammer outside your window isn't maliciously drilling into your head but into the sidewalk, which will soon be a nice, smooth place for you to walk.
2. Headphones can be a lifesaver for blunting or drowning out excess noise. You can play music or, if you find that too distracting, white noise or a recording of ocean waves or other natural sounds.
3. If you can't block out an irritating repetitive noise, switch strategies and deliberately focus on it for short periods of time. Relax and try to slow your breathing as you listen to the sound over and over, allowing it to enter your consciousness exactly the way it is. Think of the sound as your friend, not something to push away, and over time, you'll become more comfortable with it. The same approach works for bad smells.

4. If bright lights bother you, talk to your boss and/or facility person about whether the intensity might be decreased by mechanical means. If not, discuss the problem with an eye doctor, who may recommend antiglare glasses, and, in the meantime, wear sunglasses for short periods to give your eyes a break.

5. Talk to your boss about alternative work situations. Perhaps you can work somewhere outside your area for part of the time.

6. Take regular breaks away from your workstation to give your senses a chance to recoup.

☐ "My _____ hurts": Ergonomic Issues

In manufacturing organizations, the office has historically been regarded as the locus of mental activity for the organization, while the physical activity takes place on the factory floor in the form of "deskilled" jobs. Mind and body are kept in two totally separate spheres, and thus the body is seen as having no place in the office. In such circumstances, it's easy for office workers to all but forget that they have bodies, even when their bodies hurt—until the pain becomes nearly incapacitating. Our bodies aren't, after all, doing much, but that's just it: Maintaining one position for too long can be almost as bad for your body as backbreaking labor. And even small repetitive movements can cause damage, especially if done without the right support.

For the most part, the pain office workers are likely to experience is from the lower back on up: in the back, neck, shoulders, arms, wrists, fingers, head, and eyes, though what you do with your legs and feet can affect these areas. Much of this pain can be eliminated by taking proper ergonomic measures. However, these are in no way a substitute for medical treatment if that's what's needed. If you follow the suggestions given here and your discomfort continues, see your doctor.

Along with the discomfort produced by stagnation and repetitive movements, workers may also feel uncomfortable because of temperature, lighting, and ventilation issues, especially in today's energy-conscious world, where conservation often comes at the expense of workers' comfort and health. Temperature is an especially common source of complaint. The practice of turning on the air-conditioning on a certain date, ignoring actual weather conditions, carries with it the depressing message that employers could care less how their workers feel, though employers may be doing this to try to save energy.

Blues and Battleshock Busters

1. Tune in to your discomfort. Sit at your workstation and type. Starting at the top of your head and working your way mentally down to your toes, notice what areas feel most stressed. Does anything hurt? Everything is connected to everything else, so notice how different areas affect one another. For example, does your neck hurt because you're hunching forward to see your computer screen in response to vision problems?

2. Think about your chair, desk, mouse, computer screen, and document holder as a whole system, not just as individual parts. Arrange these components so as to provide maximum support and minimal strain. If you don't have an adjustable office chair, ask for one *now*. Adjust the back to support your back and the arms to support your arms without pushing them upward. Adjust the height of your chair so your wrists rest on the edge of the desk, at or below elbow height. From an ergonomic perspective, it's bad for arms, hands, legs, and feet to hang in the air, and this should be avoided as much as possible. If your CPU is under your desk, make sure it doesn't prevent you from putting both feet flat on the floor with your knees at ninety-degree angles. Any kind of twisting with your legs can have a murderous effect on your back after a while. Your knees should be at or below hip height. If you can't put your feet flat on the floor, use a footstool to raise them to where you can.

3. Never hunch forward as you type, but instead, lean as far back in your chair as you can, as you would in a rocking chair, to reduce stress on your discs. Special ergonomic reclining chairs are now available that will allow you to do this more easily.

Bring a cushion to work or order one from an office-supply store to support your back if you need to. If you have trouble seeing from this position, see number 7.

4. Move. Anytime you maintain the same position for too long, you put your muscles at risk for getting insufficient blood flow and cramping up or experiencing fidgety feelings. Circle your head, shoulders, or hands, or wiggle your fingers while you think about the next thing to type.

5. Make periodic changes to give your muscles a rest. If you're right-handed, train yourself to use your mouse with your left hand, which requires less reaching due to the placement of the keyboard numbers pad on the right side, and move your document holder from one side to the other now and then.

6. Pay particular attention to the height of your computer screen, which should be at eye level. Are you tilting your head downward all the time in order to see it? If so, how does this make the muscles in your head and neck feel? If you wear bifocals and are looking through the top sections, your screen may have to be higher than if you don't.

7. Take care of your eyes. Make sure your glasses are the right strength for looking at a computer screen in the middle distance. Some of us require an extra pair just for the computer. Whatever glasses you have should have antiglare treatment. Even if your glasses are good, use the Zoom function in your View menu to enlarge the type so it's easier to read. Develop the habit of taking your eyes off the screen at least every few minutes and rolling them up and down and from side to side. Once you've established the habit, you can do this even while you're on a roll and don't want to stop typing.

8. Read *Office Yoga: Simple Stretches for Busy People*, by Darrin Zeer, and do some of the exercises each day.

9. Get a therapeutic massage once a month during your lunch break. If that doesn't help, see your doctor, as you may need physical therapy.

10. If you have neck pain, buy a buckwheat-filled pack at a health-food store and take it to work. Heat it up in the microwave and put it on sore muscles to make them feel better.

11. How do your feet feel? If you're a woman, unless you work for a fashion-magazine cult that requires four-inch heels, wear comfortable shoes to work. High heels don't just affect your feet but throw your whole body off-kilter. If you have to wear them, but sit all day, take them off under your desk.

12. If your office is too cold, bring in a shawl or blanket to wear, which has the advantage of using no energy (unlike space heaters, which are energy black holes). Don't be deterred from taking care of your warmth needs by the fear that this may look "unprofessional"—help make your office culture a little saner by doing what makes sense instead of suffering.

13. If your office is too hot and stuffy, wear the lightest clothes you decently can, find out if you can bring in a small fan, drink lots of cold drinks, and let the management know how the heat affects your productivity.

14. If your organization offers ergonomic consultations to employees, take advantage of this service. If it doesn't, you might want to talk with your boss about whether such services could be added.

❏ "The *&^%@#! _____ is broken again!": Equipment Issues

When I was first in my current job, the only copier I could use was a geriatric machine in a dark storeroom that was some distance from my own office. Even if I had only one page that needed copying, I'd have to get up, walk to the storeroom, punch a code into the machine, and stand waiting in the gloom through a series of rumbles and groans until the copy finally emerged from the machine's innards. All the time I was standing there, I'd be visualizing the long to-do list on my desk and muttering curses to myself. This shows just how much they value my work, I'd think. They load me down with too much to do and don't even care enough to give me the right equipment.

One day it occurred to me that instead of just fuming, it might be a good idea to tell my boss about this problem and the amount of my time it was wasting. Before long I had a beautiful all-in-one machine in my office that served as not only a copier but also a printer, scanner, and fax machine. The effects of this change on both my efficiency and my job satisfaction were huge.

Having to do your job with less-than-optimal equipment can feel demeaning as well as frustrating. And at times, electronic malfunctions can be downright infuriating. According to Dan Stamp, founder of the training company Priority Management Systems Inc., 83 percent of IT managers report having to deal with enraged workers. Some technical problems you may be able to fix yourself, but in most cases you're dependent on others to either fix or replace ailing equipment. Thus, what determines how well you'll be able to solve tech problems is less your own mechanical skills than your communication and persuasion skills. You need to be able to state clearly to others exactly what happens when you do what. You also need to be able to persuade your employer to get you the equipment you need to do your best work.

Blues and Battleshock Busters

1. Don't wait to get help from a tech person when you need it. Contact the tech by e-mail, which is the way tech people were born communicating, rather than by phone. The tech person won't necessarily have to come to your office; many tech people at large companies can log on remotely to users' computers in order to fix problems.
2. When a problem occurs with a machine, write down exactly what happened in your Work Companion. Write down any error messages that appear on the screen as well as any corrective measures you try and their results. Then pass this information on to the tech person whose job it is to fix the problem. You can also write down how the problem makes you feel, but you don't have to tell the tech person about this.
3. Take a screen shot of the error. Tech people like to see the error as it appeared on the screen. This helps them to see not only the error text but also the surrounding environment, including what else was running and what the error window looked like.

4. If, when a tech person tries to explain something to you about a machine, your mind tends to go blank, take notes as the person speaks and go back and make sense of them afterward. Don't be ashamed to ask the tech person to repeat his or her explanation in simpler terms. Tech people are used to nontech people not understanding them, and you'll look like even more of a fool if you pretend to understand when you don't and have to call the person back when you still can't make the machine work.

5. Keep track of how much time a broken, archaic, distant, or overused machine costs you and give the resulting statistics to your boss. Most managers love numbers and are likely to be more influenced by them than by melodrama.

6. Figure out just what you would need a new machine to do, should one be purchased. Then ask a tech person to recommend some good models and support your request to your boss. Along with numbers, many bosses also love technology, and the tech person's enthusiasm for a state-of-the-art machine can be contagious.

7. Link your request for new equipment to the start of a new project. Your boss may be more open to spending money when he or she is gearing up for a new challenge.

8. State your request clearly and simply, supporting it with stats and technical information. The boss is always thinking about how decisions will appear to his or her boss, and statistics and tech info will make him or her feel well armed and safe.

9. Make sure that you always keep extra cartridges, disks, and other supplies on hand for your electronic equipment.

11

Peace with the Chaos

As a psychotherapist/organizer who's watched a lot of folks grow cheerier as their homes or offices became more orderly, I've come to believe that organizing your physical and informational environment can have a positive effect on your mood. In the modern office world, this means organizing not only the papers in your office but also your e-mail directories and the files on your hard drive. Most important, it means having easy access to the information you need to do your job so you aren't constantly thrown into turmoil while you struggle to fill in information gaps.

Many disorganized people think that they can get organized if some genius just gives them a "good system." This is not the case. If you struggle with chronic disorganization, the only way to change this is to figure out what's behind the disorganization and address the underlying causes. This can vary from person to person. For some people the problem may simply be the result of having too much to do in too little time; for others, the underlying problem is a difficulty in making decisions, sorting, or categorizing; for still others, it's about shame, depression, hopelessness, and the erroneous belief that they have no control over their surroundings, that the clutter will always "come back" no matter what they do. For many of us, office disorganization is a result of two or three of these underlying challenges combined, and perhaps others as well. If you have organizing problems and would like to understand their causes more fully, see my books *Making Peace with the Things in Your Life* and *One Thing at a Time*.

☐ "I can't find that report": Paper Management

You're on a roll, putting together all the materials you need for a big proposal that has to be turned in by five o'clock. Everything's going great until it's time to scan in that handwritten letter from so-and-so. You're sure it must be at the bottom of the pile on top of the credenza, but it's not. A frantic search begins, and an hour later you finally find the letter in a folder you'd thought was empty.

Poor paper management can be a major source of stress at the office, wasting huge amounts of precious time. A few papers thrown carelessly on top of a desk have a way of swelling into process-crippling piles and even, in some cases, to gargantuan oceans that may have serious emotional as well as vocational repercussions. Once your office is thoroughly deluged, you may get into a vicious circle, in which you waste so much time looking for things that you have no time to declutter. This is one of the few situations in which I would recommend actually giving up a weekend or two of precious personal time; the sacrifice may be worth it if an organized office saves your sanity and maybe even your job.

Over the years, I've come to believe that for most of us, simple is best where papers are concerned. Too many people have the idea that some fancy paper-management system that takes a whole book to learn will save them from paper problems. Others spend tons of money buying top-of-the-line equipment, somehow believing that genuine mahogany file trays come equipped with little hands that will reach out and pull the papers into them. Unfortunately, this is not how it works. The way to organize papers is not only to set up the simplest possible system for the different types of papers you deal with but also to establish the habits required to keep putting them there day after day. This can take awhile, but most people can manage it if they approach it in phases.

Blues and Battleshock Busters

1. For the first round of paper organizing, I recommend pioneer organizer Stephanie Winston's classic TRAF system. Get four boxes and label them in large letters with a thick felt-tipped marker: TOSS, REFER, ACT, and FILE. The Toss box is your recycle box (you may need an extra box if you deal with confidential materials that you have to shred); the Refer box is for papers that go to someone else besides yourself; the Act box is for papers that require some type of action; the File box is for papers you just need to keep.

2. Once you've finished TRAFing all the loose papers in your office, get rid of the Toss and Refer items, then set up a paper-flow system for incoming papers (those in your Act and File boxes will also be sorted into it). In today's fast-paced office environment, this is what I recommend. Go to an office supply store to get a desktop sorter—which is simply a box with four cubbies, one on top of the other—put it together, and set it on top of your desk. Set a wire basket on top of it, which makes a fifth cubby. Label the cubbies from top to bottom in large bold type as follows: SUPERURGENT, URGENT, NON-URGENT, HOLD, FILE. To qualify for Superurgent status, a paper must require action today or something bad will happen. If the bad event won't happen until tomorrow, put it in Urgent. If nothing bad is likely to happen for a long time or maybe not at all if you don't do it, put it in Non-urgent. Hold is where you put papers that you can't move along until someone calls you, a certain date arrives, you arrive at a decision, or some other future event occurs. File is for the papers you just want to store away. If you try to empty your File cubby at the end of every workday, maybe you'll at least manage to do it once a week.

3. Now get your file folders in shape. Use colored folders even if you have to buy them yourself. Don't worry about color

coding—just use different-colored folders so you can identify them easily, as in "It's in that yellow folder." Print out file folder labels in bold, highly legible 12-point Ariel font, all caps, with no more words on a label than will fit easily. Poorly labeled file folders—with too much type on them that's too small to read— are, in my opinion, the number-one cause of lost files. If you've inherited a big set of poorly labeled files, take the time to replace all the labels with ones you can read—this will pay off!

4. Once your file folders are all nicely labeled, sort them into piles using two criteria: frequency of use and category of information. Separate folder groups that you use many times per day from those you use less frequently. Use a desktop tiered vertical sorter for the minute-by-minute files. For example, as I monitor expenses for various grants in my job, I keep a folder for receipts coming in for each grant in a vertical sorter on top of my desk. The folders you need a few times per day should be within arm's reach, perhaps in your desk file drawer. The rest you should file according to category wherever you have space.

5. Now set up your hanging folders. Print out labels for each category of file folders, stick them on white strips, and force them into the little plastic holders. Attach each holder to the left side of the hanging folder. Place the hanging folders in file drawers and label the drawers so you can read them easily. Then set the file folders inside the hanging folders.

6. Put all the loose papers in your TRAF Act box into your paper-flow system and file all the papers in your TRAF File box in your new file system. Now all you need to pay attention to is maintenance.

7. Each time you finish a task or put it on hold, put the associated papers into your system. Make sure you *always* do this, which will be difficult if you're constantly in a hurry. (When people are rushed, what they tend to do is save three seconds not putting this away, four seconds not putting that away, then waste three hours digging through paper piles later.) At the end of each day, file all the papers in your File cubby and look through all the papers in the other cubbies, making sure they're in the right places. That's all you need to do.

8. Purge your files at least once a year during the slow times, assuming there are any. If there aren't, take a half hour each day and purge a few folders at a time. Get rid of duplicates, outdated manuals, early drafts of things, product solicitations, brochures and invitations for events that have already happened, and anything you can easily replace.

9. Break the habit of leaving papers out on your desk to remind yourself to do a task. Instead, write the task on your to-do list (we'll discuss that in chapter 12) and put the papers in the appropriate cubby. Take a slow, deep breath as you watch them disappear. Remember: In today's world, there are few papers that can't somehow be replaced.

10. In sorting papers, don't get stuck on making decisions. To speed up your decision making—a skill that's easier for some people than others—time yourself when filing and try to beat your record.

11. Be selective about what you print out and what you deal with only electronically. Print out things that are really important to give yourself extra protection from loss, but leave everything else in your computer. If paper management is difficult for you, try to move in the direction of a paperless office, though in that case you may need help organizing your hard disk.

12. Don't be ashamed if you find paper management difficult. It's like math in that some people have an aptitude for it and some people don't, and you don't have to be good at everything.

13. If you have difficulty managing papers on your own, consider hiring a professional organizer to help you. Referrals are available from the National Association of Professional Organizers (www.napo.net) or the National Study Group on Chronic Disorganization (www.nsgcd.org). This will not be cheap, but if your job is in danger from paper overwhelm, it may be worth it.

❏ "I have 400 unread e-mails": E-mail Overload

You come into the office, open Outlook, and fifty-seven new e-mails are waiting in your in-box. By the time you've dealt with three of them, six more have appeared. Without a first-rate strategy for managing e-mails, you can feel as if you're struggling to shovel out a driveway during a blizzard that never ends.

E-mail overload is one of the most stressful challenges of contemporary office life. Yet somehow, many workers do manage to stay on top of it. Managing e-mail is all a matter of triaging, the way medical staff in an overloaded ER triage patients. Once you've got a logical system of directories, some good spam software, and a few habits in place, you'll be able to calmly contend with whatever comes through your in-box, no matter how excessive the quantity.

Blues and Battleshock Busters

1. Many of us feel most stressed when going through multiple e-mails, which may contain demands, criticisms, and other unpleasant types of text. To counter this, do what Zeer, in *Office Yoga*, calls e-mail meditation, focusing your attention on one e-mail at a time and breathing extra slowly, making each outbreath twice the length of each in-breath.

2. Model your handling of e-mail on your handling of paper mail. Create e-mail file drawer directories in whatever program you use for each hat that you wear. As soon as it becomes difficult to find files in a directory, break the contents into subdirectories, which are like the hanging files in the drawers. When new messages come in that don't fit into an existing directory or subdirectory, make a new one, just the way you would make a new folder. As much as possible, try to use the same labels for your e-mail system that you use for your papers.

3. Create an action directory labeled AAA for incoming e-mails that require some type of action or follow-up—comparable to your top three cubbies for papers—and mark superurgent/urgent

messages with red flags before moving them into this directory. (Labeling the directory "AAA" will make it appear at the top of your directory list, and thus make it easy to see.) Leaving e-mails in your main directory to remind yourself to do something is just as counterproductive as leaving papers out on your desk. Whenever you move an e-mail into AAA, enter the task on your to-do list (see chapter 12); take a long, slow breath; and let go of the message as it disappears. When you've finished the action or received the response you're waiting for, move the file into the appropriate file drawer directory.

4. Resist the temptation to instantly answer each e-mail as it comes in. Instead, decide on a time each day for what I call E-mails and Shorties, when you deal systematically with accumulated e-mails and perform those actions in response to individual messages that can be done quickly. My E-mails and Shorties time is when I first get to the office, mainly because my e-mail box often contains instructions from my boss. Some workers prefer to do their E-mails and Shorties later in the day so they can get project work done first.

5. Establish a regular E-mails and Shorties routine. First, make a TASK checkbox in your Work Companion followed by E-MAILS AND SHORTIES. This frames E-mails and Shorties as a finite task that you can finish. Then, starting with the oldest messages in your in-box, read each e-mail, delete or file messages you don't need to respond to, and send a brief response to those that require this, if only to let the sender know you received it. If the message requires some type of action that you can do in five minutes or less—looking up a date, for example—do it then and there, before moving on to the next e-mail. If it's going to take more time than that or you'll need to follow up on it, flip to your task list and enter it, then file the message in your action directory, AAA. This is how I handle e-mail on normal days, and it usually takes me about an hour.

6. You also need a routine for days when you're unusually flooded with e-mails, as when you come back after a vacation, for example. When you're flooded, instead of beginning with E-mails

and Shorties, begin with a Read-Only Round, during which you're only allowed to read, delete, or file e-mails, but not to respond to them or take any actions. After you've gone through all the e-mail this way and have dealt with any urgent matters, then go back and do E-mails and Shorties.

7. Talk with your computer support person about what antispam programs to use, without which you'll quickly find yourself buried no matter how much e-mail time you spend.

8. Never open spam, as it may contain viruses, and delete all suspicious e-mails immediately. Change your passwords frequently for extra protection. Be careful when you forward a series of messages not to include confidential information, and never send your social security number through e-mail.

9. Send e-mails asking to be removed from nonspam e-lists that you don't want to be on.

10. Set some policies about what types of e-mails to file and what types to delete. Some good candidates for deletion are messages the text of which is contained in a later message, thank-you messages, scheduling messages for past appointments, and any spam that sneaks through.

11. When you send someone a message, CC yourself so you can file a copy of the message into the proper directory. If you forget to do this or if you already have a zillion e-mails in your Sent box, don't worry about it. Sent messages are automatically filed by date, making them relatively easy to find if you've got the other half of the correspondence filed in directories, and you can always use the Search command to locate lost sent messages.

12. Do *not* make your life more stressful than it already is by using Instant Messenger or any sort of notification that beeps at you every time a message comes in, which will only distract you when you're trying to get work done.

13. If you're in a high-level position where you receive unusually large quantities of e-mail, have an assistant screen your e-mail and send out routine responses. If you can't do this, you may have to send out automatic responses that let people know that you aren't able to answer individual e-mails and suggest they contact you by fax or snail mail.

14. Take the time to regularly empty Junk and Deleted mail folders, as your system may slow down if too much junk mail accumulates in them.

15. Be considerate in not overloading other people's mailboxes by sending messages only to the appropriate individuals, not to a group, and never forward questionable e-mails to others.

☐ "Oops! I lost that file": Hard Drive File Problems

At one time, an organized office simply meant logically filed papers. Alas, that is no longer the case. Now we all have to keep track not only of paper files but also of files that don't really exist, being nothing but artificial constructs for making electronic superpatterns of 1s and 0s comprehensible to mere mortals, but the disappearance of which can nevertheless put our livelihoods in jeopardy. To make matters worse, these "files" are in constant danger of being wiped out by diseases that don't really exist either but that nevertheless threaten the survival of everyone on the planet.

To work in an office these days is to live in fear of losing computer files. Although such mishaps can't be totally prevented, setting up a sensible system of hard-disk directories and developing a few regular habits may at least keep the danger at a minimum. Doing this can also allow you to access information quickly when your boss is at your back.

Blues and Battleshock Busters

1. Assuming you're using some version of Microsoft Windows, open My Documents and look at all the loose files that aren't in a specific directory. If you already have some directories set up, move any files that belong in them into the appropriate directory or subdirectory. Now look at the files that are left. Create directories or subdirectories for files that seem to belong together, until no vagrant files are left.

2. Now open each directory, one at a time, and purge any files that are no longer relevant to your work, or copy them into an Archive

directory. Look at what's left. Could the contents of several directories be combined? Do some directories contain so many files that you need to create subdirectories to make the files easier to find?

3. Set up directories on a principle of efficiency. When you're looking for a file, you don't want to have to look through a whole slew of others in the same directory, nor do you want to have to go through level after level of subdirectories. In most cases, more than three tiers of directories are too many.

4. Back up your files. Most employers will provide file servers where you can save your files and they will be backed up on a regular schedule. If your employer doesn't do this, consider getting an external USB hard drive and setting up a schedule when you copy your files to it. You can buy a large-capacity USB hard drive for less than a hundred dollars. Some employers also offer a backup solution where you install backup software on your PC and, for a small fee, it automatically backs up your data to an off-site server on a schedule of your choosing.

5. To streamline your information, use the same categories for your computer file directories as for your hanging file folders.

6. If you're working off of a network and have access to various drives, develop clear policies about what types of files you keep on which drives, and talk to your boss if you're not sure what you should and should not share with others. Change your password frequently to provide maximum protection for your information.

7. Talk to your computer support person about what regular maintenance activities you need to perform such as Disk Cleanup or Disk Defragmenter, getting rid of cookies, etc.

❐ "I don't have the information I need to do my job": Information Access Issues

It happens all the time. You're progressing smoothly on a project until suddenly you encounter a situation where you don't know something you need to know to finish it. This is especially likely to happen if you're a "person Friday" or a head something-or-other who performs many different types of tasks.

There are two types of information you may need to use in the course of your workday:

1. **Information you can obtain without involving anyone else:** This includes information in your own paper and computer files, manuals, books, and other publications. It also includes information on all Web sites and libraries to which you have access. Gaining access to this information is just a matter of finding it.

2. **Information you need someone else's help to obtain:** This includes information you can only obtain by contacting somebody who has either knowledge or access that you don't have. This person may be an expert in an area in which you aren't an expert. In today's computerized world, accessing information involves high degrees of interdependency with others, a situation that can tempt you to procrastinate if you're a shy person who hates to ask others for help. It can also make other people's vacations and illnesses problematic when only they have the information you need right now. Sometimes you can strategize around this, and other times you simply have to deal with the anxiety of putting a project on hold until the information is available.

Blues and Battleshock Busters

1. When meeting with others, make notes in a stenographer's notebook that is easily distinguishable from your Work Companion. Write out the date and underline it before each day's entries. Print clearly and label entries so they'll be easy to find later.

2. After a meeting, use a highlighter or Post-its to make important information in your notebook more visible. Copy any to-dos you were assigned or volunteered for during the meeting into your Outlook to-do list.

3. Make a list of the tasks you frequently do in your job and, opposite each of them, write down the information you need to do the task and where it is. For example:

1. *Task: Reconcile business credit card statements.*
2. *Information: (1) How to reconcile credit cards—in manual; (2) account numbers—list in folder; (3) information on hosting—who was there, purpose of event, etc.—e-mail host; (4) what account to charge what expense to—e-mail boss.*

4. Put all the handouts from trainings in a binder with dividers for each type of task and keep it handy, or file the handouts in a drawer next to your desk, where you can easily grab them.

5. Start putting together a procedures cheat sheet for your job—not just for others, but for yourself when you're asked to do the same task eight months from now and your boss expects you to remember how to do it because you've "done it before." Every time you do a new type of task, write down the required steps as well as whatever sources of help you used, including phone numbers and e-mail addresses, on the chance that you may come this way again. Copy information into the cheat sheet from the twenty-seven different manuals, Web sites, and notes from private conversations that you had to use to find out how to do the task, so that most of what you need is in one place. This takes time, but it will be worth it if it keeps you from having to start from scratch next time around. Print your procedures cheat sheet on brightly colored paper so you can grab it easily when you run into trouble, and update it whenever you do the task again to reflect procedural and technical changes.

6. Make a list of the key people to whom you might turn for information in different departments you frequently interact with, such as human resources, accounts payable, or marketing. Put together a directory of these people's phone numbers and keep it by the phone for quick access.

7. If you call one of your key-information people and the person is out of the office, don't just give up. Instead, call the department number and ask if someone is filling in for the person who might be able to supply the missing piece.

8. If you're not sure who can give you the information you need, start with some ballparking, calling people whose area of expertise relates in some way to what you're looking for even if it's

not exactly on the mark. The ballparked person can almost always refer you to the right person.

9. If you need information that's publicly accessible, ask a librarian. If your organization doesn't have its own library, contact your local library or visit a bookstore.

10. Take the time to perfect your Web-browsing skills and keep a list of Internet "Favorites" that you use regularly. A librarian can help you with online databases.

12

Peace with the Overwhelm

I'm hopelessly overwhelmed at work," you tell a confidant. But what do you mean by that? If you were going to draw a picture of your overwhelm, what would it look like? A tornado? A whirlpool? A mythological monster with a hundred hands? When we feel overwhelmed, we tend to think of problems in great big globs rather than breaking them down into parts. If you've been keeping a Work Companion and have begun putting together a Job Transformation Plan, hopefully by now you've started to think in more specific terms about the more stressful aspects of your office job and to problem-solve for ways of dealing with them. This chapter will help you continue this.

☐ "I never get caught up": Unrealistic Workload

Every day your to-do list gets a little longer, and your in-box a little fuller. You're either constantly hurrying or staying later at work every night; skipping lunch; skipping breaks; skipping life; neglecting yourself, your family, and your friends in a desperate struggle to "get on top of things."

It's no fun to feel like a rat in a wheel, and it can also be a setup for making serious, job-endangering mistakes as a result of constantly having to cut corners. If this is your situation, the first thing you need to do is stop and do some serious thinking about what's really going on here. There are two possibilities: Either your employer is giving you too much work or you're not working as efficiently as you could. Your best bet is to assume that both possibilities are true and proceed accordingly.

Blues and Battleshock Busters

1. Resist the temptation to deal with an excessive workload by working ever harder. This will only inflate your boss's expectations so you end up even more buried than you are now.

2. Don't allow yourself to work more than an hour per day of overtime except under extreme circumstances (when a big project has a deadline, for example). While it's reasonable to come in a few minutes early or stay a few minutes late to prove your dedication to your supervisor or finish something you've started, putting in more extra time than that becomes counterproductive. If you limit the number of hours you allow yourself to work, you'll work more efficiently during those hours. If you do work a significant amount of overtime and your job is nonexempt, make sure you get paid for your time. And consider whether the money is worth what it costs your health, family, and friendships.

3. Don't let hurrying become habitual. It's okay to rush once in a while, but making it into a lifestyle is bound to take its toll on you, and the faster you go, the more mistakes you're likely to make. If you're behind, rethink your strategies in order to work smarter rather than faster.

4. Don't get into a sick competition with coworkers to see who can abuse him- or herself the most by working the longest hours, taking the fewest breaks, or rushing around fastest for the sake of the company. If this is going on, talk to coworkers about it and point out how much you all have to lose from it. If you're

afraid that you'll lose your job if you don't play the self-abuse game, go along with it for now, but start looking for a job someplace where the work expectations are more reasonable.

5. After going through your e-mails every morning, make a to-do list in Outlook or a comparable program, categorizing tasks. Enter *everything* you have to do, large and small, and continue to add to the list throughout the day. Doing this religiously eliminates the fear of forgetting to do something that fuels office battleshock.

    Next to each entry, put down the date when you plan to perform the task (not the date when it's due), breaking large tasks into steps. Go back over e-mails and notes from meetings and make sure you haven't forgotten anything. Add some extra blank lines for each category so you can write in new tasks by hand that come up during the day. Print out your list and use a highlighter to mark each task with today's date on it. Put an exclamation mark opposite each task that must be done today and do these superurgent tasks first whether you like them or dislike them.

    Keep the printed-out list next to your computer, cross off each task as you do it, and write in new tasks as they come up. The next morning, return to your list in Outlook, delete the completed tasks, and type in the new ones. Write the date at the top of the previous day's printout and file it away to serve as a useful record of work that you've done. This may come in handy at performance-review time or if you should become involved in a dispute with your employer.

6. Depending on what your relationship with your boss is like, print out your fancy, highlighted to-do list and show it to him or her, asking for help with prioritization. Bosses who give orders unsystematically throughout the day may not realize how the tasks add up, and presenting it in black-and-white can make a powerful statement.

7. While doing your quantitative analysis of your Work Companion, look at what kinds of snags are costing you the most time. Is there something you can do about them? If, for example, a printer keeps jamming up, a call to a tech person might save you big chunks of time. Pay particular attention to error snags—

situations where you have to do things over because you did them wrong. The fewer mistakes you make, the faster you can work.

8. Pool tasks and errands that can be done together—for example, taking all your mail to the mailbox at once.

9. Do some creative thinking about what structural changes in your workplace might reduce your work overload, and consider presenting a proposal to your boss. How many work hours are realistically needed to keep up with your current workload? Could you convince your boss to let you hire a subordinate to help you? Would you be willing to cut back your own hours so that a second person could be hired to share the workload? Could someone from another department be brought in to help? Time such suggestions to your boss with new projects starting or funds coming in from a new source.

☐ "I'm not allowed to make a mistake": Unrealistic Quality Standards

Sometimes the problem isn't that you're given too much to do but that you're expected to meet standards of quality that are unrealistic. Worse yet, you may have to deal with both an unrealistic workload and unrealistic quality standards, which tend to go hand in hand, the second often being a response to declining quality due to the first. In addition, part of the legacy of political ideologies in recent decades has been an attitude of harsh, unforgiving perfectionism throughout our society, including the office.

In their clinical classic *Interpersonal Psychotherapy of Depression*, Gerald L. Klerman, Myrna M. Weissman, Bruce J. Rounsaville, and Eve S. Chevron state that cultures that condition people to be self-critical, achievement-oriented perfectionists tend to preprogram them for depression: "Internalization of such expectations renders these patients sensitive to the gap between wish and reality and therefore prone to consider themselves weak, inadequate, and helpless during depressive episodes." In an age in which whole careers are wiped out every day by a single oversight or slip of the tongue, it can be hard to relax. Perfectionist management fads play into this toxic mindset, ignoring the fact that our brains are highly imperfect organs, everyone's has some glitches, and we all have days when the neighbor's dog was barking all night or we're coming down with the flu or that person looking over our shoulder makes us too nervous to concentrate. The critical question, then, isn't whether or not you'll screw something up, but how you'll deal with it when you do.

Blues and Battleshock Busters

1. The harsher others are to you about your mistakes, the more self-forgiving you need to be. If you feel bad because you made a mistake, pick up your pencil and write the following quote from Alexander Pope in your Work Companion ten times: "To err is human, to forgive divine." This will help to protect you from the toxic effects of critical attacks.

2. If the harsh perfectionist in your life is you, ask yourself whose critical voice you've internalized. Is it one of your parents? A former teacher, coach, or boss? Talk back to that voice. Tell it that you don't have to be perfect, you just have to be good enough. Rather than striving for perfection with a particular task, strive for continuous improvement, with doing it a little better all the time. Excellence is a matter of degree, not an absolute.

3. Enter each error you make in your Work Companion as an error snag. Along with the error, write down feelings, automatic thoughts, counterthoughts, and how you dealt with the error. Tally up the number of error snags at the end of each month and work to reduce them rather than to please an insane boss who demands perfection. As they say in 12-step groups, "Progress, not perfection."

4. If you make a mistake your boss needs to know about, never try to cover it up. Making errors is one thing; being dishonest is another. Chances are you can make errors from time to time and keep your job, but lying will put your future in jeopardy and is also bad for your mental health. Fess up and get it over with.

5. Cultivate the art of reporting an error to a perfectionist boss. A few dos and don'ts: Don't make a bigger deal out of the mistake

than it is. Do empathize with your boss's frustration about the effects of your mistake. Don't flagellate yourself. Do tell the boss if there's a legitimate reason you made a mistake. Don't make up excuses or blame others for errors that really were your fault. Do tell your boss what you plan to do to prevent the mistake from happening again.

❏ "I'm getting it from all directions": Conflicting Demands

When you open your e-mail, you encounter three messages from different people asking you to check on why they haven't been reimbursed for travel expenses. There's also a message from your boss telling you she'll need your report by this afternoon, and another from her partner, an obsessive-compulsive crazymaker, fuming in big block letters about your not yet having ordered the food for a meeting scheduled to take place three months from now. Meanwhile, a coworker comes in and tells you there's a weird buzzing sound coming from the light fixtures that's getting on his nerves and will you please call maintenance and get someone up to check it ASAP?

Today's office professionals often feel assaulted by conflicting demands between different people, all of whom act as if they're on the verge of bleeding to death. Faced with such circumstances, it's easy to panic and start trying to do everything at once. There are better ways to respond than this. Learning how to calmly triage others' "emergencies" can be a giant step in reducing office battleshock.

Although multitasking can be stressful, some people enjoy the challenge of it. Psychiatrist Edward M. Hallowell, in *CrazyBusy*, writes about working as a short-order cook at a roadside dinner between 3 and 6 A.M., when he was the only one at the grill, struggling to simultaneously cook "burgers, hot dogs, grilled cheese sandwiches, eggs, bacon, sausages, hash browns, pancakes, French toast, western omelets, and the occasional cube steak." He survived by setting his own rhythm rather than simply reacting to circumstances, allowing his instinct to tell him what to do first, second, and third. In juggling many conflicting demands in the office, the same approach of keeping control of your choices no matter what and relying on your instinct to help you prioritize may make the difference between feeling overwhelmed and feeling exhilarated.

Blues and Battleshock Busters

1. Repeat this sentence three times: "I am not an EMT." No one is going to die if you don't do something instantly, though *you* may die from a heart attack if you constantly buy into others' emergency mentalities.

2. Try not to experience people's requests as attacks. When many requests come in all at once, you may feel as though missiles are raining down on you, but that's not the case. All that's happening is that people are asking for what they need, which they have a right to do, just as you have a right to make them wait.

3. Whenever you start to feel overwhelmed, close your eyes and breathe slowly, then open them again and write down what you're feeling in your Work Companion. What are you afraid might happen? How would you deal with it if it did? Enter your worries as clouds and do what you can to reduce or eliminate them.

4. Prioritize for survival, using the Outlook to-do list described in the "Unrealistic Workload" section of this chapter. After printing out your list and highlighting today's tasks, decide which of them to do first according to the following criteria: If there's an urgent task on your list that you can do in five minutes or less, start with that. If not, start with your boss's requests, then move on to the others in decreasing order according to the probability of someone complaining to your boss if you don't do the task (assuming you believe that the boss will take the person's complaint seriously). This strategy will best protect you from being fired for not getting things done, the fear of which, for most people, is at the root of job stress. In the example with which we began this section, according to these guidelines you would:

1. Call maintenance about the buzz (takes less than five minutes)
2. Do the boss's report
3. Order the food for your boss's partner
4. Check on the reimbursements

    Yes, you may feel bad about the people waiting for their money, but when you're drowning you have to take care of yourself first or you won't make it. The name of the game is survival.

5. Write down the first task in your Work Companion and put a checkbox next to it. Deal with your anxiety about other undone tasks by entering them as clouds. Once you've done that, you can let go and focus fully on the task at hand. If you have trouble doing that, focus on the first step. Try to think of it as the only task in the world. Keep working on the task until it's either finished, you hit some sort of roadblock that forces you to put it on hold, or your workday ends.
6. If you can't do something for someone immediately, manage the person's expectations by letting him or her know when you'll have it done, and do your best to fulfill your commitment. If it looks as if you're not going to be able to meet a deadline for some reason, try to give the person advance warning.

☐ "I'm constantly hitting roadblocks": Obstacles

It's three o'clock and you're only now starting the report your boss needs for her four o'clock meeting. Things are going fine until you realize you need to get some numbers from a coworker who's gone to a meeting, or you try to sign on to an online system and it won't accept your password, or you realize the report has to be signed by the chief something-or-other, currently at a conference in Beijing, or you get an e-mail from the building watch telling you the National Weather Service has issued a tornado warning and ordering you to report to the basement immediately.

    Obstacles are a part of life, especially office life. They don't, however, have to cause you stress. It's all a matter of learning how to think about them and how to respond to them.

Blues and Battleshock Busters

1. Assume that your progress on every task you undertake will be blocked by obstacles at some point. Then, upon those rare occasions when everything goes smoothly and you pass through door after door unmolested, you'll be pleasantly surprised.

2. Develop an Obstacle Routine that you calmly follow each time you come to a stumbling block. First, close your eyes and take a long, deep breath. Then enter the obstacle as a snag in your Work Companion. Next, put the paperwork in your Hold cubby with a sticky note to remind yourself what happened. If you're waiting to reach someone, add a to-do to your task list to try the person again tomorrow if he or she doesn't contact you in the meantime. Finally, decide what task to work on while you're waiting for the obstacle to go away (which it will).

3. Let go of the idea that you have to do whole tasks from beginning to end, with no obstacles. That would be nice, but it's not always how life works. It's fine to shift back and forth from one task to another all day long, while waiting for others in your organization to act. People in organizations, especially large bureaucracies, are interdependent. While this at times means you're at the mercy of others, at other times it means they're there to help you out.

4. Think back through times when you've encountered obstacles while working on other tasks. How many of them never got finished? Probably very few, if any. If you wait, sooner or later you'll always feel a lurch and the train will start moving again.

5. Many obstacles are missing-person snags. If you try to reach someone and he or she is unavailable, contact anyone else you can reach in the person's office, explain your situation, and find out if someone else there can help you.

6. If you feel yourself panic when you hit an obstacle, you may need to walk away from the situation for a few minutes. Walking will help release the tension, and you'll be able to look at the problem with fresh eyes when you come back.

7. When it becomes clear that you're going to miss a deadline because of an obstacle, let the people who will be affected know

ASAP. Say what the obstacle is, but without unnecessary detail, which makes it sound more as though you're making excuses. Remember that most people—with the exception of the federal government (grant proposal deadlines *are* written in stone) and personality-disordered individuals (see chapter 5)—understand that the universe isn't entirely under your control, and will be willing to wait so long as you let them know what the problem is and what to expect.

☐ "People keep barging in on me": Interruptions

In *Finding Time: How Corporations, Individuals, and Families Can Benefit from New Work Practices*, Harvard business ethnographer Leslie A. Perlow describes a study of the work patterns of a group of engineers, many of whom worked eighty-hour weeks, to try to figure out why they were unable to complete their assigned tasks within more sensible working hours. In doing so, one of the things she discovered was that they were constantly interrupting one another. She suggested to their supervisor that they establish regular "quiet times" during which no one was allowed to interrupt anyone else. As a result, many of the engineers began working much shorter hours.

In office workplaces, interruptions (I call them "interrupts" for short) are a serious cause of frustration, overwhelm, and wasted time. They can also have a detrimental effect on the quality of your work. When an interrupt occurs, it triggers a person's autonomic nervous system, creating heightened arousal, which has been shown to have negative effects on memory, attention, and the efficiency of complex thought processes.

Interrupts can be divided into three types: *Mandatory interrupts* are simply part of a job in which the worker's primary responsibility is to respond to the needs of someone else—while acting as a receptionist, for example—although he or she may be given tasks to fill the empty time between requests that may be interrupted at any time. *Interdependency interrupts* are the result of workers frequently needing one another's help in order to complete their own tasks. *Social interrupts* serve to build relationships, which may be beneficial to the group but also make it difficult to get things done. What strategies you choose in dealing with interruptions depends on which of these three types of interruptions you most often have to deal with.

Blues and Battleshock Busters

1. For a few weeks, log all interrupt snags into your Work Companion with the name of each person and his or her reason for interrupting, then go back and look through them to determine the type and identify patterns.

2. If your job involves mandatory interrupts to tasks that are mere filler, label each of these interrupts in your Work Companion as a service task along with the name (or if you don't know it, role) of the person you're assisting and a Task checkbox, thus:

    ☑ *Service task—Tim—Take Bronson report down to the Director's Office and get signature.*

    Dealing with mandatory interrupts/service tasks this way will help you to keep from becoming overly focused on filler tasks that are not your primary responsibility and to experience more of a sense of accomplishment in responding promptly to the needs of others.

3. If you're someone's assistant, he or she may assign you a long-term project, as opposed to just filler, then interrupt you as you work on it with short-term requests, i.e., service tasks. When this happens, ask your boss if you should address the short-term requests before continuing on the long-term project. This will protect you from anxious feelings about being blamed for not finishing a long-term project due to your boss's constant interruptions with short-term requests.

4. To cut down on the number of interdependency interrupts, ask other workers to contact you by e-mail rather than in person, and check your e-mail several times a day.

5. If a worker interrupts you excessively for social reasons and you like the person, invite him or her out for lunch or a break so as to spend time together, but set boundaries politely when he or she drops by one time too many—"Sorry, I really have to get___

done." Practice a few catchphrases to use in this situation. If the interrupter doesn't take the hint, consider yourself at liberty to speak more frankly about the problem. Note: Setting boundaries to excess social interrupts doesn't mean you shouldn't spend any time building relationships at work, which can be healthy for both you and your organization. Social interrupts are only a problem if they cause you stress or keep you from doing your best work.

6. If you're having trouble getting major projects done due to interruptions and you're normally expected to be available to others, ask your boss if you can have some closed-door or quiet time, during which coworkers cannot interrupt you. If you're part of a group that meets regularly, you may want to propose such a scheduled quiet time to the whole group, bringing up the example of Perlow's engineers.

7. Finally, there's always the good old DO NOT DISTURB sign, which you can either tape to the door or, if you have a cubicle, hang in a prominent place on the outside wall.

13

Peace with the Tasks

No matter what your physical surroundings are like and no matter how organized you are, you're not going to be happy if you're at odds with the actual tasks that you're doing. There are, of course, some naturally lethargic folks who find any kind of work aversive regardless of circumstances, people who need to either marry for money or get psychiatric help. For the rest of us, job satisfaction may be affected by a multitude of task characteristics such as variety, quantity, wholeness or fragmentation, suitability to one's talents and education, control over how and when a task is performed, and measurability of outcomes. Every job is different, and the more task challenges you have to contend with, the harder it may be to like your job. The good news is that task problems can usually be addressed. The key to greater happiness is to identify the issues and do some good brainstorming—preferably with your boss and coworkers—for solutions.

☐ "I hardly ever do the same thing twice": Excessive Task Variety

In today's office world, too much variety of required tasks is probably more common than too little. Variety, up to a certain point, keeps your brain alive and allows you to develop new skills. Beyond that point, however, variety produces constant stress from your being asked to do things you don't know how to do, having to depend on helpers who may or may not be available, and having to use programs and online systems you've never seen before. Even if you've done a task sometime in the past, you may have forgotten how to do it, and even if you haven't forgotten, the way to do it has probably changed by now.

Finally, even if you know how to do all of the different tasks that are part of your job description, frequent transitioning from one task to another can eat up a lot of time, as has long been noted. Adam Smith, the eighteenth-century Scottish economist and inventor of the term "division of labor," in an essay on that concept, wrote that "a man commonly saunters a little in turning his hand from one sort of employment to another." While the general thrust since the Industrial Revolution has been in the direction of greater division of labor for both blue- and white-collar workers, in recent decades this has been reversed to some extent in the office due to electronics and downsizing, which have led to many workers' routine tasks being combined under a single job description.

While it might seem that an employee doing four different tasks that take two hours each should be able to get as much done as an employee doing two different tasks that take four hours each, this isn't the case, as Smith divined. Excessive task variety is especially likely to be a problem for the employee who is the only office support person for a program, department, or small business—what's commonly known as a person Friday.* If you're looking for a job,

---

* The term "person Friday" is derived from Daniel Defoe's eighteenth-century novel *Robinson Crusoe*, in which the narrator, stranded on a desert island, refers to his sole companion and servant-of-all-work as "my man, Friday." In the mid-twentieth century, the term "gal Friday" referred to female assistants who served as sole supports, but more recently, this has been replaced by a gender-neutral version.

you may want to take that into account and think twice before accepting such a position. Such jobs can be rewarding, but they're often also a recipe for role conflict, exploitation, and stress.

Blues and Battleshock Busters

1. Start putting together a procedures cheat sheet for your job ASAP, as described in the "Information Access Issues" section in chapter 11. This could save your life!
2. Make a list of the hats you wear and the best people to go to for help in each role, together with their phone numbers, e-mail addresses, and when they're likely to be available.
3. Rank your hats in order of importance, then show your list to your boss and ask how it compares with his or her priorities, adjusting your list accordingly. Make use of this list in deciding what task from your to-do list to tackle next.
4. If you experience role conflict, don't waste time and energy in a state of inner debate about what to do next. See the "Conflicting Demands" section in chapter 12.
5. Be fair to yourself. Don't blame yourself if you don't remember how to do a task you haven't done in a long time. Most people's memories need refreshing now and then. If your boss is on your case, you might want to look up the date in your Work Companion when you last did the task and remind him or her of this.
6. Sign up for refresher or update trainings to relearn skills you may have lost over time.

☐ "I'm afraid I'll get fired if I don't look busy": Task Insufficiency

In the 1980s, I spent several years as a part-time secretary for a chemistry professor. It was a job in which there wasn't always enough to do. My boss kindly told me it was fine with him if I spent my spare time doing my own work. He would come in and dictate a few letters, then leave me to work on my novel for an hour or two while he went off to teach a class. This made it any writer's dream job. Alas, such jobs in today's office world are few and far between. Not that people always have enough to do, but in a global economy of massive layoffs, if you're not up to your neck in work, you'd still better look as though you are if you don't want to wind up on the street.

Task insufficiency is often a negative consequence of seasonal and economic slowdowns combined with the practice of paying workers for their time rather than for the fruits of their labors. This gives both employers and employees security: The employer needs to know that workers will be available when needed, and employees need paychecks even during slow seasons. There have always been slow seasons in most industries, and if they don't last too long, they may come as a welcome relief, times when workers can clean out files, attend staff-development workshops, and build relationships. But when idle times go on and on, either because the organization has too many workers or because business is slow, the dual task of keeping one's neurological circuits charged and looking busy to the boss becomes almost more stressful than having too much work to do, leaving you exhausted and empty at the end of each meaningless day.

Not having enough to do causes time to pass far more slowly than when you're struggling to keep up with a real workload. Every hour becomes a desert you have to cross, and unless you have a boss like my chemistry professor, office blues frequently ensues. The question is, how can you get through such times and stay sane?

Blues and Battleshock Busters

1. Use the slow period for a good office cleanout. Get your files in tip-top shape, including archives, both paper and computer (see chapter 11). Clean out your desk drawers, sorting paper clips, rubber bands, and other small supplies into compartments, getting rid of pens that don't write and dried-up bottles of Wite-Out. Get special cleaning supplies for your computer and spend

half a day cleaning each individual key on your computer keyboard with a Q-tip. Move all the stuff off the top of your desk and scrub it clean. Rearrange knickknacks and update your bulletin boards. Take papers down to the shredder and empty your recycle box.

2. Now do what you can to develop your skills. Sign up for workshops and online trainings. Read through technical manuals, policy and procedure guides, or substantive materials relating to the work that your organization does. Ask coworkers to teach you skills that you haven't yet mastered. Tell professionals you support that you'd like to learn more about their work and ask for suggestions about what to read. Take a job-related course and ask permission to do some of the homework at work. Become part of the in-crowd that knows what's really going on.

3. Just because you don't have enough to do, that doesn't mean no one else does. If coworkers are overloaded, offer your help. You and your coworkers may want to talk with your boss about how work could be redistributed more equitably.

4. Use your time planning your next career move. Update your résumé and rethink your options and what you can do to make your skills more marketable. Treading water is okay for now, but you're probably not going to want to do it forever, and if you wind up laid off you'll need a Plan B to start swimming again.

5. Spend time chatting with coworkers and provide support to each other. Empathize with others' anxieties and share information.

6. Do anything rather than just sit for long periods of time letting your brain cells die. Your first duty to your employer is to stay healthy, and if you have to engage in nonwork activities to keep your mind alive, so be it. In that case, approach your nonwork tasks systematically. Set a goal for the day and work toward it, even if it's only to read *War and Peace* on the Internet, listen to every recording Miles Davis ever made, or speed up your proficiency at Sudoku.

7. If and when you're given any actual work to do, welcome the opportunity to work on it slowly and improve the quality. At a slower pace, you may be able to streamline your work process, cutting out illogical or unnecessary steps.

☐ "I do the same things day after day": Repetitiveness

Even when your in-box is perpetually full, you may become bored if your work is overly repetitive. If all you do all day is enter data, proof uninteresting manuscripts, or fill out online accounting forms, you may begin to feel antsy after a while, or just dulled out. Repetitive office work is less common in today's world, but it is by no means gone from the planet.

The good thing about a job with lots of repetitive work is that it's usually less stressful than work with more variety, as tasks become easier when you do them frequently. You're also less likely to get behind when you don't have to spend time transitioning from one type of task to another. If the work requires no more conscious thought than driving, you may even be able to do something else at the same time, such as listen to an audiobook or chat with co-workers.

The challenge of repetitive work is to keep your brain alive. Neurons that aren't used have a way of atrophying. If you don't do anything to stimulate your mind, you may feel dull and depressed. Employers who forbid neurologically stimulating activities such as Web-surfing breaks while keeping intelligent workers chained to a mental treadmill are working against their own interests. Do they really want a lot of brain-dead employees on the payroll?

Blues and Battleshock Busters

1. Play "Beat the Clock," challenging yourself to get as much of the repetitive task done in as short a time as possible, setting the timer on your computer and being careful not to allow the quality to suffer as you work more quickly. Keep the outcome statistics to show your boss at performance-appraisal time as evidence of your improved efficiency.

2. Each time you repeat a familiar task, try to do it a little better. The Japanese call this *kaizen*, which means "continuous improvement."

3. Try to look at the same old work in new ways by learning more about its larger significance. If you enter research data, for example, learn everything you can about the study it relates to.

4. Use headphones to listen to your favorite radio station on the Internet while you work. In addition to keeping your mind just a little busier, music can also be therapeutic if you crave more emotional stimulation than your work environment affords. I like to listen to piano music while I type and pretend that I'm a concert pianist as I hit the keys on my keyboard along with the recording.

5. Approach any repetitive task as a kind of meditation in which you try to be as present in the moment as possible. Pay attention to your posture, your breathing, and the thoughts that float through your mind as you work. If a particularly creative thought comes to you, take a break and note it down as a flash in your Work Companion.

6. If your workload isn't heavy, offer to take on more intellectually demanding tasks. Volunteer for trainings that will enable you to move up the career ladder to a more challenging, less repetitive job. If you're an administrative assistant, for example, you might want to take a course in graphic design, grant writing, or management.

7. If your work consists of several different repetitive tasks, rotate from one to another each time the boredom becomes unbearable.

8. Notice how each time you do something, it's a little different. Jeffrey Brantley and Wendy Millstine, in *Five Good Minutes at Work*, quote an old saying: "You cannot step in the same river twice."

❑ "I'm working on an assembly line": Task Fragmentation

When I was a research secretary back in the 1980s, I spent most of my time typing manuscripts. Although the work itself was unexciting, finishing a letter, an article, or a grant proposal gave me a certain sense of accomplishment. It felt good to hand a nice clean copy to my boss or stick a manuscript in an envelope and send it off. Alas, this is a type of pleasure that office workers rarely experience in today's world. Instead, we often spend our days performing individual steps in a task that someone else gets to finish, even though research has shown that workers experience greater job satisfaction if they can accomplish whole projects from beginning to end.

As technology has advanced, beginning with the assembly line and scientific management in the early twentieth century, employers have progressively engaged in an emotionally idiotic practice known as de-skilling, the breaking down of large projects into small steps for rank-and-file workers to mindlessly repeat while only their bosses are allowed to think. While at one time, a few factory workers might make whole large chunks of cars or even whole cars, now all they did was stand next to a conveyer belt and put in one piece, which required far less skill. Although this made production hugely more efficient, if "use it or lose it" is the rule, as neuroscientists tell us, the damage this practice has done to the human brain over the last century is unimaginable. And emotionally, it has resulted in factory workers becoming "alienated," disconnected from work they might once have enjoyed.

While in the electronic age, increases in task variety may have helped to counter some of the brain-damaging effects of de-skilling for rank-and-file office workers, the same alienation effect has become very much a reality for those forced to type meaningless bits of information onto online forms all day—forms they may never even see completely filled out—before sending them on to the next person on the assembly line. Often, too, completing work simply means sending something off online rather than printing out a manuscript you can hold in your hand. In such circumstances, it can be hard to feel that your work is meaningful. Any sense of wholeness that you do have about your job you must create yourself. This is difficult, but not impossible. The key word here is "interconnection."

Blues and Battleshock Busters

1. Make it your business to find out who performs the steps before and after your own on the projects in which you're involved. Make a list of these people in "assembly line" order. Contact the people who immediately precede you in the sequence and let them know what they can do to make your job easier, and contact the people who follow you and find out what they would like you to do.

2. Spend enough time schmoozing with others whose duties intersect with yours that you experience them as real people, not just wheel cogs.

3. Use your imagination to visualize the chain of activities you are a part of and their ultimate realization in concrete terms. If you work in a payroll office, for example, imagine an employee going to the bank and withdrawing money on payday, then taking it to the store to buy groceries to feed his or her family. Feeling yourself a part of this process will help to make your work more meaningful.

4. Talk to your boss about what projects you might take on that you could complete from beginning to end. If you're good at writing, for example, could you produce articles for the organization's newsletter?

❑ "Why did I go to college?": Intellectual Deprivation

In *Work in America*, a report issued by a task force to the Department of Health, Education, and Welfare in 1974, one college graduate wrote,

> I didn't go to school for four years to type. I'm bored, continuously humiliated. They sent me to Xerox school for three hours. . . . I realize that I sound cocky, but after you've been in the academic world . . . and someone tries to teach you to push a button you get pretty mad. They even gave me

a gold-plated plaque to show I've learned how to use the machine.

While bookish types may find office work a little more challenging now than it was in the seventies, if you're one of those people who loves history and philosophy, psychology and literature, chances are you'll still find most types of office work pathetically undernourishing. Job trainings on how to set up a better balance sheet or use a database program do little to satisfy a mind that yearns to be analyzing the Cuban missile crisis, paraphrasing a speech from *Othello*, or discoursing on Leonardo da Vinci's *Virgin of the Rocks*. While graduate school is the obvious place for scholarly types to head, academic life is highly competitive and suits some liberal arts enthusiasts better than others. Meanwhile, even people who've read *Beowulf* in the original old English have to eat.

These folks rarely complain to their office coworkers about their intellectual cravings for fear of sounding snobbish, but their suffering is real, as is liberally documented in poems, novels, and films. Throughout history, office employers have failed to recognize that academically and artistically gifted people may be as much in need of accommodations as people with learning disabilities. Such individuals may become depressed and underproductive when denied the mental food they crave, and mere technical education is often not sufficient. If this is you, your best bet is to look for a boss with a good academic brain. If you're working for a professor or a journalist, it may be a lot easier to explain your cravings than if you're working for someone with only practical types of intelligence, who may not be able to understand why you're not thrilled by training in using a new copy machine.

Blues and Battleshock Busters

1. If, for practical reasons, you have to get an office job, look for one in an academic department, a publishing company, an arts organization, a library, or someplace else where you won't be the only liberal arts type within a hundred-mile radius.

2. Make sure you get plenty of intellectual stimulation away from the office. Take courses, read, write, listen to audiobooks while commuting or exercising, or watch interesting films. Spend your lunch hours going to lectures or museums.

3. Start a lunchtime book discussion group. Don't be discouraged if the people who show up have less sophisticated literary tastes than you do. All minds have something to teach us.

4. Keep your eyes open for people at work who share your interests. If you see someone reading a book during lunch that intrigues you, ask the person to tell you about it.

5. Once you've mastered your job, reframe it as some type of research project, whether for a book, a piece of art, or a scientific study; take notes; and do some related reading outside of work. Be careful, however, that you don't become so preoccupied with your project that you fail to attend to your work duties.

6. Make it your business to learn as much as you can about your organization, the type of work it does, and the history of that type of work. Consider whether you might want to do the type of work that the professionals you support are doing, and what type of education that would require. If your boss is an academic, ask permission to sit in on his or her classes.

7. Listen to public radio or recorded books while doing repetitive tasks.

8. Take five-minute Web breaks every few hours to read something short that interests you. This is not time theft any more than going to the bathroom or getting a drink of water is; it recharges dying neurons.

9. If someone in your workplace is fluent in a language other than English, ask him or her to practice conversing with you in it. If English is the other person's second language, you may be able to help each other.

☐ "I just can't do this": Daunting Tasks

Nothing can be scarier in the workplace than being assigned a task that you expect to be difficult for you, if not impossible. If you're like most people, what you'll want to do when that happens is procrastinate. You'll somehow convince yourself that if you put the daunting task out of your mind, it will go away, but it won't. You might not be thinking about it anymore, but your boss still will be, and sooner or later he or she will ask, "How's that project coming?" and you'll have to admit that you haven't even started it yet and deal with the consequences.

Rather than putting off a daunting task, you need to face up to it and figure out exactly why you expect it to be so difficult. There can be five possible reasons for this:

1. You've never done the task before. It might not be hard at all, but you're afraid of the unknown.
2. You don't know how to do the task because you were never given the necessary training and aren't sure how to get it. This is particularly scary if you foolishly let your boss think you knew how to do whatever it is when you were hired, in which case you'll need to scramble around and find some way to pick up the new skill before the truth comes out.
3. You've done the task before but you've forgotten how. In this case, you may be afraid to ask someone else—especially your boss—for help for fear the person will say, "You should know how to do that by now—you've done it before."
4. You know how to do the task, but you have trouble doing it. In this case, you may have a glitch in your brain wiring that makes it hard for you to perform a particular type of operation that the task involves, such as writing text, organizing information, or keeping track of a lot of details. You can be brilliant and still have brain glitches that make certain types of tasks difficult. For example, you might be great at reconciling accounts because you have good problem-solving wiring, but find travel arrangements difficult because your brain doesn't hold lots of details in working memory.
5. It's a big, long task, the kind of task that makes you feel like the miller's daughter in the fairy tale "Rumpelstiltskin" who was given a big pile of straw to spin into gold, thanks to her father's bragging. Big projects are especially overwhelming to big-picture

thinkers whose brains don't automatically break them down into steps. If this is you, it's easy to forget that you can work on a project a little at a time and may not have to do it all yourself.

What strategies you'll use to deal with daunting tasks depends on which of these five possibilities are at the root of your problem.

Blues and Battleshock Busters

1. If your problem is simply that you're afraid of doing something you've never done before, then enter your fear as a cloud in your Work Companion and get busy doing whatever it is. As soon as you've done it successfully once, your fear will be gone.
2. If you lack adequate training to do a particular task, talk to your coworkers and find out who can help you. If your organization offers formal trainings either in person or online, ask for permission to sign up. Discuss your training needs with your boss on a regular basis. Face up to gaps in your knowledge and make a plan for filling them.
3. If you don't remember how to do something you did a long time ago, don't be ashamed to ask questions. Most humans aren't designed with perfect memories. Once you've retrieved the information you need, add it to your procedures cheat sheet so it will be available next time around.
4. If you believe a brain glitch is the problem, try to pinpoint exactly what operation is hard for you and think of ways of compensating. If you have trouble remembering lots of details for a project, for example, you might create a memo file. If you find that compensating for a particular brain glitch doesn't enable you to succeed at it, don't blame yourself for this. Instead, admit to those you work with that you find the task difficult and ask for their help. It may be that you can trade tasks with someone who has different strengths or delegate the task to a subordinate. If not, talk to your boss, assuming that he or she isn't a crazy-

maker. (If he or she is, review chapter 5.) Admit that the task is hard for you and ask for his or her help. Making your boss a part of your self-improvement team is always good job insurance.

5. If you're dealing with a long project, you might need to do a Long Project Plan, especially if it involves other people besides yourself. Here's how: Make a list of all the tasks that the project involves, and next to each task, write the name of the person you expect to execute the task. For example, suppose your project is to produce a big annual report. Your task list might look something like this:

- *Gather information—me*
- *Write specific project and program descriptions, provide photos—contributors—Joe, Ann, Sue, Lisa, Bill, Leon, Jack, Bob, Fred, Jane, Herman, Ricardo*
- *Enter information and photos into computer—me*
- *Format camera-ready copy—me*
- *Create cover design—hire graphic designer*
- *Print report—hire printer*

Now set intermediate deadlines for yourself and others. Work backward from your deadline for the whole project, basing deadlines on how long different parts will take. It's okay to set false deadlines for yourself and others that are earlier than the real deadlines—everyone does this, and it helps get you to the finish line on time. Thus, your project plan might look something like this:

September 1: Make list of items I need, send e-mails to contributors, get bids from graphic designers and select one

October 1: Meet with graphic designer and choose cover design

November 1: Preliminary deadline for contributors to turn in materials

December 1: Final deadline for contributors to turn in materials

January 1: Final deadline for cover design

February 1: Send formatted copy and cover design to printers

April 1: Report is released

☐ "I have no control over how I do my job": Autonomy Issues

In the era of scientific management, industrial engineers talked about there being "one best way" to do any task, a term which has been recycled in the electronic age as "best practices." These are terms I don't care much for, because while they make sense in terms of the flow of papers, things, or information, they don't make sense where workers are concerned. This is because they assume that we're all identical twins rather than individuals whose brains are wired in many different ways, whose emotions are intertwined with their thinking processes, and who instinctively know how to make best use of their particular neurological and physiological equipment in accomplishing tasks.

In a routine office job, being forced to do things using a method that doesn't feel right to you can take all the joy out of work. Nevertheless, in the office world, constraints are often placed on the methods workers use to complete tasks due to the need for standardization. When this is the case, you may have no choice but to do your work the company way. If you're a copy editor for a publisher, for example, to decide to use your own private symbols for when to capitalize, when to delete, etc. would only confuse the printer, who has to read symbols written by many different copy editors. In such situations, simply letting go of your own way of doing things is going to cause you the least stress.

However, the need for standardization is not the only possible reason why you may not be doing your job as you see fit. You might have an anxious, micromanaging boss, or you yourself might be afraid of the possible consequences of experimenting with a new work method. How to respond to a lack of task autonomy, then, will depend on what's really going on.

Blues and Battleshock Busters

1. If you have to do something the company way due to the need for standardization, focus on the choices you still *can* make. The

copy editor who has to use standard symbols still makes important choices in improving the writing in the text.

2. If your boss is a micromanager, read the section "Micromanagement" in chapter 15, which deals with this issue.

3. If the culprit is your own fear of trying a new approach to a task, you need to overcome that fear, but do it gradually, taking small risks and experiencing the benefits before you move on to bigger ones.

4. In tasks where standardization isn't required, think not in terms of "best practices" but of "best practices for you," experimenting to find the best way to accomplish a task, given your own particular set of strengths and weaknesses.

5. Talk to as many coworkers as possible who do the same type of work you do and compare notes on your work methods. Try to find out why they choose the approaches they do and reevaluate your own in accordance with what you learn. Then try some of theirs.

6. If, in the course of experimenting, you come up with a new way of doing something that you think works better than the prescribed way, share your discovery with others, including your boss if you think he or she will be open to it. Be circumspect, however: While good bosses welcome and reward creative suggestions from employees, insecure bosses may take it as an attempt to undermine their authority, and coworkers may not want to make the effort that change requires.

❑ "I can't tell if I'm doing a good job": Lack of Measurable Outcomes

In *The Three Signs of a Miserable Job*, management consultant Patrick Lencioni uses a parable about a corporate manager taking charge of a small-town restaurant in which all the employees hate their jobs to illustrate the value of "measurable outcomes." He asks each employee to figure out what he or she could count that would reveal if the person was doing a good job or not. The head cook counts customers' comments about the food and the minutes it takes him to prepare it. The waitress counts tips. The dishwasher counts the number of clean dishes he has ready to be used at certain points. In other words, the manager makes the work into a game in which each employee continually challenges him- or herself to get a better score. Soon all the employees are happily working to improve their scores, and the restaurant becomes a success. All because of measurable outcomes.

In the real world, this may not be the answer to everything, but it's at least a piece of the puzzle. One thing workers of all sorts, including office workers, need in order to be happy is some kind of feedback that comes not from a boss—whose praise or blame may have more to do with his or her personality or moods than the worker's performance—but from the work itself. This feedback can be quantitative, i.e., measurable outcomes, but it can also be qualitative. The worker who enters data, for example, can track the number of data sheets entered. The copy editor can look at how significantly he or she was able to improve the quality of the text.

In some office jobs, however, this can be difficult, especially in jobs with highly various and fragmented tasks or in assistantship positions where one simply does whatever one is told. Still, as Lencioni's example illustrates, where there's a will, it's not impossible.

Blues and Battleshock Busters

1. Ask yourself the key question that Lencioni's corporate manager asks the restaurant workers: How do you know if you're doing a good job? Spend some time writing in your Work Companion about this.
2. Ask some coworkers the same question and see what you can learn from their answers.
3. Then ask yourself a second question: Is there something here I can count? This may or may not be a question you can answer easily. If your job is to sort checks into piles all day in a bank office, for example, you can simply count the number of checks you sort. If your tasks are more varied or fragmented, it can be more difficult.

4. For those in the second group, here are some things you can count: (1) The number of times each week that someone tells you or you discover yourself that you've made a mistake—this is easy, as they should all be recorded as error snags in your Work Companion. (2) The number of items left undone on your to-do list at the end of each week. (3) The number of papers left in your top three paper-flow trays—Superurgent, Urgent, and Non-urgent—at the end of each week.

5. Note that in many cases what you can count is what doesn't happen. If you're a clerk in a government office who checks over certain tax forms before sending them on to another office, your measurable outcome may be the number of forms that come back because you missed a red flag you should have noticed, a score that you try to make as low as possible, as in golf.

6. If you're somebody's assistant, you'll know if you're doing a good job by how your boss seems to feel and how much he or she seems to be getting done. Good assistantship is about relieving someone else of tasks and stress so the person is free to accomplish more of the tasks he or she was hired to do. This may be hard to quantify, but not impossible. At the end of each workday on which you interacted with your boss, ask yourself what the person's mood seemed to be like. Did he or she seem sad or happy? Tired or energetic? Frantic or relaxed and in control? Give the person's mood a score on a scale from 0 to 10. Then ask yourself how productive your boss seemed to be and do the same thing, ending up with a boss's productivity score. Do this each day and chart your findings on a graph.

7. If you're an assistant but you're not a numerical type, you may prefer to take a more qualitative approach, simply noticing how your boss seems to be feeling and working in order to get a feel for how you're doing yourself. And your boss's "I feel" statements count too. The highest praise I received from my current boss was when he ended a performance appraisal with the words "I feel better having her here." Such words are music to an assistant's ears.

8. No matter what measures of outcome you use, remember that they can never be more than rough measures, because they may

be affected by many factors beyond your control. If you're counting errors, for example, you're likely to make more mistakes if you're forced to work faster due to a heavy workload than if you can take your time. If you're counting the number of to-dos left on a list, the results can be drastically affected by a single time-consuming assignment. If your boss's mood or productivity are your gauge, it's obvious that these can be hugely affected by factors you may know nothing about.

9. In evaluating your measurable outcomes, look mainly at the big picture. Charting them on a graph, which is easy to do in Excel, will help you to do this.

10. When your numbers falter, try to figure out the reason and develop a plan to overcome whatever problems have arisen.

14

Peace with the Disconnect

M ost office workers don't work alone. Yet many complain of loneliness, isolation, conflict, and lack of communication with other workers. Human beings need to feel emotionally connected to families, friends, and communities, though until recently this fundamental psychological fact has been largely ignored. Psychiatrist Edward M. Hallowell writes, "When people comment on the perils and possibilities of modern life, they usually skip over these crucial ones: the damages done by disconnecting as well as the benefits conferred by connecting."

Research shows that feelings of social connection are vital to health and well-being, making the lack thereof in workplaces and elsewhere a serious public health issue. This is less a matter of how many people you have around you than how meaningful your relationships feel. In *Loneliness: Human Nature and the Need for Social Connection*, psychologist John T. Cacioppo and coauthor William Patrick write that chronic feelings of loneliness can have devastating effects on people's health, compromising their immune and cardiovascular systems and even accelerating the aging process. "Over time," they write, "these changes in physiology are

compounded in ways that may be hastening millions of people to
an early grave."

Along with feeling connected, people also need to feel that others
appreciate them and that they can be proud of the roles they play
within their groups. They need to feel that when they speak, at least
some people understand them and value what they have to say.
When these emotional needs aren't met at the office, office blues and
depression can result.

❏ "I miss the people I love": Separation Issues

One of the greatest challenges of confinement to a traditional office
is separation from loved ones, who may spend their work, school,
and at-home days far away. Part of the sadness we may feel at work
may just be the result of needing more contact with family and close
friends than office life affords. In addition, many office workers feel
cut off from their own communities. While at one time, most office
buildings were located in downtown districts that also contained
shops, restaurants, churches, and other types of buildings, many
have now been banished to the no-man's-land between cities, where
no place is available for workers to walk, eat, or socialize with anyone outside their own organizations.

The structure of present-day office workplaces makes connection
with families, nonwork friends, and communities difficult but not
impossible. Although you may not be able to bring loved ones to
work every day, you *can* find ways to connect with them, however
imperfectly. All this requires is a little extra effort.

Blues and Battleshock Busters

1. Explore the possibility of doing all or part of your work from
   home or changing your hours to allow for more contact with
   loved ones.
2. Bring photos to work of the important people in your life, past
   and present. Don't bring just head shots but photos from vaca-

tions and happy times, or of your loved ones at work or school. Make sure you put your photos where you can see them, and yes, it's okay to talk to them when you're alone. An artist friend of mine made a big, beautiful photo collage of his family members that is on the wall opposite his desk.

3. Make videos or ask other family members to do so, and put them on a disk or Web site where you can play them. These days, I take a "baby break" every afternoon. While snacking, I go to the blog my son and daughter-in-law set up to share videos of my twin grandchildren, Charlie and Rachel. After watching them splashing in the bathtub, banging on the piano, or struggling to take their first steps, I always return to my work revitalized.

4. If you have an infant, talk with your boss about other alternatives than separation from your child for eight or more hours every day, which isn't ideal for either child or parent. If you work for a large organization, day care may be available in the building where you work so you can look in on your little one every now and then. (A few employers even allow workers to bring infants to work with them.) If you're a nursing mother, taking an extralong lunch hour to breast-feed your child or using a breast pump so your child can receive your own milk will be good for both of you.

5. If at all possible, connect with those you love at least once a day by telephone or e-mail. Any employer who forbids this shouldn't be surprised at high job turnover. Though chatting on the phone with friends all day long is likely to interfere with work and shouldn't be allowed, a few brief calls to loved ones may make the difference between a depressed, underproductive worker and a happy, productive one.

6. If you have young children, ask if you can set up a Web camera so they can see you from a distance when you communicate.

7. Connect with your loved ones in person as much as possible during your workday. If you have family at home and work near enough to go home for lunch, do so whenever possible. If you don't, meet family or nonwork friends in restaurants for lunch. If you live close enough to where you work for older children to visit you, allow them to do so if your employer permits this. You

may be able to put your child to work doing little tasks such as sorting papers or stuffing envelopes, which will make the child feel grown up and important. Make use of "take your child to work" days and lobby for more of them.

8. If you don't already work for a family-friendly employer, look for one and consider changing jobs, though you may need to wait for the economy to improve. This is too important an issue to let pass if you have a choice.

9. If you work in an isolated building, if at all possible, drive to someplace where there are shops and walk around at least once a week during your lunch hour. Form a connection with a favorite bookstore, coffeehouse, or restaurant and get to know some of the people there.

10. If you feel cut off from your community at work, do something to counter this on your own time: Volunteer for a charity, a political or religious organization, an arts group, or a professional society and stay with it until you experience people there as family. Everyone needs a village.

☐ "I don't really know the people I work with": Isolation

In today's office world, you can work with people for years and never get to know anyone well at all. I can think of three reasons for this:

1. Office workers today are often struggling to keep up with unrealistic workloads and have little time to chat.
2. Having to continually compete just to keep their jobs, workers often find it difficult to trust one another.
3. Office cultures have evolved to minimize conflict by discouraging personal communication and making many topics of conversation taboo in the workplace.

The result is that people who see one another daily often feel as if they scarcely know one another. To change this requires conscious effort. Finding out about people's hobbies and outside interests is often a good place to start. When I was first in my present job, I simply saw a lot of anonymous people that said hello to me in the hallways. Over the years, however, I've learned that one of those people draws fantastic cartoons, another trains guide dogs for the blind, another recently did a tour of duty in Iraq, another is a fine actor in community theater, and another raised twins as a single mom. While at first I felt that I had nothing in common with anyone, as I've gotten to know people, I've found many with whom I have common interests—even a few social workers and writers!

Blues and Battleshock Busters

1. Even if you're dealing with an unrealistic workload, give yourself permission to spend a little time socializing. In the long run, this may save you time, as you'll be more likely to get help from others when you need it.
2. Make a point of inviting at least one person to lunch per month. During lunch, try to find out everything about the person that he or she is willing to tell you, and be alert to evidence of common interests.
3. Start a group. Do you like to read? Organize or join a book group. Are you interested in genealogy? Look for others who are also tracing their family roots. Do you like to play a particular sport, knit, or garden? Look for others who share your interests and team up with them.
4. Join a committee. Large organizations usually have committees that plan social events, represent workers' interests to management, or engage in charitable projects for their communities. Though joining a committee can mean sitting through some boring meetings, it can also mean getting to know more people and feeling a part of something larger than yourself.
5. Look for a true friend or two at work you can be yourself around. Think about what qualities you'd like your soul mate at work to have. The person shouldn't be someone you feel the need to compete with. What's important is that you feel good around him or her.

6. Find a mentor, a more experienced worker who's willing to advise you not only about how to do your work but also about how to deal with the various political and social challenges of office life.

7. If your workplace has a newsletter, volunteer to write stories. Interviewing other workers can be a great way to get to know them.

8. Volunteer for a peer counseling program. Helping others to solve problems can be emotionally rewarding to the helper as well as to the person receiving the help.

9. While building relationships at work, also try to relax and enjoy whatever solitude comes with your job.

❐ "I'm nobody, who are you?": Status and Identity Issues

Do you ever feel as if you're just a cog in an organizational machine composed of anonymous workers? Is there a class system where you work in which an "upstairs" group such as doctors, lawyers, engineers, or professors treats a "downstairs" administrative and technical group as something less than full-fledged humans? Are you an assistant to someone who makes you feel invisible? In such situations, it's easy to lose yourself, buying into others' assumptions that you are of no consequence rather than the uniquely gifted human being that you are. This is not good for your mental health. While Emily Dickinson might have seen being nobody as a positive thing, remember that she herself spent most of her life as a recluse writing poems about death—great for literature, but maybe not so great for her. Barbara Ehrenreich, in *Nickel and Dimed*, relates her dismal experiences in low-wage service jobs to research showing that when animals such as monkeys and rats are forced to assume a subordinate position relative to others, this has a depressing effect on them. Such circumstances cause the serotonin levels in their brains to diminish as the animals become progressively more anxious and withdrawn, even failing to defend themselves against attacks.

In other words, to hold office blues and depression at bay, it's best to feel that you're somebody, not nobody.

Blues and Battleshock Busters

1. Put up a Personal Identity Board in your office, a bulletin board to which you can pin photos of your family and friends, your favorite poems and other writings, programs from events in which you performed, pictures that you love, or other things that remind *you* of who you are.

2. Outside of work, take up one of the performing arts, even if you're a beginner. This will both give you a creative outlet and boost your self-esteem. Singing is especially therapeutic for those who feel they have no "voice" in their workplace.

3. Write. The written word is a wonderful tool for identity building. Use it. Write in your Work Companion. Write in your journal at home. Write for your organization's newsletter. Post articles on a blog. Write just for fun. Write poems, stories, plays, or essays and send them out to literary journals. Or write a book and start looking for a literary agent.

4. Don't waste your energy trying to make people who see you as part of the furniture acknowledge your humanity. If they want to cheat themselves of all that you could offer them as a person, that's their problem. Look for people who value your company and ignore the rest.

5. If you're an assistant, remind yourself that just as a therapist doesn't typically tell his or her problems to a client, you can't expect your boss to pay as much attention to your needs as you pay to his or hers. The assistant role is inherently asymmetrical. To keep from losing your identity, it helps to do some things outside of your job where you can be front and center and to find an outsider you can talk about your boss with. Don't allow yourself to become a codependent worker-martyr.

6. Remember what Gandhi said: "They cannot take away our self-respect if we do not give it to them."

☐ "I just had a huge fight with so-and-so": Conflict

Many people in workplaces have the idea that conflict and fighting are the same thing. This is not the case. Conflict, which simply means people wanting different things, exists in all relationships and organizations. However, people deal with it in different ways. People who equate conflict with fighting are often conflict-avoidant. These are the "I don't want to talk about it" types. Others assume they can only deal with it by fighting, and do so. Still others face up to the conflict, consider logically who wants what, and problem-solve. This is by far the best option.

Blues and Battleshock Busters

1. When a conflict arises, stay outwardly calm even if you see the other person becoming agitated and feel that way inside. Breathe slowly and deeply and walk away for a few minutes if you need to.
2. Say, "We have a problem," and then reframe the conflict in problem terms: "The problem is, you think we should use overheads and I think we should use PowerPoint. How can we work this out?"
3. If someone blows up, suggest that the group takes a break, which should give the person a chance to cool off.
4. Don't blame others for things that are your fault or yourself for things that aren't your fault. Take responsibility, but be fair to yourself.
5. Use "I" statements rather than "you" statements: "I need you to get the mail to me sooner" rather than "You *always* wait until right before you leave to give me my mail."
6. Empathize, empathize, empathize.
7. If necessary, ask someone else to mediate the conflict, usually either a manager or an HR person. Many large organizations have special mediation professionals.
8. Without dwelling on the possibility, be aware that occasionally conflict can escalate into violence. If you overhear a conversa-

tion that seems to be headed that way, find some trivial excuse to interrupt—"Do you know what time the building closes?" for example. This can often help to defuse conflict. Keep emergency phone numbers handy and don't hesitate to contact security personnel anytime you feel unsafe.

☐ "So-and-so and I got our wires crossed": Communication Problems

Often when we think others are being mean, the problem is simply one of miscommunication. Just knowing that you and someone else "don't communicate well" isn't enough to change things, however; you need to troubleshoot for the specific problems involved. While you don't have the power to improve someone else's communication skills, you can work to improve your own, both oral and written. Communication is a complex subject, which is why I've subdivided suggestions in this section.

Blues and Battleshock Busters

General Communication Skills

1. Listen, listen, listen. You can't listen too much in the workplace. Listen actively and with an open mind. This means asking questions and, if you're listening for information, taking notes. It also means making empathy statements—"You sound sad" or "You seem anxious," for example—rather than judgmental ones, as in "You shouldn't feel sad" or "Why are you always so anxious?" when the speaker is expressing feelings.

2. Monitor how much you're speaking relative to the other person, never allowing your conversation to turn into a monologue. If you're talking too much, be quiet and listen. If the other person is doing all the talking, try to be more active and don't be afraid to interrupt if necessary to hold your own. Conversation should feel like a game of catch: back and forth. If the back-and-forth isn't there, do something about it.

3. When miscommunications occur, troubleshoot for the communication glitch. Who said what to whom? Where did the misunderstanding occur? Did somebody read in a message that wasn't there? Was something left out? Do this not to assign blame but to learn.

4. Pay attention to nonverbal communication. Conversation doesn't take place purely on a verbal level. We also communicate through voice tones, nonverbal noises such as "uh-huh," facial expressions, body language, and overall actions. If you see a disparity between someone's words and someone's nonverbal messages, point out this disparity to the other person—"You say I did a great job, but your voice tone says you think I could have done better," for example. In most cases, nonverbal communication will be more trustworthy than verbal communication. Note, however, that some people in the workplace are unable to "get" nonverbal communication or underlying verbal messages, and communicate only on a literal verbal level. These people may be a little autistic, or perhaps even suffer from Asperger's syndrome, a high-functioning form of autism that is common, though generally unacknowledged, in a working world that values technical capabilities more than emotional intelligence. If you work with someone this applies to, you need to say things very clearly and concretely rather than expecting the person to "get the hint."

The Art of Persuasion

1. When you want to persuade someone of something, choose your moment carefully. Don't ask the boss for a raise right after he or she has just lost a big contract.

2. Know exactly what you want before going into the conversation. If you're not sure, take time to figure it out. Gather facts, figures, and stories ahead of time that might support your case.

3. Rehearse what you plan to say before going into the conversation, perhaps with a friend who's willing to role-play.

4. Give the other person your full attention. Turn off your cell phone, and, unless you know this person's culture would regard this as rude, make eye contact while you speak.

5. Take time to build rapport, listening first to what the other person has to say, validating feelings, and sharing relevant experiences.

6. Explain where you're coming from, using "I" statements and giving enough details that the person can identify with you.

7. Put yourself in the place of the person you're speaking to. Try to imagine what's most important to the person and what concerns he or she might have.

8. Don't be discouraged if you don't immediately get what you want. Just as it takes time for seeds to grow, it often takes time for people to "hear" what you're trying to tell them.

9. If someone refuses to take no as an answer in trying to persuade you of something unreasonable, use the "broken record" strategy of repeating the same few words over and over until he or she gives up.

10. Don't expect the preceding suggestions to work if you're dealing with a crazymaker. In that case, review chapter 5.

E-mail Communication Skills

1. Pay attention to what you put in the subject line, and include the most important facts that you want the recipient to grasp quickly.

2. In a world that communicates routinely by e-mail, grammar is personal hygiene. If yours is weak, take a refresher course or study *How Not to Write: An Office Primer for the Grammatically Perplexed*, by Terence Denman. Write important e-mails in Word and use the Spelling and Grammar check before sending them off.

3. Try to put yourself in the place of the person receiving the e-mail and think about how he or she might feel reading the words you've written. Soften things that sound too harsh, and add thanks wherever appropriate.

4. Keep your messages brief, but be careful not to sound too abrupt, which can make the reader feel attacked.

5. When giving instructions in an e-mail, be clear, but don't insult your reader by putting words in all caps or by being overly repetitive.

6. Be considerate about not flooding others' e-mail in-boxes with announcements. Whenever possible, try to combine them into a single e-mail.

7. As a rule, don't communicate using instant-messaging. If you want to have a back-and-forth conversation, use the phone, and if you want to write, send a regular e-mail.

8. Don't make the mistake of trusting e-mail blindly. Technical mishaps do happen, and many a friendship or project has foundered on someone's belief that another person received a message that never arrived.

Telephone and Voice-mail Tips

1. When recording your own voice-mail greeting, respect the fact that your callers are busy people and keep it brief but friendly. You don't need to tell the caller that you're not there, which is obvious. Do, however, say when you're likely to be in the office and ask the person to leave you a message.

2. Don't assume when you call someone that he or she will answer. It's much more likely that you'll get a message system, so be prepared.

3. When you call someone and he or she does answer, or when another person calls you, always begin by expressing your delight. Direct contact is rare these days, and the more you reward a behavior, the more likely you are to get it.

4. If you make a business call, write down the name of the person you speak to so you can refer to that person if you need to call the same place again.

5. Think twice before saying something nasty to someone when you get frustrated by a user-unfriendly phone system or a lengthy wait. Just because the listener doesn't know you doesn't mean he or she has no feelings, and you never know when you might need the person's help again.

6. When you leave a voice mail, be sure to leave your name, phone number, and some good times to call you back. Repeat the number a second time before you hang up.

7. If you want someone to return your call, don't say everything you have to say on your voice mail—leave a mystery that will make the person curious. Also, try to sound positive and upbeat so the person won't dread the emotional downer of calling you back.

Public Speaking Made Simple

1. Use as few words as possible for what you have to say. Remember Abraham Lincoln's Gettysburg Address. Keep it simple, but don't talk down to your audience.

2. Make an outline of your talk, and use it if you need to, but don't write it out and read it word for word unless this is standard practice for the situation.

3. Practice your talk in front of a friend or imaginary audience, timing it to make sure you don't go over the limit.

4. Make your talk as user friendly as possible, incorporating many concrete examples, stories, and metaphors, as well as visual aids, to illustrate your points.

5. Do a dry run whenever possible to make sure all the technology you're going to use in your talk actually works, and always have backup options in case it doesn't—a set of overheads as well as a PowerPoint file, a story you can tell to replace a video that fails to play.

6. Get some training in learning to use PowerPoint—a basic skill in today's business world—but don't feel you always have to use it. Using slides is a plus if you have a lot of information you want to communicate quickly, but it can get in the way if you're trying to connect more personally with your audience.

7. Don't put too much information on slides or overheads.

8. Be bold. Don't be afraid to reveal yourself, including weaknesses. If you have a sense of humor, let it show. If you have an interesting story to tell, do so.

9. If you use PowerPoint, don't use templates and generic photos or clip art but your own creative ideas and pictures. Speak in a genuine voice, not some anonymous perfect one.

10. If you do a lot of public speaking, consider joining Toastmasters International, an organization that helps people not only to improve their public speaking skills but also to feel more comfortable in front of a group.

☐ "I hate serving on committees": Meeting Issues

Do you feel disconnected and unhappy in workplace meetings? If so, try to pinpoint exactly what it is you find so unpleasant. Meetings are, after all, just gatherings of human beings, but they're gatherings that seem to affect a lot of us in a negative way. The reasons for hating meetings can vary, but the four big ones are irrelevance, understimulation, loneliness, and frustration. The trick is to do specific things to address each of these specific factors that you believe relates to you.

Blues and Battleshock Busters

1. If the meeting is irrelevant to your job, you might want to ask if you can be excused. If you're asking your boss, say what work you'll be using the extra time to get done. If skipping the meeting isn't possible, occupy yourself by mentally relating what's said any way you can to your job, or offer your services as a disinterested party to those in conflict.

2. Does the mere thought of sitting through a meeting make your hands and feet start to go numb? If you need a lot of sensory, intellectual, or emotional stimulation, you won't get it in most meetings, where you can't get up and walk around but are forced to sit in a chair while your most boring coworker sprays the room with colorless, odorless office-speak. Worst-case scenario: It's after lunch. In that case, try a little constructive fidgeting: Tip back in your chair, drum your fingers, doodle, knit, or sip something cold—a little extra motion may help keep your body awake. Also, think what you might do to liven up the conversation. You are, after all, part of the group. Could you ask a speaker to give an example of a point he or she is making or offer one from your own experience? Many people fall into office-speak in meetings not because they're stupid but because they think their own ideas have no value. Make it your challenge to draw others out and you'll never be bored. Only connect!

3. Is loneliness the issue for you? Do you feel different from everyone else in a meeting that you regard as a waste of time and that they all seem to take seriously? Don't be fooled by other people's poker faces. Chances are you're not the only one who'd rather not be there. Talk to others after the meeting and find out how they felt about it. You might be surprised by what you learn.

4. What about frustration? Does your group go around in circles talking about issues they never seem to resolve? Do they love to philosophize, but never accomplish anything concrete? Or are they so overfocused on details that they miss the big picture? Are you bothered by the leader's failure to keep the meeting on track or to interrupt a dominant member who monopolizes the meeting? Tactfully voicing your frustrations with "I feel" statements to the leader or to the whole group can help make your group function more effectively.

15

Peace with the Boss

It always amazes me how, whenever something catastrophic happens—even a natural disaster such as a hurricane, an earthquake, or a flood—most people immediately look around for a single individual to blame. As humans, we find it easier to attribute our problems to our favorite superjerk than to figure out what's really going on or, better yet, do something to cope with the mess. This is no less true in the workplace than anywhere else, and may partially explain the bad marks employees often give their bosses when surveyed.

Partially, but by no means totally. In a 2007 survey of seven hundred employees, management professor Wayne Hochwarter of Florida State University found that 39 percent of employees said their supervisor failed to keep promises, 37 percent said their bosses didn't give them credit when credit was due, 31 percent said their supervisors gave them the silent treatment during the past year, 27 percent said their supervisors bad-mouthed them to other employees, 24 percent said their supervisors invaded their privacy, and 23 percent said their bosses blamed others to cover their own errors. Most of these sins cannot be accounted for by mere context but do seem to relate to individual failings. Thus, it would seem that, for whatever reason, a good boss is hard to find.

Furthermore, good bosses can sometimes fall into not-so-good behaviors. In this chapter we'll talk about some common complaints that office workers have about their bosses and offer suggestions for coping with them.

☐ "My boss expects me to be a mind reader": Unclear Instructions

When your boss doesn't give you clear instructions, this puts you at risk for doing your job wrong, for which your boss will probably then blame you. If you point out to the boss that his or her instructions were unclear, unless your boss has a good, solid, observing ego, he or she is unlikely to hear you and may even accuse you of insubordination. Thus, if you want to keep the peace as well as your job, you may need to learn how to get the information you need out of a boss who expects you to read his or her mind. This may require some special strategies.

Blues and Battleshock Busters

1. No matter what your boss is like, be clear about your communication needs. You don't have to act like your boss's boss to do this, nor do you have to put yourself down. Just say something like "I tend to do best when people put things in writing" or "I'm sorry—I need you to repeat that."
2. Before you ask a question, be sure there isn't some way you can find out the answer without asking your boss. It can be annoying to bosses when workers automatically ask them questions without even thinking about where else they could get the information they need. Remember, bosses are busy people!
3. If you decide the only way you can get information is to ask your boss, continue asking questions until you have the information you need. Don't worry about looking stupid because you

don't know something. It's better to look stupid by asking a question than to screw up. Don't be put off if your boss becomes impatient, talks to you as if you're a first-grader, sighs noisily, or otherwise treats you like an idiot. Calmly and professionally ask for clarification until you get it, then do the task right.

4. Rephrase what you think your boss's instructions are in your own words, then ask if that's what the boss means. Keep asking until you're sure you have it right.

5. If your boss is a high-speed instruction giver, perfect the art of note taking. Use a stenographic notebook (not your Work Companion) and write on only one side of each page, which will make your notes easier to review. Before you meet with your boss, print the date and "Meeting with so-and-so about such-and-such" in your notebook and underline it.

6. After taking notes, go back and transfer tasks to your Outlook to-do list. Put in headings and use highlighters or tabs to make it easier to find things in your notes, which you will inevitably need to do. When your notebook is full, print the first and last entry dates on the outside and file it where you can find it easily.

7. Ask your boss to send you instructions by e-mail. Written instructions are better than spoken ones for three reasons: First, writing them forces the boss to slow down a little, which makes him or her likely to be clearer and more complete; second, you don't have to try to remember the boss's instructions or decipher your own speed writing; and third, once instructions are in print, you have concrete evidence of what was said to use for self-defense if you should be unjustly accused of incompetence.

8. When you start to do a task and then realize there's something your boss forgot to tell you that you need to know, ask yourself if there's some way you can find this out without bothering him or her. Has someone else in your office worked for your boss longer than you have? This person may be able to help you fill in the gaps.

9. If possible, arrange to meet with your boss regularly so that you can check over instructions, ask questions, and provide progress updates.

❒ "My boss watches every move I make": Micromanagement

Micromanaging makes people nervous. The feeling of being watched sets off the employee's arousal system, and when people get anxious, their performance often suffers. Also, because our brains are all wired differently, each of us naturally has his or her own way of doing things. Micromanaging can be particularly hard on creatives, who are constantly thinking of better ways to do things than the ways the micromanager demands, and feel frustrated in consequence.

Not everyone micromanages for the same reason. Many micromanagers have trust issues, believing they have to control everything around them to keep something bad from happening. Some, but not all, are obsessive-compulsive crazymakers. Also, micromanagers may be inexperienced, poorly trained, or emotionally unintelligent and have little idea of how their behavior affects their employees' performance. How you deal with a micromanaging boss is going to depend a lot on what you think is going on behind the micromanagement.

Blues and Battleshock Busters

1. If you believe your boss is micromanaging out of inexperience and is open to feedback, it may be beneficial to tell the person how you feel and that you believe you work better when you're allowed to do more things your own way.

2. If you believe your boss is micromanaging out of anxiety, your best strategy may be to try to gradually win the person's trust. Express your appreciation for the amount of time the boss is willing to devote to "training" you, and tell the boss you really want to get to be great at your job and that you hope, after such great supervision, you'll eventually be able to work more independently. Honey rather than vinegar.

3. If your boss is an obsessive-compulsive crazymaker, don't expect that he or she will ever stop micromanaging you or getting upset about even your most trivial mistakes. Don't make yourself

crazy trying to please someone who is unpleasant. Instead, clarify your own internal standards and work to please yourself. Just say to yourself, I'm going to keep doing the next task, large or small, to the best of my ability, no matter what this nitpicking lunatic throws at me. And update your résumé—you deserve better!

4. Never make the mistake of pointing out that something your boss thinks is important is trivial, even if it is. If your boss demands that you spend hours perfecting details that could just as well remain unperfected, don't argue—just perfect the next detail.

5. Think of a micromanaging boss as a Zen master who is helping you to develop the discipline you need to live a more rewarding life. Believe it or not, when you leave this person's employ, you will be better off for having made the effort to meet the micromanager's standards, however unreasonable.

☐ "My boss is an idiot": Incompetence

In the TV series *The Office*, Michael provides a perfect illustration of a boss who isn't up to the job. The ultimate doofus manager, he continually makes bad, politically incorrect jokes, plans Mickey Mouse activities, and subtly bullies his employees, which may explain why most of them appear to suffer from office blues. Alas, the Dunder Mifflin employees aren't alone. According to organizational psychologist Robert Hogan, 50–60 percent of managers are considered incompetent by their employees, lending support to Scott Adams's Dilbert Principle, that "the most ineffective workers are systematically moved to the place where they can do the least damage: management."

In considering how to deal with an incompetent boss, it's helpful to recognize that he or she may not be incompetent across the board. Some bosses are extremely knowledgeable about the tasks the workers do but have poor supervisory skills. Others may be great at the people stuff but know nothing about things they're supposed to teach others. It's also important to consider the boss's situation within the organization, as what looks like an incompetent boss may simply be incompetents higher up forcing a potentially good boss to act like an idiot.

Working for someone you believe to be less intelligent than yourself can be frustrating, especially if the person is unwilling to accept your input. You can just see that the contract he or she is negotiating is a road to disaster for your organization or that everything your boss is saying to a client is turning the person off, and yet be unable to do a thing about it. This requires both tact and the ability to let go of what you can't change.

Blues and Battleshock Busters

1. Don't make things worse by obsessing over your boss's stupidity and blabbing about it to coworkers. If he or she says something that makes you cringe, take a few slow, deep breaths before you respond. Keep one fact firmly in mind: None of us—including your boss—chose the brain we were given.

2. Assess your boss's difficulties and the reasons for them to determine whether there's anything you can do to help and how welcome help would be. Some mediocre bosses get by because they're smart enough to listen to the wisdom of more competent subordinates. Being one of these people can be rewarding.

3. Make a list of specific difficulties that your boss is having that cause you and your coworkers distress. Make creative suggestions, but be tactful, always speaking as a respectful subordinate, especially if your boss seems insecure. Does your supervisor, for example, have no idea how to run a meeting, allowing one person to monopolize the discussion? Tell the boss how you feel when you can't get a word in edgewise and ask for support in dealing with the discussion hog. Does the boss have little competence at a computer program you know well? Offer to show the person "a few new tricks" you've learned.

4. If you believe in your organization's mission, try to put it first—before either yourself or your boss—in deciding how to respond to incompetence. Don't try to aggrandize yourself by starting a

campaign to get someone fired. In most cases, this will be a losing battle that could easily backfire, and even if you succeed, there's nothing heroic about subjecting a fellow human being to this sort of humiliation. If you truly feel that your boss is doing something dangerous or hurtful, then and only then should you consider taking the issue to your boss's boss.

5. Beyond that, practice letting go of what you can't change. Your boss is, after all, the boss.

❏ "My boss doesn't know what I look like": Avoidance

Have you ever worked for a ghost? Some of us have. Perhaps he or she hires you and gives you instructions only through a subordinate. Or perhaps the boss doesn't deal with you at all, failing to give you the instructions you need to do your job. Or maybe the boss has at least spoken with you and given you instructions but is rarely around and fails to answer e-mails or phone calls. If you ask questions, the boss promises to answer them but never does. If you confront the boss, he or she may express confidence in your ability to "work independently," but you fear being blamed if what you do isn't what he or she wants.

Blues and Battleshock Busters

1. Do some detective work to try to ascertain the underlying cause of the avoidance. It may just be because the boss travels a lot, is exceptionally busy, or has something challenging going on in his or her personal life such as a divorce, a serious illness, or a recent death. Or perhaps it is simply a matter of personality: You may be working for someone who is exceptionally shy, doesn't like people, or is afraid to face up to problems.

2. Talk to coworkers and ask them how they've managed to communicate with the ghost boss. Is he or she ever responsive to e-mails—a favorite mode of communication among avoidant types? If so, what do your coworkers put in the subject lines?

3. Resist the temptation to take it as a personal insult if your boss communicates with you only through an assistant rather than directly. This is about your boss—not about you. If the arrangement doesn't work well for you, ask the assistant to schedule a meeting where you can talk directly with the boss about it.

4. If your boss fails to give you instructions, then do the best you can without them. Ask coworkers and others in your office about what they think you could do to benefit your organization and your boss, and carry out some of their ideas, sending periodic reports about your activities by e-mail to your boss. Be glad that you have the freedom to create projects that suit your abilities.

5. When performance-appraisal time rolls around, write out a list of the things you've accomplished and give it to your boss. Don't expect that he or she will know what you've done, though you might be surprised by what your boss has observed.

☐ "My boss is a crook": Ethical Issues

In the memoir and movie *All the President's Men,* *Washington Post* reporters Bob Woodward and Carl Bernstein investigate the Watergate burglaries and their cover-up during the Nixon administration. In the course of their investigation, the reporters visit various administrators, secretaries, and other office workers at all levels, some knowing more than others about what is going on. Some of these employees are more loyal to the individuals they worked for, while others are more loyal to the American public, believing the public has a right to know the truth. Those who know what's going on are often confronted with an agonizing choice: Should they betray their bosses and put their own jobs at risk, or should they keep what they know to themselves even if it means betraying their own principles and risking being punished as accessories?

Working for someone you suspect might be doing something illegal or unethical can be painful, especially if the person puts pressure on you to collude with his or her activities. A boss who behaves like this may be an antisocial crazymaker, or he or she may simply lack the moral strength to stand up to an antisocial individual or group. In either case, you're in a dangerous situation, and you need to get out of it ASAP and in the best way you can.

Blues and Battleshock Busters

1. If this is your situation, use your Work Companion to document everything, and don't leave it lying around where others can read it. Keep it with you at all times and take it home with you at night.

2. Keep your eyes and ears open and gather as much information as possible. Use your instincts. Talk to coworkers and ask if they've noticed anything, without betraying confidentiality or giving them information that could implicate them.

3. Share your concerns with your boss, but only if your gut tells you this is safe. He or she may be able to provide you with a reasonable explanation for the suspicious behavior. If your organization has a hotline where workers can express ethical concerns, use it to run your boss's explanation by someone who might be able to help you understand the situation more clearly. If you trust your HR department, you might want to talk to someone there about it, though be careful—this could have negative repercussions. It's safer to talk to a therapist, counselor, or friend outside the work situation, though these people may not understand the situation as well.

4. If you're convinced your boss is guilty, go to someone at a higher level in your organization and let the person know what's going on. If you're not satisfied with the response you get, talk to an attorney or someone at the appropriate government agency.

5. Do *not* let your boss persuade you to do anything illegal or unethical, whatever the consequences. It's better to be fired than to wind up in jail. If your boss tries to fire you, once it's on record that you reported the infraction and you've documented this yourself, you'll have evidence for a lawsuit.

☐ "My boss is a wuss": Lack of Authority

Maybe your boss is a nice person, someone you'd be glad to have as a neighbor or a sibling-in-law. The only problem is, he or she isn't your neighbor or sibling-in-law but your boss, though the person doesn't seem to know it. Instead of acting like a boss—i.e., a leader—this person tries to be everyone's pal, even the pal of nasty, manipulative crazymakers, failing to notice the pain the crazymakers cause others and providing no protection from them. Nor does the wuss boss do anything about poor work performance. The wuss boss gives excellent appraisals and raises to everyone, even those who accomplish next to nothing while others carry the load. And when a big decision is called for, the wuss boss convenes a committee meeting and has the committee vote on what to do rather than just getting their input and making an autonomous decision. This person is not a leader; if a crisis occurs, rather than putting together a bold action plan, the wuss boss simply throws his or her hands up in despair and waits to be rescued.

Working for a boss whose authority you don't respect can be an uncomfortable situation that requires some special strategies.

Blues and Battleshock Busters

1. Make use of the plus side of the wuss boss, which is his or her openness to suggestions from subordinates, to let the person know how you feel when he or she fails to protect you from a crazymaker or rewards incompetence. ·

2. If the boss tries to get you to make a decision that the boss should make, say the words "You're the boss—you decide." Or offer a number of different options from which to choose. Help your supervisor to clarify his or her own values by making statements like "I get the sense that what's most important to you here is such-and-such—is that right?"

3. If a crisis occurs where bold leadership is needed, don't be afraid to ask for it, with some encouraging words such as "You can do this—now's your chance to turn things around. Go for it!"

4. Nurture your boss's strengths by regularly pointing them out and expressing admiration whenever your employer does something decisive. Sometimes people just have to grow into being bosses.

☐ "My boss is the boss from hell": Bullying

Does your boss regularly lecture you in a demeaning fashion, call you names, insult you, threaten you, physically attack you, get in your face, invade your space, tease you with promises and then fail to keep them, publicly shame you, subject you to unjust "inquiries," or engage in any other behaviors that leave you feeling helpless, violated, impotent, and enraged? Does he or she have a track record of employees leaving because of such abuse? If so, you're working for a bully-type crazymaker and need to take action *now*. The longer you continue to work for a bully boss, the more likely you are to begin to believe that you deserve such behavior—you don't—which puts your mental and physical health at serious risk.

Blues and Battleshock Busters

1. Ask yourself if it's really worth putting up with daily attacks for what you get in this job, and what your other options might be. It's better to take a pay cut or a loss of status or opportunities than to stay too long in a situation where your health may begin to suffer. You may have great skills for handling a difficult boss, and these will stand you in good stead short term, but bullying will take its toll even on people with great coping skills. No one should stay with a bully boss long term, but many people feel they have to while looking for a new situation or in order to gain valuable experience. The rest of these suggestions are for these folks.

2. Minimize contact with the bully boss and try to deal with him or her face-to-face only when witnesses are present. Whenever you have to deal with the person, try to do so by e-mail if possible or, if not, by telephone rather than in person. The more proximity you have, the easier it is for the boss to upset you.

3. If you have to deal with the bully boss face-to-face, look the person in the eyes at all times and speak in a louder, clearer, and calmer voice than his or hers. No matter what you're feeling inside, always maintain a calm, self-assured demeanor.

4. Document all incidents carefully in your Work Companion and keep it with you at all times. Do not show your Work Companion to your boss.

5. Keep your expectations realistic. Never expect a bully boss to change. Just take care of yourself.

6. In your Work Companion, keep a record of your boss's attack behaviors and give yourself plus points for each thing you did right in response, whatever he or she did back. For example, "Bully behavior: Told me I was empty-headed. What I did right: Remained calm—5 points; acknowledged that I can sometimes forget things but said I would prefer not to be called names—10 points." Don't give yourself any minus points for mistakes—just points for the good things—and stay focused on what you do, not the reaction you get. Work to improve your total scores for the week. Make this into a game and give it a silly name, which will help deflate your boss's importance in your mind.

7. Watch for signs that the bully boss is behaving hurtfully to others and offer support to them discreetly after you see this happening. Before long you may have a whole network of covert allies. Management scientist Robert I. Sutton, in *The No Asshole Rule*, talks about a group of university secretaries who regularly met to pray that a certain dean would have something happen to him that was just bad enough to end his tenure. This didn't work—he continued as dean—but they found it therapeutic nevertheless.

8. Discuss the bully boss with someone outside of your work situation whom you trust to provide positive feedback and suggestions. While it's okay to vent, spend most of your conversation plotting realistic strategies for dealing with the person.

9. Do things away from the office that bolster your self-esteem. Anything that gets you applause, status, or praise will do.

10. Bring things to work that you can look at to remind yourself of your own value after a dressing-down—a trophy or ribbon you

won in a sport, a program from a concert or play you performed in, a letter from a loved one telling you how wonderful
you are, a picture of a child you're terribly proud of.

11. Above all, don't stop looking at other options and get out as
soon as you can. You're in the red zone!

16

Peace with the Coworkers

Coworkers can be the best part of office life, the one aspect that saves your sanity amid a sea of troubles. However, they can also be major contributors to that sea of troubles. It's the luck of the draw. In most cases coworkers can't fire you the way bosses can; all they can do is irritate you, depress you, compete with you, gossip about you, gang up on you, exploit you, whine to you, mess up your space, and take forever to give you things that you desperately need. Nor can they give you raises, though they can give you information, empathy, support, companionship, wisdom, and ego boosts. And life isn't simple: The same people who sometimes make you crazy can at other times keep you from coming unglued.

In this chapter, I'll address some of the most common complaints office employees have about one another and offer some ideas that will enable you to coexist more peacefully or even to connect.

❏ "If my coworker does that one more time . . .": Annoying Little Habits

Bruce makes that awful scraping sound with his chair day after day. Nancy *always* has to say the thing about money not growing on banana bushes at least once at every budget meeting. Leo tracks in mud every time it rains. Shonda piles papers on your chair for you to sign even though you've asked her forty-seven times to put them in the box on your door. Yang borrows your Scotch tape and never remembers to give it back. George drives everyone crazy with his weird, tuneless whistle.

Even most kind, well-intentioned people can do things at work that get on your nerves. Little behaviors that wouldn't bother you at all when someone does them once or twice become torture when repeated on a daily basis within the confines of an office. You know the person doesn't mean to be so annoying—it's not as though he or she is purposely trying to propel you into a screaming tantrum. Furthermore, you want everyone to see you as a team player, which means you can't risk starting a war in response to what is, after all, no big deal. Yet you also know that if you just keep putting up with it, sooner or later you may snap and say or do something you'll regret. What to do?

Blues and Battleshock Busters

1. Accept the fact that you have no control over your coworker's annoying little habit. You cannot make the coworker's mouth stop saying something or body stop doing something you dislike. However, you can find ways to influence your coworker to change the behavior. These include asking the person to make the change, changing the environment, changing your own actions in response to the behavior, or asking someone else to intervene.

2. Make a decision about whether to try to build your tolerance for the annoying little habit or to influence the person to change it. Either way, you'll wind up happier, but you need to decide.

Don't waste your precious energy arguing with yourself about whether to speak up.

3. If you decide to build your tolerance for the annoying little habit, simply note it down in your Work Companion whenever it occurs, along with a short description of what you felt in response. Then go back and write a less intense version. Change "My coworker left greasy food bags on the kitchen counter again. Why can't she pick up after herself? I could kill her when she does that!" to "My coworker left greasy food bags on the kitchen counter again. It irritates me when she doesn't pick up after herself."

4. If you decide to say something, don't expect that mentioning it just once will get a person to forever change an annoying little habit after he or she has already done it a zillion times. Don't initiate a sit-down talk or make a speech in which you state your request and expect that that will settle things once and for all. Accept the fact that you'll probably have to ask the person multiple times before anything changes. The offender will be all apologies, then will probably forget and do it again. Instead, assume that the annoying behavior will reoccur, but deal with the next incident and every subsequent incident as if each time is the first time it's ever happened. Keep your request brief—"Would you mind putting your bags in the trash?"—preferably as soon as the behavior occurs. If you can head off the behavior with a request as soon as you see it coming, that's even better.

5. When you ask a coworker to change an annoying little habit, frame it in terms of consequences: "Could you please use the box on my door rather than leaving papers on my chair? I don't want them to get lost in the shuffle" or "Don't forget to put your bags in the trash—I heard the boss grumbling about the kitchen the other day."

6. If you can, change your environment or your own actions so as to make the behavior less likely. Keep the Scotch-tape dispenser in your drawer so Yang can't take it. Bring a mat to put down where Leo can wipe his feet. Put some rubber casters on the legs of Bruce's chair.

❑ "I can't get my coworker to do anything until the last minute!": Procrastination

You're putting together materials for a brochure. Everything is all set to go except the part on the training program, which is your coworker's responsibility. You've already asked your coworker for it six times, and each time he or she promised to have it to you by the end of the week. You have a deadline, and you're going to miss it if your coworker doesn't come through. Although you can tell the boss why you're late if your coworker fails you, you don't want the boss to see you as a person who can't get people to do things, as you're hoping to apply for a supervisory position next year. What can you do?

Working with people who continually procrastinate can be stressful. When dealing with a procrastinator, it's easy to get caught in a vicious circle, in which the more you pressure the person to do the task, the more he or she avoids it, which increases your anxiety so you pressure the person even more. How can you keep this from happening?

Blues and Battleshock Busters

1. When asking someone to commit to a project, give the person a specific deadline—"I'll need this by noon on Wednesday, August 1"—and explain why you need it on that date. For example: "We want to have these ready to hand out at the next conference."
2. Be shameless about setting false deadlines. If you really need something by August 1, build some time into the due date and ask for it earlier.
3. If your coworker promises to have the job done "by the end of the week," pin him or her down more specifically by saying, "I'll expect it by Friday at noon."
4. If your coworker is late meeting a deadline, ask what the problem is and offer to help. The coworker may be putting off the task because he or she doesn't know how to do it. A few simple instructions may be all that's needed. Or your coworker may just

have too much to do and not see your project as a high priority. What can you do to make it one? Or he or she may just dislike the task and need a little empathy to get past the aversion.

5. Ask if your coworker has started the project and if you can see what he or she has already done. It could be that your coworker has hit a stumbling block that you might be able to assist him or her in overcoming.

6. If your coworker hasn't started the project, ask the person to do so even if he or she can't do the whole thing right now. Once the ball is rolling, the coworker may feel like continuing until the project is done.

7. If your coworker doesn't complete the task by your false deadline, don't wait until your real deadline is looming to take action.

8. Warn your coworker before you involve your boss. "If I don't get this from you by Friday at noon, I'll have to turn the matter over to Jim, and I don't think he's going to be too happy." This will probably take care of it, but if it doesn't, follow through and let your boss know what's going on.

9. If you have to involve your boss to get someone to complete a project, don't say, "So-and-so is being a jerk about this" even if you think that's the case, but something like "I need your help in getting so-and-so to move on the training brochure. I've already reset the deadline three times, but he/she hasn't come through, and I'm not sure what else to do. Do you have any suggestions?"

❑ "My coworker always has to win": Competitiveness

You and your coworker are meeting with your boss. At first it's okay, but then your coworker launches into a long spiel about a project that is supposed to be mostly yours, reeling off details at the speed of light. When she's finished, she offers to e-mail you all the information she's gathered. "I always try to be helpful when I can see someone's struggling," she says. Now she's going on and on about what a fascinating project this is and how excited she is about it. You're not worried about your job, as you're sure that your boss can see through the coworker's tactics. But you're glad the wastebasket is next to you in case you have to vomit.

And you have to admit, the coworker does work hard. She's always there when you get to work and always there when you leave and rarely takes a break. A few times you've tried to chat with her, but usually it ends with her saying something that's a veiled put-down, so you don't do it anymore. Sadly, you remember a time when you looked forward to coming to work with the coworker's predecessor, a friend who could enjoy a good laugh but still get the work done and who always supported you in meetings with the boss.

In free-market economies, healthy competition between peers is part of organizational life. Competition does have the effect of energizing people, and it can feel good to work hard, enjoy your achievements, and be rewarded with a promotion that someone else is denied. However, cooperation is also important in accomplishing organizational missions. And when people who are determined to win at all costs resort to unfair games like the one your coworker plays in the meeting, this can be downright toxic.

Blues and Battleshock Busters

1. Remember that it takes two to compete. Acknowledge and accept your own competitive side. If a coworker's competitiveness gets to you, this may mean that part of you also wants to win rather than just cooperate. That's okay. Ask yourself what winning means within the context of your organization. More praise from your boss? A promotion or a raise? A plaque on your wall? Do you think the prize is worth competing for? If not, it's okay to let the coworker win. If so, give it everything you can without putting your health at risk, or don't play.
2. Make a list of your own strengths. Remind yourself that there are a lot of ways to be good at your job, and that just because your coworker is good at his or hers doesn't mean you're not good at yours.
3. In talking with a competitive coworker, focus on defining differences, the underlying message being, "We're both great at

our jobs—we're just great in different ways." Once differences have been defined, respect your coworker's task "territory" and respond calmly but firmly to his or her attempts to invade yours: "Excuse me, I believe I'm supposed to be in charge of that project."

4. Cultivate your strengths and make them stronger. Take pride in your achievements and give yourself credit for them whether anyone else does or not.

5. Don't let competition for a specific reward be the elephant in the office. Talk to your coworker and bring it out into the open in simple words, such as "Look, I know you'd like to become branch manager and so would I, but that doesn't mean we can't work well together." Don't be fooled if your coworker denies his or her ambitions.

6. If your coworker behaves competitively in a meeting with your boss, show your boss that you know how to be a supportive team player. "Wow, she really knows her stuff, doesn't she?" If the coworker offers you "help" that you don't need just to impress the boss, graciously accept it.

7. Point out to your coworker how much you have to gain by cooperating in dealing with management, and ask for help in negotiating. For example, say, "Would you be willing to go with me to talk with Jack about our work schedules?"

❑ "My coworker always does things by the book": Rigidity

You and your coworker are going over the department budget and are trying to decide whether to authorize a trip to a convention where the travelers could make some valuable contacts. "We don't have much left for travel," you say, "but we've hardly spent anything on computers this year, so it should be okay."

"No, it's not," the coworker says. "Travel is travel and computers are computers. We can't spend funds on travel that the budget designates for computers. What if somebody's computer crashes before the end of the year?"

"But the end of the year is two weeks away!" you say. "And the company could really benefit from sending those people to the XYZ convention. Budgets aren't supposed to be carved in stone. Everybody moves money from one category to another. Everybody."

"Not me," says the coworker. "I was taught that you stick to your budget or else."

It isn't the first time you've locked horns with your coworker in situations where the person wanted to interpret the rules literally while you favored a more flexible approach. Your coworker's by-the-book attitudes are driving you crazy. If only the person would get a job writing directions for board games and leave me in peace, you think. What can you do?

Blues and Battleshock Busters

1. Recognize that organizations need both "strict constructionist" and "loose constructionist" elements to survive and thrive, though often these are combined in the same person or people. Thus, your coworker is playing a valuable role and so are you.
2. Step outside the box and say something to your coworker like "This company is so lucky to have two people like us. You make sure we follow the rules, and I make sure we bend them enough to grow." Defining differences is nearly always constructive.
3. Reframe conflict between you and your coworker as a good thing, not something to be feared. Although conflict makes many of us uncomfortable, it doesn't have to mean fighting. It can just mean weighing both sides of a question in order to make a decision. Share this view with your coworker: "This is an important decision and it's important for us to talk it through until we can come to some consensus."
4. Choose your battles. It's okay to let a coworker win sometimes, especially when the prize is insignificant. To rigid thinkers, small matters are usually just as important as large ones. Such thinkers lack perspective, which you need to supply with statements like "This isn't worth arguing over, so okay" or "This is really important, so I can't let it drop."

5. Suggest that you go to someone you both respect who may be able to see both sides of the argument.

6. When you feel you can do so in good conscience, take a strict-constructionist view of an issue and let your coworker know about it. Don't be surprised if you find the coworker arguing on the side of flexibility in order to maintain the balance between you. Over time, this may help to depolarize your interactions and make them less combative, though it won't work if the rigid coworker is an obsessive-compulsive crazymaker. In that case, see chapter 5.

☐ "My coworker doesn't toe the line": Laziness

"Oh, sure, I'll take care of everything," says your coworker in the staff meeting. You know, however, that a few days before the big event he or she still won't have scheduled the room, ordered the food, printed out the programs, arranged for the audio-visual equipment, or sent out the notices, and you'll have to jump in and do most of the work in order to avert disaster.

Most of us have at some point had to work with someone who contributes far less than we do to the completion of tasks. The more you do, the less the other person seems to do, and as time goes on, you become increasingly angry and resentful at all you have to do, while the other person accuses you of being a control freak. Laziness—which is important to distinguish from mere busyness or forgetfulness—also often frustrates groups, where one or two members often do most of the work while the others sit around and criticize the way it's being done.

Blues and Battleshock Busters

1. If possible, try to find out the underlying cause of the laziness. Your coworker may simply believe that you would rather do most of the work yourself because you're taking such an active role. Or the person may be suffering from a medical problem

that affects his or her energy, or going through something difficult outside of work such as a recent death or a divorce. It's
also possible that your coworker could be a passive-aggressive
crazymaker. All of these possibilities require different responses.

2. If a coworker appears sad, becomes tearful, has trouble concentrating, doesn't eat normally, seems to take little pleasure in social
activities, or looks as though he or she isn't getting sleep, the
person may be suffering from office blues or even full-blown
depression that requires medical help. If you think it's serious,
don't pressure your coworker to do more, which will only make
things worse and might even be dangerous. Instead, discuss the
situation with someone you think will be receptive. This could
be your boss, a coworker who does crisis counseling, a workplace
counselor, someone outside the workplace, or the coworker him-
or herself. Every situation is different, and use your instincts in
deciding whom to approach. Don't, however, just keep the problem to yourself. Depression is a life-threatening illness and
should be treated as such. Meanwhile, you may have to pick up
the slack for your coworker, perhaps asking others to help too.

3. If you find out that a coworker is grieving a loss or going
through a difficult time outside of work, express your sympathy
or offer your support as appropriate, including being willing to
do some of the coworker's work until the situation resolves. This
may make your job more difficult for a while, but if you're there
for your coworker now, he or she is more likely to be there when
life gives *you* a nasty blow.

4. If you think your coworker is a passive-aggressive crazymaker,
it's essential to set strict limits and get support from others. Re-
read chapter 5 for a fuller understanding of crazymakers, and
take care of yourself!

5. Are you caught in an overfunctioner-underfunctioner dance in
which the more you do, the less your coworker does? If so, it can
be helpful to talk to your coworker about this dance and ask for
his or her help in breaking out of it.

6. When you commit to a task, negotiate with your coworker
about who will do what and let the person know you'll only do

what you've agreed to. If you've played rescuer in the past, make it clear that you're not going to do that this time, and your co-worker will have to deal with the consequences. "I'll make the room reservations and get the programs printed, but it's up to you to order the food. If you don't do it, you'll have to explain to Jack why there's nothing on the table when the guests show up." Once you've issued such a warning, make sure you stick to it if your coworker doesn't toe the line.

7. If all else fails, go to the boss and complain about the problem. Tattling on a coworker isn't usually the best route, but sometimes it will be your last resort. If you decide to take this approach, be as neutral and objective as possible, sticking to a recitation of documented facts, and leave out the melodrama!

☐ "My coworker is an idiot": Incompetence

In any large organization, encounters with incompetence are part of everyday life. You try to explain a simple spreadsheet to a coworker and the person looks at you as though you're speaking Greek. You call your computer-support line with a problem and the person on the line has never heard of the system you're using, even though everyone was trained in it last week. Incompetence causes workers almost as much stress as nastiness and is far more common. The question is, how can you keep those who don't know how to do their jobs from affecting your well-being?

Blues and Battleshock Busters

1. Don't expect most people to be consistently intelligent. The human brain is an unreliable organ, people frequently change jobs, training isn't always the best, and the technical knowledge one needs for any given job continually changes. If you expect a certain amount of incompetence, you'll be better prepared to deal with it, and when you run into somebody who really knows his or her job, you'll be pleasantly surprised.

2. Know who the most competent people are at work and seek those people out. Know who the least competent people are and go around them whenever possible.

3. In deciding how to respond to incompetence, make sure you differentiate between lack of ability and ignorance due to inexperience. If you're dealing with someone who's simply inexperienced, offer your help if it's appropriate and expect that in a few weeks this person may be fully competent. If the problem is lack of ability, try to be compassionate but also try to find someone else to deal with on a permanent basis, as the situation is unlikely to change.

4. When a coworker's stupidity makes you cringe, take a slow, deep breath and remind yourself that the person did not choose his or her brain, that it's only luck that saved you from being given one just like it, and that people who have difficulties in one area may be highly intelligent in others.

5. If you work with an incompetent coworker daily, try to get to know the person well enough to find out (1) what this person's specific strengths and weaknesses are; and (2) whether this person responds better to talking or to e-mails. Take your findings into account in deciding how to deal with the coworker's shortcomings.

6. Adjust your own communication style to the level and favored mode of the person you're speaking to. Don't talk technical jargon to technophobics, and don't send e-mails to people who are barely literate—call them instead.

7. Remember that most of us become less competent when we feel anxious. Thus, it's important not to engage in behaviors that might make your coworker feel tense and have trouble concentrating. These include hovering over the person's shoulder; micromanaging; talking in an impatient, domineering, or disrespectful voice; demanding why a coworker did something; using the word "should"; or raving about how wonderful a coworker's competitor is.

☐ "My coworker is a slob": Messiness

You can't help it. It's the way you were brought up. Every night before you leave your office, you clear your desk, file your papers, and lay out everything you'll need in the morning. When someone asks you for information, you know just where to find it in your paper or computer files. Your office mate, however, is a different story. Your coworker's desk is buried under stacks of papers mixed with dirty paper plates, articles of clothing, and year-old newspapers. Any request you make to the person for information results in an episode of frantic scuffling through the stacks followed by a shamefaced apology. You like your coworker, you really do. There's no one more likely to help out in a pinch or bring you a casserole in a time of need. If only your coworker weren't such a slob!

Blues and Battleshock Busters

1. Understand that creating order is like math—some people have a greater aptitude for it than others. Your coworker didn't choose his or her brain and neither did you.
2. Try to identify the underlying causes of the messiness. What's really going on here? Your coworker could just be struggling with an unrealistic workload and trying to save time by not putting things away. He or she could be suffering from an energy-depleting illness. The coworker could have ADD or some type of learning disability that makes sorting or categorizing difficult. Or the person could simply like the way messiness feels (like a nice comfy nest), in which case the coworker will probably be as bothered by your neatness as you are by his or her messiness. My books, *Making Peace with the Things in Your Life* and *One Thing at a Time*, offer helpful solutions for dealing with the messiness issue.
3. Try to talk to your coworker about the problem, but in terms of differences rather than blame. "I've noticed you don't seem to have the same need for order that I do. Do you believe that 'A clean desk is a sign of a sick mind'?"

4. People with clutter problems can feel incredible shame in the workplace. If your coworker seems ashamed, empathize with the shame and let the person know that you understand that this isn't a simple problem. "I used to think that messiness meant people were just lazy, but that was before I read this great book that explained how hard organizing can be for some people." If—and only if—your coworker acts interested, offer to lend him or her your copy of the book.

5. Offer help and support, but only in helping the coworker to organize his or her space—don't step in and do it for the person. If he or she says something self-critical, counter it with encouragement. If the coworker seems overwhelmed by the task of cleaning up, suggest that the person focus on one small project—a particular pile, a certain file drawer—and deal with one piece of paper at a time.

6. If a coworker asks for help in setting up a filing system, don't set up one just like yours, which may be more complicated than he or she can handle. Instead, try to make things as simple as possible, and respect the person's need to control decisions about how paper should flow.

7. If you're unable to help a messy coworker, suggest that the person hire a professional organizer to come in after hours.

8. If you try to talk with a coworker but he or she is unwilling to do anything about the clutter and it continues to bother you, set clear boundaries between the coworker's space and your space and try not to look at the coworker's part. If his or her stuff continually creeps over into your territory, tell the person that if things don't improve, you're going to have to ask your boss to intervene, and then do so if necessary.

9. Consider asking your boss for a change of offices, saying that you feel your organizational styles are "incompatible" rather than blaming a coworker outright. Someone who's just as messy as your coworker is unlikely to mind the person's clutter, and you'll be happier with someone as neat as yourself.

☐ "My coworker is a whiner": Griping

During this age of personal responsibility and corporate irresponsibility, the term "whiner" has often been unjustly applied to employees who dare to register a legitimate complaint about unacceptable working conditions. Telling someone in your office that you don't think you should have to regularly work twelve-hour days (a serious health risk that many office cultures are in denial about), that you don't have an adequate work space, or that a copy machine that keeps breaking is driving you nuts isn't whining—it's simply drawing people's attention to a problem that needs to be solved.

This does not mean, however, that real whining doesn't exist, and that it isn't irritating to deal with. The real whiner isn't interested in solving problems but in expressing negative feelings, regardless of whether the listener wants to hear about them. All of us, of course, may need to vent at times to a willing friend or counselor, and workplaces these days give us plenty to vent about. But in a healthy interchange, venting is a phase that the speaker passes through on the way to being open to positive suggestions from the listener. When the speaker stays stuck in the venting phase, dismissing every proposal with a "Yes, but . . . ," then venting becomes whining. Real whining is not only depressing to listen to but also contagious. If you're exposed to it on a daily basis, watch out: Before long, you may start whining too!

Blues and Battleshock Busters

1. Make sure that what you're hearing is genuine whining and not constructive complaint registering. The only way to know the difference is to offer help in dealing with the problem and see if your coworker rejects it or not.
2. Resist the temptation to try to fix the problem that your coworker is whining about. This will not work, and it's not really what the person wants. What your coworker wants is to know that someone else can hear how unhappy he or she is. Instead of saying "Have you tried . . ." or "You might want to . . . ," say

something like "I'm sorry you're having such a hard time—you sound pretty miserable. Is there anything you'd like me to do to help?"

3. Watch for signs that your coworker is suffering from depression, and don't be afraid to ask questions. "You know—I get the sense you're going through a difficult time. Have you been sleeping okay lately?" Possible signs of depression include sleeplessness, change in appetite, sadness, hopelessness, crying, inability to experience pleasure, and, in severe cases, suicidal thoughts.

4. Take care of yourself. If you feel yourself becoming depressed from someone's perpetual whining, end the conversation politely whenever it starts and, if possible, leave the room.

5. Resist the temptation to label someone "a whiner" in talking about him or her to others. Doing so is counterproductive gossip. Instead, say that your coworker seems to be having a difficult time and do some problem solving about how to help the person.

17

Peace with the Culture

In chapter 3 we talked about various aspects of office culture, that unique set of customs, rules, values, and beliefs that workers often come to accept as "regular" when they've worked in a place for a while, even when to an outsider some of these may seem downright bizarre. If you're a creative, individualistic person, you may be less inclined than those around you to buy in to your organization's culture. Something inside you resists pressures to conform even when resistance has negative consequences for promotion and monetary gain as well as social connectedness. All of us have to decide how much of ourselves we're willing to give up for the sake of salary, benefits, and friends, and this can be difficult. In this chapter we'll look at some of the specific dilemmas posed by office cultures and suggest some ways of dealing with them.

❐ "I have to wear a mask": Anonymity

How similar is the person you feel obliged to become when you walk in the door of your office to the person you are when you walk out?

For some of us, the difference isn't all that great. For others, it's huge. Feeling that you have to display a false self all day long just to hang on to your job can be hard on you, especially when you have to pretend to feel things you don't feel and not to feel things you do, as sociologist Arlie Russell Hochschild points out in her classic work *The Managed Heart*. Hochschild talks about the stress of "emotional labor" and maintains that the clash between felt and displayed emotions—which she calls emotional dissonance—can adversely affect the worker's mental health. As an illustration, she provides the following example:

> A young businessman said to a flight attendant, "Why aren't you smiling?" She put her tray back on the food cart, looked him in the eye, and said, "I'll tell you what. You smile first, then I'll smile." The businessman smiled at her. "Good," she replied. "Now freeze and hold that smile for fifteen hours."

While workers who serve the public, such as flight attendants or tour guides, might be most at risk for these effects, office workers in environments where one is expected to look positive and upbeat no matter how unjustly he or she is being treated may be able to relate to their experiences.

But in the office world, negative emotions are not all that workers may be required to hide; they may also feel they have to keep whole chunks of their personalities out of sight. The pressure to keep the real you hidden is one of the most stressful aspects of office life and takes many different forms from employee to employee. You may be a scholar who can't afford to let your learning show for fear of being seen as an elitist. You may be a person from a culture that values closeness and community who has to act like a rugged individualist. You may be a natural follower who has to act like an authoritative leader. Or you may think your company's mission is bunk but have to pretend it's the most important thing in the world to you. All day you walk around with your mask in place, knowing that if you let it slip for even a moment and they see the wonderful person you really are, this might put your job in jeopardy, because in this crazy office world that wonderful person would be considered unacceptable. Instead, what your office world seems to prefer is a man or woman in its version of the gray flannel suit, a suit you're afraid will sooner or later become you. In the words of the twentieth-century humanist and social psychologist Erich Fromm: "Today we come across an individual who behaves like an automaton, who does not know or understand himself, and the only person that he knows is the person that he is supposed to be, whose synthetic smile has replaced genuine laughter, and whose sense of dull despair has taken the place of genuine pain." The question is, how can you wear whatever mask you're forced to wear at the office and still keep your real, authentic self alive beneath its disguise?

Blues and Battleshock Busters

1. Consider whether you might be disguising more of your personality than you really need to at work. I believe this is often the case. Many of us, realizing we can't afford to be totally ourselves at work, go to the opposite extreme. Try letting a little more of yourself show at work and you might be surprised by people's responses.

2. "All the world's a stage," wrote Shakespeare in *As You Like It*, "and all the men and women merely players." In other words, it's impossible not to playact, no matter where you are. Ask yourself what acts you put on outside of work, even with those you're most intimate with, and how these acts relate to your office mask. Doing this will help you put your work "act" in perspective.

3. Outside of work, indulge those sides of yourself that you have to keep hidden at the office. If you have to act serious all day, be as silly as you like at night. If you hate having to keep your politics to yourself at work, do some campaigning in your community once you get home.

4. Consider taking an acting class or becoming involved with a theater group away from the workplace. If you have to be an actor, you might as well learn how to be a good one.

5. Be careful that in playing the roles that your work requires, you don't fall into doing something unethical. It's one thing to feign

confidence you don't feel when you're doing a presentation in front of a group, and it's another to falsify information to try to impress your audience or because you didn't care enough to do adequate research.

6. When you've had to keep your real thoughts hidden during an interchange, express them in your Work Companion afterward, or with a trusted soul mate.

7. Remember the words of Ralph Waldo Emerson: "Nothing is at last sacred but the integrity of your own mind."

☐ "Why do even the smart people talk like idiots?": Office-speak

You know the people you work with aren't stupid. Some of them are quite intelligent, even creative, when it comes to doing their jobs. So why do so many of them, especially managers, walk around spewing out foggy concoctions of totally predictable word mush? Deloitte Consulting managers Brian Fugere, Chelsea Hardaway, and Jon Warshawsky, in *Why Business People Speak Like Idiots*, decry the gap between the warm, colorful way most of us speak at home and the "office-speak" people fall into at work. "Between meetings, memos, and managers," they write, "we've lost the art of conversation. *Bull has become the language of business*." Fugere and his co-authors cite several possible causes of this disconnect. These include fear of liability, political correctness, business consultants who "make a living repackaging old concepts as something 'new,'" and the influence of technology. The result may sound something like this:

> A comprehensive study of the multiple economic challenges currently impacting our industry has led us to conclude that we have no other alternative than to undertake a total restructuring if our organization is to remain viable. A committee has been appointed whose mission is to develop a plan for implementing the essential changes needed to create a more dynamic, competitive, and client-focused company.

Reading through the previous paragraph, how do you feel, physically? Do your eyes glaze over or do your hands and feet go numb? What you're experiencing is a semihypnotic state, designed to put the higher centers of your brain to sleep so they won't think critically about anything that's being said. It's also the mindset of the unreal, just-get-through-the-day, zombielike office existence that I call office blues. It is, in fact, an unthinking state that is more likely to make you accept the unacceptable, which is exactly what the speaker intends.

Now contrast the paragraph with this "translation":

After taking a good, hard look at what's been going on in our industry, we've decided that we're going to have to make some changes in our workforce if we're going to stay in business. We've set up a committee to figure out whom we need to hire, fire, or transfer and have come up with a plan for putting these changes into effect. Hopefully, the end result will be a company that both makes money and serves clients' needs while continuing to grow.

This version is not exactly poetry, and it may be almost too blunt, but reading it after the original, you can feel the fog lift and the gears of your higher brain centers engage. If you want to pull out of the office blues and start taking better care of yourself, paying attention to language is extremely important.

When you turn a critical ear to the language around you, one of the first things you'll notice is buzzwords and pat phrases. In the office world, conformists try to use certain words and phrases as often as possible as a way of proving that they're willing to sell their souls to the company and thus deserve to be made CEO. If you're a nonconformist, however, expressions like "pursuit of excellence," "mission critical," and "strong organizational culture" may make your skin crawl, and you'd rather be roasted over an open fire than use one of them yourself.

Sometimes business gurus capitalize on a pat phrase and make it into a new expression such as "Total Quality," "Participative Management," or "Best Practices," which becomes the focus of seminars for which they're paid thousands of dollars. Then they go on to sell books in which they say the same things businesspeople have said for centuries, but in terms of the new expression. The people who come to the seminars and read the books then go back to work and impress their bosses by using the new expression and proposing an "initiative" to start a program based on it. Soon everyone in your organization is using the new expression, except perhaps you, the nonconformist, who feels progressively more nauseated every time you hear it.

But at least new expressions are words. Sometimes, however, office types talk not in words but in letters, though whenever possible they try to put these letters together to form words that collectively stand for a group of words, smiling at their own cleverness during their PowerPoint presentations as they reveal that the acronym for "Catastrophic Action Team" is "CAT," or "Health Unit Lifeline" is "HULL." The purpose of acronyms is to make language more efficient, presumably because the less we talk, the more time we'll have to take action. This may be justified in some situations, but the speedup of language in the form of acronyms also contributes to the manic pace that plagues contemporary office life. Personally, I'm a believer in "slow language."

Blues and Battleshock Busters

1. If the way others in your workplace speak bothers you, acknowledge these feelings to yourself, but be respectful. People have different thresholds for creativity of language, and there are probably things others are sensitive to that you barely notice, your obliviousness driving them equally crazy.
2. Don't force yourself to conform to others' speech habits if this feels like selling out. A good boss won't be fooled by pretentious language, and anyone who punishes you for speaking clear, jargon-free prose instead of office garble isn't worth working for.
3. Be aware that by making a decision not to use phony jargon or silly acronyms, you're setting an example for others and helping to improve your workplace's linguistic environment.

4. Never use language to humiliate someone less educated than yourself. If someone seems to have a limited vocabulary, make creative use of simpler words, which will be good for your own prose style.

5. Express your appreciation any time someone says something in a particularly colorful, creative way. Enjoy others' diverse dialects and encourage people to talk the way they do at home rather than using office-speak.

6. If someone releases an incomprehensible torrent of abstract verbiage, tell the person you don't understand it and ask for a simpler version. Or say, in your own terms, what you think the person is getting at and ask if that's what he or she means.

☐ "I hate having to wear a tie": Clothing Issues

Have you grown so fearful of wearing the wrong thing to work that you've lost touch with your own clothing preferences? If so, it's time to reconnect with them, first considering how they relate to what's required or expected in your workplace.

One advantage of working in a university, as I do, is that there is no real dress code. Faculty often choose to express their individuality by dressing down rather than up, sometimes to the point of scruffiness. This makes things confusing for new support staffers who used to work in "the real world" and had to dress up every day. Many start out wearing suits and gradually work their way into Eddie Bauer and L.L.Bean—the gray flannel suits of the academic world.

In a corporate environment, things may be very different. There the classic business suit with its ridiculous padded shoulders—designed to make everyone, male or female, look like a male bodybuilder the way bustles and falsies once were used to make every woman look like a statuesque Venus—is still a common feature of office life. In addition to radiating a message of physical prowess, these suits serve as portable boxes in which workers hide their personalities from one another and from bosses who feel threatened by individual differences. Along with these suits, men, though not women, are traditionally expected to wear nooses called ties around their necks which the boss can presumably hang them from if they become troublemakers. Some people mind such dress codes more than others. Those who like their jobs may feel energized when they put on their work uniforms; for others, however, getting dressed for work is an office blues trigger.

Take a moment to think about the clothing aspect of your job. Does your organization have a dress code? What are its rules, spoken or unspoken? Do people in different roles dress differently? How do the clothes you wear to work make you feel? Are they comfortable or uncomfortable? Do you like the way you look in them? What could you change without breaking any code rules that might make you feel better?

Then, setting dress codes aside, consider whether you're exercising whatever level of wardrobe freedom you have. Do you choose clothes that are comfortable, or are aesthetics more important to you? Do you feel that your clothes are "you," or have you long since ceased to care what you wear, so long as it conforms to the office code? And how aware are you of what the people around you are wearing? If you're not very aware, tune in, especially if you're suffering from sensory deprivation. In a sterile office environment, bright, interesting garments—assuming they're allowed—can serve as a welcome source of color, stimulation, and conversation.

Also consider your hairstyle and makeup. Have you made any compromises regarding these for the sake of your job? Do you feel that your chances for advancement would be seriously threatened if you grew a beard, or let your hair grow a certain length, cut it in a particular style, or dyed it an unusual color? Could too much eye makeup cost you a promotion? What would happen if you got a tattoo or a piercing in a visible place?

There's nothing wrong with making clothing, hairstyle, and makeup concessions for practical reasons, but you need to think about how the need to "dress for success" makes you feel.

Blues and Battleshock Busters

1. When you're at home, take all your office clothes out and lay them on your bed, including shoes and undergarments. Now look at them. Screen them for downers and tormentors. Downers are clothes that make you feel ugly enough to spoil your day: the sweater that makes you look twenty pounds heavier, the wild tie you got for your birthday that isn't you, the checked jacket that refuses to wear out. Tormentors are clothes that cause you discomfort or anxiety all day long: pants or pantyhose that cut you in half at the waist or feel as though they're about to fall down, bras that pinch, shoes that crinkle your toes. You may have been taught that it's okay to wear clothes that hurt if they also make you feel gorgeous, but beauty and pain don't necessarily have to go hand in hand.

2. If the clothes your dress code requires cause you discomfort, do what you can to adjust them when the clothing police aren't looking—loosen your tie during closed-door time, take off uncomfortable shoes under the table, give your hose a discreet yank.

3. If you're not sure if something's acceptable to wear to work, ask your boss. Don't spend the days you wear a questionable garment worrying about whether someone is seeing it as inappropriate.

4. Don't be a hairstyle martyr. If your goal is to advance your career in a conservative organization, accept the reality that the wrong hairstyle can have a huge effect on your prospects for promotion. If, on the other hand, you don't care about being promoted and your noncorporate hairstyle makes you feel beautiful, keep it—just make sure you're good enough at your job to make them want to keep you, Mohawk and all.

5. Talk to your coworkers about your organization's dress code or norms and find out how they feel about them. Point out the financial advantages of working together on this issue rather than competing for advancement by buying a more expensive outfit than your coworker's.

☐ "I don't know what the rules are": Romance and Sex

I grew up watching TV shows and movies that treated romance and sex as a standard part of office life, much as the new series *Mad Men* does. Offices in those days, at least according to the movies, were populated by attractive young secretaries who, if they were "nice girls," might end up marrying their bachelor bosses, or, if they were "bad girls," were likely to have affairs with their married bosses. Some extremely bad girls were known for sleeping their way up the career ladder, which may have once been the only way a young woman could move up at all. In other cases, a nice-girl secretary would succumb to a boss she thought was a bachelor only to discover, too late, that the jerk had a wife; and, if she refused to continue the liaison, she would end up with no job. There were no taboos against dating people you saw at the office, nor were managers who went out with their employees considered unethical. And if somebody at work chose to make your life miserable by hounding you with suggestive comments and unwanted passes, there was nothing you could do about it except get a new job elsewhere.

Fast-forward four or five decades and we now have a totally different set of norms. In most present-day offices, bosses are considered monsters if they date their employees (though some manage to discreetly do it anyway), and workers have learned that dating co-workers can be dangerous. Meanwhile, though sexually harassed workers can now file complaints or sue, many people are confused about exactly where they need to draw the line. Whether you're a single person looking for the love of your life, a not-so-single person struggling to make a marriage or partnership work, or just a person who wants to do his or her job without being hounded by sexual predators, the question is, how do you cope?

Blues and Battleshock Busters

1. Be aware that attraction and attachment are just feelings. That doesn't mean you have to act on those feelings if the circumstances are wrong. In most cases in the office they are, especially

if one of you is otherwise attached or is the subordinate of the other.

2. Don't allow yourself to become involved with your boss, at least not until you've found a way to alter the power balance between you by getting promoted or by pursuing a new career.

3. You may find yourself falling into a relationship with a "work spouse" at the office, someone who can supply some closeness and emotional support, but without the sexual element. This can often work out well, especially when both parties are married and the spouses are friendly, though it can be risky if either of the work spouses feels attracted to the other.

4. If you do become romantically involved with a coworker, it's best to keep your relationship private.

5. In the event that someone hounds you with unwanted sexual attention, protect yourself, but don't overreact. If someone you're not interested in lets you know in a civilized fashion that he or she is interested in you, be kind but firm in saying no. If the person refuses to take no for an answer or behaves offensively, put your foot down. Say that no means no and that you'll file a complaint or take legal action if the behavior continues. Document all incidents, tell friends who might be willing to serve as witnesses to what's going on, and carry out your threat if the behavior doesn't change.

6. Be aware that in some cultures, certain types of touching—grasping an arm or patting a shoulder, for example—are a standard part of most conversations, and be careful not to misinterpret this behavior as a sexual advance when it isn't. This doesn't mean you shouldn't tell the person if it bothers you, but you may need to frame it in terms of your cultural differences, not sexuality. Also, be aware that cultures vary in terms of how closely people normally stand to one another when conversing.

☐ "It's just because I'm . . .": Discrimination

At the age of fifty-five, Marge decided she was ready to move on to a more challenging job. She visited her organization's HR Web site and applied for some positions a rank or two above her own. Weeks went by, but she got no interviews, even though she had a terrific résumé, excellent references, and great performance appraisals. "What do you expect?" a friend told her when she expressed puzzlement. "You're over fifty."

"Why wasn't I included in the group going to Houston?" Hussein asked his boss. Brad mumbled something about "thinking Hussein had a meeting he had to attend somewhere else," but Hussein suspected it was really because he didn't want to have to fly with a man with a Muslim name.

Angela, who was confined to a wheelchair, left the meeting of the social committee feeling hurt after her coworkers voted to organize a mountain hike for the next event, ignoring the fact that she would not be able to participate.

The official policy in most organizations is not to allow discrimination and bigotry, but unofficially, this behavior is commonplace. The question the victims struggle with is, When do you make an issue out of something and when do you let it go? You want to be a team player. You want to belong. You don't want to be divisive. But when you've reached a point where you can't ignore evidence that's staring you in the face, what should you do, and where can you go for help?

Blues and Battleshock Busters

1. If someone says or does something that offends you, ask the person, in a nonaccusatory fashion, to explain what he or she was thinking. You may be surprised by the person's response. All of us misread cues sometimes. When possible, give others the benefit of the doubt. Slips of tongue and moments of carelessness can happen to good people. Patterns of intentional behavior, on the other hand, are something else.

2. Try to talk to the person who offends you about how his or her behavior makes you feel. Sharing some of your past experiences with the offender may help him or her understand why you're hurt. Unless the person is a crazymaker, there's a good chance that he or she will apologize and that will be the end of it.

3. Choose your battles. Any time you choose to fight, you exert energy you could have spent elsewhere.

4. Arm yourself. Document all incidents of discrimination or bigotry in your Work Companion. Discuss the incidents with witnesses and ask for their support.

5. Get help. Talk to someone who specializes in diversity or equal opportunity issues, either within your organization or outside of it. If you believe you have grounds for a lawsuit, consult with an attorney, but be aware that lawsuits can carry a heavy price tag. Don't allow yourself to be persuaded to take legal action precipitously.

18

Peace with the Game

Although learning to cope with challenges and tune in to day-to-day pleasures can make you happier at work, tangible rewards are also important. For some of us, work is about satisfaction at getting things done, but for most of us it's also about getting something back. There's nothing wrong with this. All of us need money to survive, and promotions, praise, and awards can all give your sense of well-being a major boost. While it's important to enjoy "playing the game" at work, it can be hard to do so if you're constantly losing, being passed over for promotions and denied raises, especially if you have a family to support. If that's your problem, it's time to make peace with the game.

☐ "They don't pay me enough for what I do": Financial Issues

I've long believed that money is one of the best antidepressants on the market. Money reduces stress, frees you from discomforts, and allows you to do things that give you and your family pleasure and hope (though what you have to do to get it may often undermine these benefits). If your boss or your company gives you a better raise than you expected, you may feel more nurtured, which is good for you. A nice raise can't always eliminate office blues, but it can help.

If, on the other hand, you're not paid as well as most people for the type of work you do, this adds financial stress to your life, denies you pleasure, and leaves you feeling exploited. Depression and feeling exploited often go hand in hand, dancing in a vicious circle. The more depressed you are, the less energy you have to demand fair treatment from your exploiter; and the more you're exploited, the more tired and depressed you become.

So let's assume you're in a job where you feel monetarily underpaid, both in terms of what you need to make ends meet and in terms of what you believe others are making for similar work. What can you do?

Blues and Battleshock Busters

1. Sit down with those in your household and figure out how much money you really need to pay your bills every month and live the way you want to, then compare this amount with what you're making. If your net household income falls short of your needs, there are two things you can do to correct the situation: Find a way to make more money or look for a way to cut expenses. Usually the first option takes longer than the second, so it's important to think about economizing.

2. Avoid the debt trap if at all possible. The desperation you may feel in response to debts gives your employer greater power to jerk you around. If you're already in debt, make getting out of it your first priority, starting with the smallest debts and working your way up to the biggest ones. Figure out what you're spending your money on and what purchases you can live without. Ask yourself if what you're buying is worth the freedom and peace of mind it costs you. Economizing, however, will only work if you and others in your household are making enough to

pay basic bills and have some left over. If this isn't the case, you need to focus first on increasing your income.

3. Try to find out the going rate for the type of work you're doing. In many workplaces, there's a taboo against sharing salary information with colleagues. One way around this is to get a bunch of professional peers together, ask everyone to write his or her salary on a piece of paper and put it in a hat, then look at all the numbers and figure out the range and mean. Put your results on a spreadsheet and share it with the participants. It's also helpful to look outside your own workplace. Web sites such as www. salary.com, www.indeed.com, www.iaap-hq.org (for administrative professionals), and other professional organization Web sites post average salaries for people in different types of jobs.

4. Learn how your organization's raise structure works. In many workplaces, raises are awarded only once a year on the basis of performance evaluations. In others, the boss can give you a raise whenever he or she feels you deserve one, though this may happen only if you ask for it. In large organizations where you have the freedom to apply for promotions outside your own department, changing positions may be the best route to a decent raise. Another alternative, if you've taken on more advanced duties than you performed when you started your job, is to ask for a title change, which should come with a higher salary. (All this, of course, can be different during tough economic times, when organizations may be forced to freeze raises or even cut salaries in order to survive.)

5. If and when you're in a situation where it makes sense to ask for a raise, do your homework first. Make a list of the ways you benefit your boss and your organization and gather data from your collected to-do lists and Work Companion. Build your case over time, taking on projects you think may give you a chance to shine. Choose your moment carefully, in terms of both your own situation and that of your boss. Good times to ask are when you've just finished a successful project, when you've just been given a good performance evaluation, or when new funds become available.

6. Consider whether promotion is a reasonable possibility in your case. Do you have a dead-end job that won't enable you to move

up or a job where promotions are routine? Do you think your boss values your work enough to give you a promotion? Would moving up in your organization mean longer hours and bigger headaches? Do you think you'd like the work you would be doing more or less than you like the work you do now? If you think a promotion would help, what could you do to make this happen? Do you need some additional training? Consider your options and *all* their possible consequences, some of which may be negative even when you move up the career ladder.

7. Aside from raises and promotions, another way to increase your income is to take on a second job or start a small business. Ideally this would be something you enjoy as a hobby, such as writing for publication, playing music professionally, making jewelry to sell, cleaning up the environment, or coaching a sports team. The worst kind of second job to get is another routine office job. If you can't do something that relates to a hobby, do something that involves physical activity such as housecleaning or waiting tables, which will help to counter the negative effects of sitting in an office all day.

8. Consider taking courses to upgrade your skills so you're qualified to get a better-paying job. However, make sure that there's really a market in your area for the new type of work so you won't waste huge amounts of time getting qualifications you can't use.

9. Don't allow loyalty to your boss or your company to supersede your own financial interests if your salary or benefits are so minimal that you're experiencing financial stress. It's one thing to sacrifice certain luxuries for the sake of genuine relationships at work; it's another to deprive yourself and your family of a comfortable lifestyle so you can keep a job you like.

❐ "I only hear about it when I've screwed up": Lack of Encouragement

Though money is important, it's not the only thing most of us work for. When you've done a particularly good job, it can feel good to receive a few words of praise from your boss or coworkers or an award for superior performance from your organization. Alas, in today's busy world, such encouragement is often either conspicuously absent or blatantly insincere, leaving workers feeling deprived and resentful. And if encouragement is offered in a demeaning fashion, this can also play games with your mind, as with the insulting "Dundie" awards that Michael doles out to his employees in *The Office*.

Blues and Battleshock Busters

1. Be honest with yourself about your needs. If you grew up in a family where you were constantly being criticized, or suffered humiliation as an adult due to academic failure or job loss, you may need more praise or recognition than other people do to feel good about yourself. In some situations, it may be helpful to share your story with your boss or coworkers or tell them you respond well to positive reinforcement. Praise, however, can be addictive. If you feel that no amount of it will satisfy you, rather than working yourself to exhaustion to get it, do some internal work on learning to be content with less.

2. Figure out ways to create measurable outcomes in the job you do and challenge yourself to break your own record (see chapter 13). Whenever you manage to do so, give yourself some kind of reward such as a short break or a cup of tea. Post graphs to remind yourself of your progress on outcomes.

3. Don't personalize others' neglect of your ego. Remember that you're not the center of anyone's universe but your own. Your boss, coworkers, and others in your organization may sometimes be too preoccupied with their own struggles to remember to express appreciation when it's merited.

4. Find ways outside of work to get praise and recognition. Especially valuable are activities where you get applause, as in the performing arts, a Toastmasters public-speaking group, or a competitive sport.

☐ "The performance appraisals aren't fair": Unjust Evaluations

Uh-oh, it's that time of year again. Your boss just sent out an e-mail warning that performance appraisals will be coming up. You know you've done a fantastic job and your coworkers know it too. A couple of times you've even saved your boss's skin. However, looking back over the years, there has never seemed to be any correlation between the quality of your work and the appraisals you've received. You wonder what you can do to get the best performance appraisal possible, and what recourse you'll have if your appraisal doesn't reflect the quality of your work.

Blues and Battleshock Busters

1. Remember that your boss is a human being, and that humans have limitations. Some bosses are better than others at evaluating those who work for them. Many are great at the technical aspect of their jobs but not at understanding people. Others are simply overloaded with too many employees to evaluate and have trouble keeping track of everyone's accomplishments. In *The Complete Idiot's Guide to Difficult Conversations*, Gretchen Hirsch points out that bosses are prone to certain errors in writing performance appraisals. These include the "halo effect" and the "pitchfork effect"—overrewarding or overpunishing the worker for one really good or really bad action instead of looking at the whole picture; the "recency error"—basing the evaluation only on what happened just recently instead of over the whole last year; and the "central tendency error"—ranking everyone more or less the same rather than distinguishing between individuals.

2. Ask for feedback from your boss every few months, and be specific in the questions you ask. This will save you from nasty surprises and enable you to improve your performance and earn a better review.

3. Help your boss by reminding him or her about all the wonderful things you've accomplished this year. A few weeks before performance-appraisal time rolls around, put together a list and give it to your boss, who will probably appreciate your making his or her job easier. Do the same thing if you're asking someone to write a reference letter for you. Be sure to include the accomplishment of helping others on your team, which is often overlooked.

4. If your boss writes something negative in your review, ask yourself if there might be some truth to it. Do some thinking about how you can improve your performance in the areas that he or she criticized. Make your boss an ally in your self-improvement program and ask for suggestions and progress reports. This makes it less likely that your boss will have the same complaints on next year's appraisal.

5. If, after intense self-scrutiny, you still feel that the boss's appraisal was inaccurate, tell him or her so and explain why in specific terms. Keep your voice calm and your approach rational. Some bosses will still get defensive, but others will listen and may even make changes based on your comments.

6. If you receive a single performance appraisal that you feel is unfair and the boss is not willing to change it (especially if it's your first one from that boss), it's probably not in your best interest to take the matter further, but if the pattern continues year after year, consider taking the matter to your boss's boss.

7. Try to find out if other employees have felt similarly disappointed with their performance appraisals. If they're dissatisfied too, then a bad appraisal means something different than if you're the only one getting slammed. If you're not alone, you can assume that your boss just believes in tough love; but if you are, you should be looking for another job, as you may be on your way to losing this one.

☐ "I'm just a secretary": Low Prestige and Rankism

Years ago, I was at a party and a woman asked me what I did for a living. "Oh, I'm just a secretary," I replied.

"Never say you're 'just a secretary,'" she said. "Secretaries do important work." She went on to talk about how secretaries are often in a position to influence people with power and about the important role they play in providing support to others.

At the time, I understood what the woman meant, but I found it no more convincing than being told that fat people are just as beautiful in their own way as thin people. Just as fat people in our society are constantly being given messages that they're ugly, people with certain job titles, such as "clerk," "secretary," and even "admin," are often looked down upon, both within their own organizations and in society at large.

Unfortunately, some people assume that if they're of superior rank to someone else, they don't have to treat their underling as a full-fledged human being. Robert W. Fuller, past president of my alma mater, Oberlin College, has a name for such discrimination on the basis of job rank. He calls it rankism, which he defines as "abusive, discriminatory, or exploitative behavior towards people who have less power because of their lower rank in a particular hierarchy." Rankist behavior can be as subtle as ignoring someone of lower rank while paying attention only to what a higher-ranking person has to say, or it can be as blatant as bullying and violence. If you feel you've been the victim of such "rank" behavior, what can you do?

Blues and Battleshock Busters

1. Even if your current job is at the bottom of the status hierarchy, make a decision to speak about it with pride when asked what you do. Instead of apologizing, educate others about the importance of the work you do and the skills it takes to do it well.
2. If someone behaves toward you in a fashion that feels rankist, tell the person how his or her behavior made you feel, using lots of "When you _____, I felt _____" statements. If the person is a crazymaker, he or she won't hear you, but many non-crazymakers engage in rankist behavior out of ignorance and simply need to be educated about how their behavior affects others.

3. Educate others about rankism and about how it feels to experience it. Point out that people have different strengths, not all of which society rewards equally, and that those who work hard at "menial" jobs deserve respect just as much as those who are fortunate enough to work at jobs with more prestige. Give them a copy of *The Mind at Work: Valuing the Intelligence of the American Worker*, by education expert Mike Rose, a study of the complex thinking processes involved in doing various low-status jobs.

4. Join a professional organization that works to improve the status of its members. Organizations such as the International Association of Administrative Professionals, for example, set standards and provide certifications, implying that the type of work their members do can be done well or poorly and is to be taken seriously.

5. Learn something about the history of your profession as well as about how it's experienced by people in different countries and cultural groups, and pass on what you learn to others.

6. Learn about some of the "greats" of your profession who've had an effect on the course of history, such as some of the past U.S. presidents' personal secretaries, for example.

7. Talk to your boss about whether your job title might be changed to something that has a more positive connotation. Would you rather be called a program coordinator than an administrative assistant? Maybe this is a possibility.

❑ "I don't believe in what this organization is doing": Meaninglessness

Part of what can make you proud of your job is pride in your organization. Identifying with your company's mission may make you willing to go the extra mile, which is why executives try so hard to get people excited about what their organization is doing. Working for a company whose products or services have the power to change the world, supporting researchers whose findings might benefit humanity, or contributing to a nonprofit or government project that could benefit huge numbers of people can make you feel important even if your job is at the bottom of the organizational chart. But what if you work for a company that makes useless toys or a government program you believe is a waste of the taxpayers' money? What should you do?

Blues and Battleshock Busters

1. If you can possibly avoid it, don't take a job for an organization whose mission you believe to be unethical. If you're a pacifist, don't get a job at a munitions plant. If you're a vegetarian, don't work for a butcher. To do so is a recipe for depression.
2. Think of a less-than-desirable job as a training ground for something better. Try to get different types of experience, and use work as a way of developing your cognitive skills such as attention, memory, language, or math. Meanwhile, update your résumé and get ready to conduct a new job search.
3. Use whatever influence you have to try to make things better in your organization. If you're an assistant to someone high in the company, for example, ask lots of questions that might get the person to rethink things and perhaps become more open to new ideas or more sensitive to workers' feelings.
4. Take pride in supporting your family or yourself. Anyone who isn't a burden to society has at least one reason to feel good about what he or she is doing.
5. Instead of focusing on what your organization is supposed to be doing, which you may find totally futile, focus on the people you work with. Get to know them as well as you can. What can you say or do that might make their jobs easier or their lives better? Make this your own personal mission, and you'll never be bored.

PART IV

Beyond Peace:
Working Together for Quality
of Life in the Office

19

Become a Change Agent

You've been using a Work Companion for quite a while, made some Job Transformation Plans, and have found ways to deal with some of the challenges associated with your own office situation. You've refigured your OCAB ratio, and the benefits number is now at least twice that of the challenges number. In other words, you're feeling a lot better. Work flows more smoothly and peacefully, you're getting along with others in your workplace, you no longer feel as though missiles are raining down on you, and the office blues have begun to lift. Having accomplished all this yourself, you'd like to take things to the next level and begin working for changes in your workplace that might benefit everyone. You're evolving into a change agent.

You Don't Have to Be a Boss to Create Change

Many people believe that change happens only from the top down. If they're not the boss's boss or at least the boss, they assume they have no power to change anything. This is not necessarily the case. A great deal of change happens from the bottom up, as when an individual who feels victimized by some form of social injustice decides to stand up for his or her rights. Rosa Parks, for example, started the American civil rights movement by simply sitting down at the front of a bus when an unjust rule said she was supposed to sit in the back. One route to workplace change is to defy office policies that you believe to be unjust. The problem with this approach is that you won't be likely to stay around long, assuming the rule you're protesting is of any significance to management, as it will probably get you fired.

If you're exceptionally heroic, and you're up against extreme injustice, you may feel it's worth risking being fired and/or challenging your employer in court in order to bring an issue to public awareness. This is what Josey Aimes did in the movie *North Country* after she and her female coworkers had been subjected to hideous abuse and sexual harassment by the men they worked with in a Minnesota mine, and management failed to protect them. Most of us in the office, however, have other priorities than sacrificing ourselves for the greater good, admirable as that might be.

Luckily, to improve conditions in your office workplace, you don't have to do anything so dramatic. As a change agent, you can start small. In fact, you may have already begun improving conditions for others by simply working to improve your own. Suppose that when you were first hired, you were struggling with an unrealistic workload that had caused several of your predecessors to quit. Instead of walking away, you managed to persuade your boss to hire a second employee to share your load. You might think this just benefited you, but that's not necessarily the case. In the first place, you've made the boss see the advantages of having adequate staff to cover the work. Second, because someday you'll be leaving this place yourself, your actions mean that your successor will likely also be less overloaded. Third, in standing up for your right to a reasonable workload, you've set an example for your coworkers.

In *Nice Girls Don't Get the Corner Office*, business coach Lois P. Frankel recommends that workers "play the game within bounds but at the edges." She suggests that you write down two rules that you've always interpreted narrowly and followed, then ask yourself if you've seen other people bend the same rules. What happened to them when they did? If nothing happened, take the risk of stretching them yourself and make the office world a kinder, gentler place. If you want to be a little braver, try doing this with a rule that you *haven't* seen anyone else stretch. You'll never know what will happen unless you try it.

The transition to becoming a change agent isn't something you're likely to achieve consciously but something that just happens, the way a child starts learning to walk at a certain point. Working to make changes that go beyond your personal needs is the natural result of growth.

Constructive change does not have to involve conflict. A simple action such as bringing a plant to your office, rearranging furniture, or inviting a coworker to lunch can sometimes have ripple effects that go far beyond what you originally intended. Not all of these effects are going to be positive, of course—change always involves risk—but if you persevere in your new role, you're almost certain to find it rewarding.

What Do You Want to Change in Your Workplace?

Imagine that this is your last day in your current workplace and your fellow employees are throwing a party in your honor. One by one, they make speeches about how you've improved the quality of their office lives. What would you like them to say that you've done? In answering this question, here are some things to think about:

Who or what's missing from your workplace that you feel needs to be there? This could be anything from plants to art to humor to coffee breaks to a better printer to a receptionist to regular staff meetings with the boss. Make a wish list of missing things.

What problems need to be solved? Make another list of recurring problems that don't affect just you, such as communication problems with a particular department, a copy machine that continually breaks, workplace bullying, or people complaining about feeling isolated. These are problems that you might propose brainstorming solutions to as a group.

What are your personal capabilities and interests? You're most likely to be successful in creating change in areas that relate to your own unique knowledge areas, talents, and interests. Are you a master gardener? You might offer to purchase and tend plants in your work area or start a group project planting a garden in a nearby public area. Do you love politicking? Maybe you could serve on a committee to represent workers' interests to management. Do coworkers often tell you their problems? How about volunteering for a peer counseling program?

What do others in your workplace see as important? In working for the common good, you need to find out what matters to your coworkers. Take an informal survey and find out what gaps need to be filled and what problems need solving. If you have specific projects in mind, run them by others and see what sort of responses you get. If no one seems interested, this doesn't necessarily mean you shouldn't try to do something, but be prepared for an uphill battle.

How much time and effort will projects you're considering involve? One trap some people fall into is becoming so busy helping others that they imperil their own personal development. For this reason, anytime your mind starts spinning out ideas for a new project, it's important to ask yourself just how much time and effort it will take and what you're going to *not* do in order to work on it.

What specific projects will be doable, given your circumstances? Make a list of five small ways you might create more quality of life in your workplace. For example:

1. Put up a bulletin board in the common area for personal displays.
2. Talk to the boss about having a brief social time every afternoon.
3. Invite a coworker to lunch and ask her if she'd like to start a monthly book group.

4. Find out if you can bring in a time-management expert to talk about dealing with e-mail.
5. Propose brainstorming about the parking situation at next staff meeting.

Once you choose a specific issue and execute your plan, be sure to write about the results in your Work Companion.

Note that change agent decisions often don't feel like decisions. You won't always make a list of possible projects, settle on one, and do it. Rather, you may encounter an unsolved problem or an unmet need that everyone's always accepted, and something tells you that now's the time to do something about it. Or you'll be talking to someone and all of a sudden one of you will get the idea and you'll be off, discovering leadership strengths you never knew you had.

Cultivate Personal Powers

Maybe you think you're powerless to enact change because you're the lowest-ranking employee in your office. Believe it or not, history and literature are filled with stories about low-ranking employees and servants whose personal powers allowed them to exert influence on and even control the behavior of their superiors. As a therapist, I've come to think that most of us have powers we never bother to use. Some of these personal powers, which you can work to develop, include the following:

The power of competence: It stands to reason that if you're good at your job, you're going to have a lot more influence in your workplace than if you're not. If you want to really increase your power, get to be good at something difficult that no one else in your office can do. Don't assume that people will be aware of your expertise if you don't let it shine.

The power of language: People who are gifted communicators have the ability to strongly influence others, even when the other person is of higher status. If you are a skilled writer, you'll be ahead of the game in communicating by e-mail, writing for Web sites, or producing documents that help spread your ideas.

The power of proximity: A certain amount of power resides in just spending time around those who have power. CEOs' secretaries or administrative assistants, for example, have long been notorious for managing their bosses and even running the organization behind the scenes.

The power of listening: When someone listens to you talk about yourself without being critical, you begin to trust the person more and more. Thus, over time, good listeners tend to gain influence with those they listen to. This is how psychotherapy typically works—by just listening to the client for a number of sessions, the therapist gains enough influence that the client may eventually be open to following his or her suggestions. There's nothing wrong with using this strategy in the workplace as long as you respect others' rights to make their own decisions.

The power of joining: By identifying similarities between yourself and someone else, you make the other person more likely to take what you say seriously. This will not work, however, if you're dealing with a narcissistic boss, as such a person will not want to think that he or she has anything in common with a subordinate.

The power of giving: The more favors you do for others in the workplace, the more likely they are to do you favors, assuming they're not exploitive crazymakers. Think of it as a bank account into which you deposit and withdraw funds.

The power of networking: Knowing people who know people who know people that might be able to help you can strengthen your position in any situation. The Internet makes this easy in today's working world.

The power of negotiation: There is an art to negotiating for what you want. Lois Frankel recommends taking a negotiation skills class or reading *Essential Managers: Negotiating Skills*, by Tim Hindle and Robert Heller, for some tips on how to negotiate successfully.

The power of creativity: No matter how lowly your position, being able to think of creative ways to solve problems can enable you to cut through red tape and skip whole groups of usual steps in influencing others and making new things happen. Erin Brockovich, a file clerk in a law firm who, after noticing a pattern while sorting some papers, investigated a public health tragedy and worked with one of the firm's associates to win a giant environmental lawsuit, is a case in point. Creativity is powerful, however, only if you're working with people who welcome it.

The power of example: In working with parents, I've seen how much more powerful the example they set is than any other kind of influence on children, and I believe the same is true in the workplace, especially the examples that bosses set for their subordinates. Even among coworkers at the same level, setting a positive example can be a significant form of influence, as some workers serve as trendsetters for others.

Take a moment now to inventory your personal powers. Which ones do you already possess and which ones could you develop? Do you have other personal powers that aren't listed here? Add them to the list!

Change Agent Strategies

As you move into your change agent role, you'll feel the increasing urge to hook up with others to work for the common good. There are a variety of ways that workers do this:

Invite people to lunch: The purpose here is not simply to combat your own personal loneliness, as in chapter 14, but to explore common interests, problems that need solving, or projects you might want to start. For example, you might invite a coworker out for

lunch who shares your interest in literature and end up deciding to
start a book club.

Join or start a committee: If you work for a large organization,
there may already be committees you can serve on that plan social
events, organize group projects, engage in charitable activities, or
represent workers to management. If a committee doesn't already
exist, you may want to start one, though bear in mind that this can
take considerable time and energy.

Find or serve as a mentor: Formal and informal mentorship is a
time-honored institution in the contemporary workplace. Many organizations have mentorship programs, but this is not the only men-
toring that goes on. Some mentors simply help the mentee with the
work itself, providing valuable information and suggestions. Others
provide guidance in career planning or in dealing with interpersonal
problems in the workplace. If you've followed this program and
found your way to a more peaceful, rewarding workplace life, you
may decide to become a mentor yourself and help someone else to do
the same.

Connect with colleagues outside your workplace: Professional associations and conferences abound that bring people together from different organizations. Joining one of these can help
you put your own workplace's problems into perspective and em-
power you with learning other people's successful strategies.

Participate in union activities: While relatively few office workers belong to labor unions, "white-collar sweatshop" conditions
have led to the growth of collective bargaining associations in certain sectors. If employees in your workplace are already unionized,
participating in union activities is an obvious way of working for the
common good. If you find that the union's primary focus is simply
on bargaining for higher pay, you may want to try to persuade others
to address quality-of-life factors as well. If you're extremely brave,
you might want to participate in organizing a new union, but be prepared for negative consequences if you do.

The Challenges and Rewards

The change agent phase of your work life can be challenging, and it may take you a while to figure out just how much change agent work is right for you. If one of your personal challenges has been work overload, you may need to say no to those opportunities that are likely to require the most time and energy and confine yourself to working for change in smaller ways. If you're doing committee work during your regular work time, make sure your boss is okay with this. If you're on a committee that uses e-mail to communicate, it's best if you can set up a special mailbox or directory to keep committee e-mails from distracting you when you're supposed to be working at your regular job.

Some types of change agent work may also put you at odds with your employer. While sometimes this may be justified, you'll always need to consider the possible consequences of your actions and whether you're willing to risk being labeled a troublemaker for whatever it is you're hoping to gain. Chief Justice Earl Warren, who presided over *Brown v. Board of Education*, once said, "Everything I did in my life that was worthwhile I caught hell for."

Nevertheless, being a change agent can also be a great antidote to office blues, as it helps to counter feelings of loneliness and gives you a reason to come to work every day. On a more practical level, you may pick up leadership experience and new skills to add to your résumé that may take your career in a whole new direction. Most of all, you'll have the experience of participating in something greater than yourself, and in this life, you can't do much better than that.

20

Break Down the Walls

I started this book talking about the office world having walls, con-straints office workers must operate within. Some limitations are part of every situation. But when external forces crush in brutally on workers, starving their spirits and leaving no room for them to breathe and grow, then the health of workers, organizations, and society begins to suffer, and something has to be done.

The question is, how can we office workers join forces to break down the barriers to health and happiness that have arisen in our workplaces? When others refuse to listen and instead dig in their heels, imprisoned by their belief that there's nothing anyone can do about even the most outrageous injustices, what recourse do we have? How can we break the cycle of defeatism being passed from one generation of workers to another? When so much needs to be changed, where shall we start? The purpose of this chapter is to sug-gest a few possibilities.

Breaking Down Inside Walls: Community Organizing in the Office

We can start by breaking down walls on the inside that separate individuals. Elsewhere in this book, I've talked about ways to form positive connections with others in your workplace through shared interests and goals. When more and more people find ways to connect in an organization, the result is a growing sense of community. While at one time, community may have developed more naturally in office workplaces, in today's world of increased competition, uncertainty, and job instability it may need to be created through conscious organization.

In the research center where I work, a couple of years ago the director's office and its staff advisory committee conducted a climate survey. One of their main findings was that many workers felt isolated and lonely. This led to in-depth conversations about what could be done and all sorts of "initiatives" by various staff groups that were designed to "build community" in our workplace. During this time, I served on several project-planning committees and helped do some of the legwork. The result of all this conscious effort was that the next year's climate survey showed a significant improvement on the isolation/loneliness issue. This didn't happen spontaneously, but through deliberate effort. By sometimes getting people to work together on common projects and other times just getting them together to talk, we were able to break down walls and create new connections between workers the way the brain creates new connections between neurons when learning takes place.

If you and your coworkers are interested in doing the same, here are some projects you might want to try, assuming your human resources department or administration doesn't already have them in place (you'll need to get permission from higher-ups to do most of these):

A movie discussion: Get people together to watch a film that's relevant to workplace life and hold a facilitated discussion afterward. Some possibilities are *Office Space* to talk about office life in general, *Crash* to talk about racism, *North Country* for a discussion of sexual harassment, or *The Devil Wears Prada* to focus on supervision issues. Refreshments and door prizes will make people more likely to come.

A get-to-know-you lunch: Organize a luncheon in which workers are seated in small groups. A trained facilitator, usually a psychologist or social worker, will then suggest ice-breaking exercises that help participants get to know one another in a more personal way than traditional office interactions typically allow. The facilitator might ask what people would do if they had three wishes, or what they wanted to be when they grew up, or how they would complete the sentence "If you really knew me, you would know . . ." Workers whose daily conversation for years might thus far have consisted only of "Hi, how are you doing, nice weather we're having" may find these conversations liberating, as though a bunch of stone statues had suddenly come to life.

A common interests event: Do some brainstorming and make a list of workers' possible common interests. Then send out a group e-mail asking for additional suggestions. Some possibilities include gardening, knitting, needlework, book discussion, creative writing, choral singing, visiting museums, golf, bowling, swimming, yoga, volleyball, martial arts, genealogy. Write each suggestion at the top of a piece of paper, with numbered blanks beneath it for signatures. Then put each sign-up sheet on a table in a different part of the room. Hold a pizza lunch and instruct participants to walk around and sign the sheets relating to their own interests. Set a time when the sign-ups will stop and groups of individuals who signed each sheet can meet in different areas to get organized. This has been an extremely popular event in my workplace, and many of the resulting groups still meet regularly.

An office read: Choose a book that you believe will be both educational and entertaining. Some possibilities include *Mountains Beyond Mountains*, by Tracy Kidder; *The Eighth Promise*, by William

Poy Lee; *Arc of Justice*, by Kevin Boyle; *The Kite Runner*, by Khaled Hosseini; or *Nickel and Dimed*, by Barbara Ehrenreich. If you can get funding, order multiple copies and make them available to those in your organization until they run out. Set up a luncheon discussion event with a facilitator, and post the date several months in advance so people will have time to read the book. If possible, arrange for the author to come and speak.

An office garden: This could be on your office grounds or in a public area. In either case, you'll need to go through official channels to get permission to landscape the space. Another possibility is creating an indoor garden in a group of large planters. During planting time, you may need to recruit people to work on weekends, but the dividends of this project can be huge in terms of workers' sense of well-being. Sometimes, gardens may even happen spontaneously. Recently, in my workplace, someone put a few boxes of African violets on a long windowsill in one of the hallways. More violets appeared along the windowsill until it was covered from one end to the other, giving workers a place to renew their connection with nature on wintry afternoons.

A charity drive: Many workplaces engage in charitable activities. Contact your local Red Cross chapter to arrange for a blood drive, put out boxes before Thanksgiving time to collect food for the local food bank or before Christmas to collect toys for a domestic violence shelter, or hold a "baby shower" for mothers at a free obstetrics clinic. All these projects provide connections between workplace and community.

A fund-raising auction: Hold an auction to raise funds either for a charity or to support the career development of workers in your organization by paying for tuition, books, conferences, or other educational activities. Suggest that workers donate items they've made or services they can offer, or that a group of workers put together a basket of items around a particular theme. This has the added advantage of revealing workers' hidden talents to their coworkers.

An office community Web site or newsletter: Create a special Web site or newsletter or expand those that already exist to report on community-building activities, present profiles of individual workers, and allow workers to share views on workplace issues. Include a calendar that will help people minimize conflict when scheduling community events.

A book exchange: Set up a shelf where people can leave books they want to get rid of and take others in exchange.

An expert lecture: Invite so.meone to speak who's an expert in an area of general interest such as diversity issues, office organizing, time or stress management, organizational relationships, "difficult people," recycling, energy conservation, ergonomics, financial issues, physical activities, or work-life balance. Or bring in someone from a local charity to talk about the work that goes on there, or from a local college or university to talk about climate change, the economy, or the latest NASA space mission.

A hidden-talents brown-bag series: This can be wonderful for workers in menial jobs who are gifted in areas outside of work. Organize a brown-bag series in which each month a different worker talks about an outside passion, and provides demonstrations whenever possible. In my workplace, an administrative assistant who trains guide dogs for the blind brought in some dogs and talked about her work. It was a hit!

A group outing: Get a bunch of workers together for a lunch outing at a nearby zoo, spend an hour in an art gallery, or get group tickets to a Saturday concert or sporting event.

A community support project: Often, it's when an individual is facing some sort of dramatic challenge—a serious illness, the loss of a home, a tour of combat duty—that community becomes most fully realized in the workplace. A few years ago, one of our computer techs, whom I'll call Fred, was called to serve a tour of duty in Iraq. Workers in Fred's department corresponded with him and collected gifts and batches of homemade goodies from other employees to send to him and his fellow soldiers. When Fred came back, he shared some of his experiences and expressed his thanks to a packed conference room that overflowed with goodwill and community spirit.

The Walls of the Office World: Together We Can Break Them Down

But what about the walls in the office world that I talked about in chapter 1, those economic, political, and cultural realities that make it hard to change anything in the workplace no matter what you try to do? While a thorough acquaintance with these realities is essential for effective coping, it can also be extremely frustrating. If you can attribute a particular problem to your boss or one of your coworkers, this might not make you happy, but at least you might be able to influence the person in some way to make things better. If, on the other hand, you can see that the culprit is something big and abstract such as the economy or technology, you may be tempted to give in to despair.

At such times, it's helpful to remember that you're not the only person in the world capable of taking constructive action. Find a group of like-minded citizens and send them a donation or volunteer a little time. It doesn't matter whether the group is a professional organization, a religious organization, a political party, a union, or a special-interest group. What matters is that you believe in the group's mission, and that it might someday make the office world and the world in general a kinder, gentler place. If you're interested in improving life for office workers everywhere by addressing some of the underlying causes of distress, what are some you might want to support? Here are a few possibilities:

Universal health care, especially single-payer health care: An awful lot of what's wrong with workplaces these days can be traced to one thing: health insurance being linked to employment. As long as employers have to pay such high premiums for their workers, they will always have to hire the fewest workers possible and overburden them in order to be competitive. Grassroots organizations such as Healthcare-NOW! (www.healthcare-now.org), the Universal Health Care Action Network (www.uhcan.org), and many physician groups are trying to change this. Help them.

Giving back time to workers: The growing movement Take Back Your Time (www.timeday.org) is working to reduce the number of hours American workers are forced to put in as a result of both mandatory overtime and insufficient vacation time. Thanks to the group's efforts, Congressman Alan Grayson recently introduced in the U.S. House of Representatives the Paid Vacation Act of 2009, a bill that would guarantee many more workers one to two weeks of paid vacation per year. A good first step if you're interested in Take Back Your Time is to go to www.timeday.org and order the book by the same title, edited by John de Graaf (the author of *Affluenza*), which gives a great overview of the movement.

Slow living: Along with those who support giving more time back to workers, various groups have arisen that focus on slowing down and reconnecting with neighbors and communities. "Slow living" originated from the Slow Foods movement, which encourages people to buy locally grown foods in non–chain stores, make things from scratch instead of cooking overprocessed foods, and eat such homemade food at a leisurely pace with family and friends. More recently, the idea of doing things the slow way and savoring the process instead of racing toward an ever-receding goal has spread into other areas of life such as travel, recreation, and even work. While it might be hard to convince your boss to let you apply slow living to the workplace, getting together outside of work with people who value slowness, and working to create more of it anywhere you can, could be hugely therapeutic to those suffering from office battleshock. Read the book *Slow Food Nation*, by Carlo Petrini, or do a Web search and find out more about the Slow Food movement.

Changes in zoning laws and urban planning: In the United States, workplaces and residential areas have become horribly separate, resulting in long commutes, sterile workplace landscapes, and extreme separations of family members from one another throughout the workday. Reducing urban sprawl by changing zoning laws would have the effect of reconnecting some workers to their communities. Congress for the New Urbanism (www.cnu.org) and other participants in the new urbanism movement are working to restructure landscapes to create more walkable, human-scale, mixed-use neighborhoods and greater connectivity. Check this out.

Child care availability: Not nearly enough quality child care is available for working parents who need it for their children. Organizations such as the National Association of Child Care Resource & Referral Agencies (www.naccrra.org) support legislation and programs that might improve the situation. They could use your help.

Better public transportation: Coming to work can be less stressful if you can take a high-speed railway rather than driving, or a bus you have to wait only five minutes for instead of half an hour. If you'd like to see better public transportation in your area, let your public officials know. You might also want to join an advocacy group such as the American Public Transportation Association (www.apta.com).

Parks, walkways, or bike paths: Most communities have parks, walkways, and bike paths. If you'd like a nicer walking route to work, do what you can to support their maintenance and construction through your local parks and recreation agency, which may collect donations or organize volunteer projects by the "Friends of ___."

Public education regarding diversity or mental health: If you're frustrated by the ignorance of people in your workplace regarding a particular diversity or mental-health issue, you might want to link up with an outside group that promotes education in this area. There's an organization for every kind of group you can imagine, and many can provide speakers, films, or exhibits for your workplace. Even if the people at your office are completely close-minded, you can have the satisfaction of doing something to eliminate a stigma in hopes that eventually even folks like them will be forced to see the light.

These are just a few causes you might support that impact the office world. I'm sure you can think of countless others, and a little Web surfing should enable you to find out whom to contact. Perhaps you think that anything you can do is only a drop in the bucket, but do it anyway, knowing that many people's drops of effort together can create rivers of genuine change. "Never doubt that a small group of thoughtful, committed citizens can change the world," wrote the anthropologist Margaret Mead. "Indeed, it is the only thing that ever has."

Conclusion: Walls and Wings

This book was born out of my own personal struggles with office blues and battleshock. Completing it, I feel not only triumphant but extremely grateful for the idea to write it—which came to me out of the blue during a dark time in my life—as well as the help that I received from others along the way. Meanwhile, my office journey continues: In a few hours I'll be at my desk scrambling to get my boss's accounts reconciled before the Thanksgiving holidays, feeling a great deal better in doing so for having learned so many wonderful things while writing this book.

As for you, if you've read the book from beginning to end, then your journey is just beginning. If you've begun to make some changes along the way and are beginning to feel better about coming to work, then I congratulate you—keep doing what you're doing. It should be apparent to you by now that with all its challenges and frustrations, office life is still mostly what you make of it. And however trapped you may feel within the walls of your own cubicle and of the larger office world, remember this: Inside, you still have the power to create wings.

When I was in college back in the sixties, I took a class in creative writing with a wonderful poet and teacher, Bruce Bennett. The following is a poem, titled "Walls," from one of his chapbooks, which I leave you with:

> *A man encountered a*
> *wall. Groped. Encountered*
> *another. Tried to turn*
> *back. A wall blocked his*
> *way.*
>
> *"Help!" he cried.*
> *"I'm trapped!"*
> *"Test your wings,"*
> *suggested a voice.*
> *"I don't have wings!"*
> *"You didn't have walls."*

Useful Resources

Professional and Personal Support

International Association of Administrative Professionals
P.O. Box 20404
Kansas City, MO 64195-0404
816-891-6600
www.iaap-hq.org
Professional association for administrative professionals

International Coach Federation
2365 Harrodsburg Road, Suite A325
Lexington, KY 40504
888-423-3131
www.coachfederation.org
Provides referrals for individuals seeking personal or business coaches

Toastmasters International
P.O. Box 9052
Mission Viejo, CA 92690-9052
949-858-8255
www.toastmasters.org
Groups that provide training and support in public speaking

National Association of Professional Organizers
15000 Commerce Parkway, Suite C
Mount Laurel, NJ 08054
856-380-6828
www.napo.net
Referrals for help with organizing issues

National Study Group on Chronic Disorganization
4728 Hedgemont Drive
St. Louis, MO 63128
314-416-2236
www.nsgcd.org
Referrals for individuals struggling with chronic disorganization

Mental Health America
2000 N. Beauregard Street, 6th Floor
Alexandria, VA 22311
703-684-7722; 1-800-273-TALK (crisis line)
www.nmha.org
*Information about disorders and a crisis line for those seeking help
and referrals*

Attention Deficit Disorder Association
P.O. Box 7557
Wilmington, DE 19803-9997
800-939-1019
www.add.org
Support network for adults with attention deficit disorder

Government Agencies

The National Institute for Occupational Safety and Health
Centers for Disease Control and Prevention
1600 Clifton Road
Atlanta, GA 30333
800-CDC-INFO
www.cdc.gov/NIOSH
Information concerning health and safety in the workplace

United States Department of Justice
950 Pennsylvania Avenue, NW
Civil Rights Division
Disability Rights Section, NYA
Washington, D.C. 20530
800-514-0301
www.ada.gov
Information on the Americans with Disabilities Act

United States Department of Labor
Frances Perkins Building
200 Constitution Avenue, NW
Washington, D.C. 20210
866-487-2365
www.dol.gov
Information concerning the Fair Labor Standards Act and other labor laws

United States Equal Employment Opportunity Commission
131 M Street, NE
Washington, D.C. 20507
800-669-4000; 202-663-4900
www.eeoc.gov
Information on discrimination and equal opportunity issues and how to file a charge

Social Justice Organizations

American Public Transportation Association
1666 K Street, NW, Suite 1100
Washington, D.C. 20006
202-496-4800
www.apta.com
Organization that works to advance public transportation

Congress for the New Urbanism
The Marquette Building
1420 S. Dearborn Street, Suite 404
Chicago, IL 60603
312-551-7300
www.cnu.org
*Organization that promotes development of pedestrian-friendly,
mixed-use environments that build community*

National Association of Child Care Resource & Referral Agencies
3101 Wilson Boulevard, Suite 350
Arlington, VA 22201
703-341-4100
www.naccrra.org
*Association that provides information for parents on child care and
works to improve the quality and make it more available*

Take Back Your Time
P.O. Box 19862
Seattle, WA 98109
206-443-6747
www.timeday.org
*Initiative that works to counter overwork, overscheduling, and time
poverty; currently sponsoring a law to guarantee paid vacation time
to workers*

Universal Health Care Action Network
2800 Euclid Avenue, Suite 520
Cleveland, OH 44115-2418
216-241-8422
www.uhcan.org
Network of organizations working toward universal health care in the United States

Useful Products

Northern Light Technologies
8971 Henri-Bourassa Boulevard West
Montreal, QC H4S 1P7
Canada
800-263-0066
northernlighttechnologies.com
Special lights to be used to treat seasonal affective disorder, seasonal depression, and winter blues

Mindfulness Meditation Practice CDs and Tapes
P.O. Box 547
Lexington, MA 02420
www.mindfulnesscds.com
Stress-reduction CDs and tapes with Dr. Jon Kabat-Zinn, to be used by themselves or in conjunction with Dr. Kabat-Zinn's books

Bibliography

Books

Adams, Scott. *The Dilbert Principle*. New York: HarperBusiness, 1987.

Albert, John. *The Working Life*. New York: Pearson/Longman, 2004.

Arnott, Dave. *Corporate Cults: The Insidious Love of the All-Consuming Organization*. New York: American Management Association, 1999.

Asch, Solomon. "Effects of Group Pressure on the Modification and Distortion of Judgments." In *Groups, Leadership, and Men*, edited by Harold Guetzkow. Pittsburgh: Carnegie, 1951.

Babiak, Paul, and Robert D. Hare. *Snakes in Suits: When Psychopaths Go to Work*. New York: HarperCollins, 2007.

Badaracco, Joseph L. "Business Ethics: Four Spheres of Executive Responsibility." In *Psychological Dimensions of Organizational Behavior*, edited by B. Staw, 229–40. Upper Saddle River, NJ: Pearson/ Prentice Hall, 2004.

Baker, Dan, Cathy Greenberg, and Collins Hemingway. *What Happy Companies Know*. Upper Saddle River, NJ: Prentice Hall, 2006.

Bennett, Bruce. "Walls." In *Not Wanting to Write Like Everybody Else.* Brockport, NY: State Street Press, 1987.

Bernstein, Albert J. *Emotional Vampires: Dealing with People Who Drain You Dry.* New York: McGraw-Hill, 2001.

Best, Joel. *Flavor of the Month: Why Smart People Fall for Fads.* Los Angeles: University of California Press, 2006.

Brantley, Jeffrey, and Wendy Millstine. *Five Good Minutes at Work.* Oakland, CA: New Harbinger Publications, 2007.

Braverman, Harry. *Labor and Monopoly Capital: The Degradation of Work in the Twentieth Century.* New York: Monthly Review Press, 1974.

Brown, H. Jackson, Jr. *Life's Little Instruction Book.* Nashville, TN: Rutledge Hill Press, 1991.

Bryan, Mark, with Julia Cameron and Catherine A. Allen. *The Artist's Way at Work: Riding the Dragon—Twelve Weeks to Creative Freedom.* New York: Quill, 1998.

Buckingham, Marcus and Curt Coffman. *First, Break All the Rules.* New York: Simon & Schuster, 1999.

Burns, David. *The Feeling Good Handbook.* New York: Penguin, 1989.

Cacioppo, John T., and William Patrick. *Loneliness: Human Nature and the Need for Social Connection.* New York: W.W. Norton, 2008.

Carroll, Michael. *Awake at Work.* Boston: Shambhala, 2006.

Caruso, David R., and Peter Salovey. *The Emotionally Intelligent Manager: How to Develop and Use the Four Key Emotional Skills of Leadership.* San Francisco: Jossey-Bass, 2004.

Cialdini, Robert B. *Harnessing the Science of Persuasion.* Cambridge, MA: Harvard Business School Publishing Corporation, 2001.

Cochran, Thomas C. *200 Years of American Business.* New York: Basic Books, 1977.

Covey, Stephen R. *The 7 Habits of Highly Effective People.* New York: Simon & Schuster, 1989.

Csikszentmihalyi, Mihaly. *Finding Flow.* New York: Basic Books, 1997.

Cullen, Michale J., and Paul R. Sackett. "Personality and Counterproductive Workplace Behavior." In *Psychological Dimensions of Organizational Behavior*, edited by B. Staw, 150–82. Upper Saddle River, NJ: Pearson/Prentice Hall, 2004.

Dalai Lama and Howard C. Cutler. *The Art of Happiness at Work*. New York: Riverhead Books, 2003.

Damasio, Antonio R. *Descartes' Error: Emotion, Reason, and the Human Brain*. New York: Avon, 1994.

Davenport, Liz. *Order from Chaos*. New York: Three Rivers Press, 2001.

Davidson, Jeff. *Getting Things Done*. New York: Alpha, 2005.

de Graaf, John, ed. *Take Back Your Time: Fighting Overwork and Time Poverty in America*. San Francisco: Berrett-Koehler, 2003.

Denman, Terence. *How Not to Write: An Office Primer for the Grammatically Perplexed*. Philadelphia: Quirk Books, 2005.

de Waal, Frans B. M. *Chimpanzee Politics: Power and Sex Among Apes*. Baltimore: Johns Hopkins University Press, 1989.

———. *Our Inner Ape*. New York: Riverhead Books, 2005.

Dutton, Jane E. *Energize Your Workplace*. San Francisco: Jossey-Bass, 2003.

Dyer, Wayne. *Real Magic: Creating Miracles in Everyday Life*. New York: Quill, 1992.

Ehrenreich, Barbara. *Nickel and Dimed*. New York: Henry Holt, 2001.

Forster, E. M. *Howards End*. London: Edward Arnold, 1910.

Frankel, Lois P. *Nice Girls Don't Get the Corner Office: 101 Unconscious Mistakes Women Make That Sabotage Their Careers*. New York: Warner Books, 2004.

Fraser, Jill Andresky. *White Collar Sweatshop: The Deterioration of Work and its Rewards in Corporate America*. New York: W.W. Norton, 2001.

Frost, Peter J. *Toxic Emotions at Work: And What You Can Do About Them*. Boston: Harvard Business School Press, 2007.

Fugere, Brian, Chelsea Hardaway, and Jon Warshawsky. *Why Business People Speak Like Idiots*. New York: Free Press, 2005.

George, Jennifer M., and Arthur P. Brief. "Personality and Work-Related Distress." In *Personality and Organizations*, edited by B. Schneider and D. Smith, 193–219. Mahwah, NJ: Lawrence Erlbaum, 2004.

George, Jennifer M., and Gareth R. Jones. "Individual Differences: Personality and Ability." In *Psychological Dimensions of Organizational Behavior*, edited by B. Staw, 3–23. Upper Saddle River, NJ: Pearson/Prentice Hall, 2004.

Gilbert, Paul. "Depression: A Biopsychosocial, Integrative and Evolutionary Approach." In *Mood Disorders: A Handbook of Science and Practice,* edited by M. Power, 99–142. Chichester, West Sussex, UK: 2004.

Gilbreth, Frank Bunker, Jr., and Ernestine Gilbreth Carey. *Cheaper by the Dozen.* New York: Thomas Y. Crowell, 1948.

Gladwell, Malcolm. *Outliers: The Story of Success.* New York: Little, Brown, 2008.

Glaser, Judith E. *Creating We.* Avon, MA: Platinum Press, 2007.

Gleeson, Kerry. *The Personal Efficiency Program: How to Get Organized to Do More Work in Less Time.* Hoboken, NJ: John Wiley and Sons, 2004.

Glovinsky, Cindy. *Making Peace with the Things in Your Life.* New York: St. Martin's Press, 2002.

———. *One Thing at a Time.* New York: St. Martin's Press, 2004.

Greenbaum, Joan. *Windows on the Workplace.* New York: Monthly Review Press, 2004.

Grint, Keith. *The Sociology of Work.* Cambridge, UK: Polity Press, 2005.

Hallowell, Edward M. *CrazyBusy: Overstretched, Overbooked, and About to Snap!* New York: Ballantine Books, 2006.

Heller, Joseph, *Something Happened.* New York: Alfred A. Knopf, 1974.

Hirsch, Gretchen. *The Complete Idiot's Guide to Difficult Conversations.* New York: Alpha, 2007.

Hochschild, Arlie, and Anne Machung. *The Managed Heart: Commercialization of Human Feeling.* Berkeley: University of California Press, 1983.

———. *The Second Shift: Working Families and the Revolution at Home.* New York: Viking Press, 1989.

Hogan, Robert. "Personality Psychology for Organizational Researchers." In *Personality and Organizations,* edited by B. Schneider and D. B. Smith, 3–23. Mahwah, NJ: Lawrence Erlbaum, 2004.

Honoré, Carl. *In Praise of Slowness: Challenging the Cult of Speed.* New York: HarperCollins, 2004.

Hughes, Langston. "Harlem." In *Approaching Poetry,* edited by Peter Schakel and Jack Ridl. Boston: Bedford/St. Martin's, 1997.

Hustad, Megan. *How to Be Useful: A Beginner's Guide to Not Hating Work.* New York: Houghton Mifflin, 2008.

Johnson, Jeff W. "Toward a Better Understanding of the Relationship between Personality and Individual Job Performance." In *Personality and Work: Reconsidering the Role of Personality in Organizations*, edited by M. R. Barrick and A. M. Ryan, 83–120. San Francisco: Jossey-Bass, 2003.

Kabat-Zinn, Jon. *Wherever You Go, There You Are*. New York: Hyperion, 1994.

Kase, Larina. *Anxious 9 to 5*. Oakland, CA: New Harbinger Publications, 2006.

King, Martin Luther, Jr. *Strength to Love*. Philadelphia: Fortress Press, 1963.

Klerman, Gerald L., Myrna M. Weissman, Bruce J. Rounsaville, and Eve S. Chevron. *Interpersonal Psychotherapy of Depression*. New York: Basic Books, 1984.

Klingberg, Torkel. *The Overflowing Brain*. Oxford: Oxford University Press, 2009.

Kusnet, David. *Love the Work, Hate the Job: Why America's Best Workers Are More Unhappy Than Ever*. New York: John Wiley and Sons, 2008.

Lancaster, Jane. *Making Time: Lillian Moller Gilbreth—A Life Beyond "Cheaper by the Dozen."* Boston: Northeastern University Press, 2004.

Lencioni, Patrick. *The Three Signs of a Miserable Job: A Fable for Managers (and Their Employees)*. San Francisco: Jossey-Bass, 2007.

Lerner, Harriet. *The Dance of Anger*. New York: Harper and Row, 1985.

Loehr, Jim, and Tony Schwartz. *The Power of Full Engagement*. New York: Free Press, 2005.

Lucas, Richard E., and Ed Diener. "The Happy Worker: Hypotheses and the Role of Positive Affect in Worker Productivity." In *Personality and Work: Reconsidering the Role of Personality in Organizations*, edited by M. R. Barrick and A. M. Ryan, 30–59. San Francisco: Jossey-Bass, 2003.

Mancini, Marc. *Time Management*. New York: McGraw-Hill, 2003.

Martel, Yann. *Life of Pi*. New York: Harcourt, 2004.

McCorry, K. J. *Organize Your Work Day . . . In No Time*. Indianapolis: Que, 2005.

Melville, Herman. "Bartleby, the Scrivener: A Story of Wall Street." In *The Piazza Tales*. New York: Dix and Edwards, 1856.

Morgenstern, Julie. *Never Check E-mail in the Morning: And Other*

Unexpected Strategies for Making Your Life Work. New York: Fireside, 2005.

Nel, Elizabeth. *Winston Churchill—by His Personal Secretary*. Lincoln, NE: Universe, 2007.

Organ, Dennis W. "The Subtle Significance of Job Satisfaction." In *Psychological Dimensions of Organizational Behavior*, edited by B. Staw, 150–82. Upper Saddle River, NJ: Pearson/Prentice Hall, 2004.

Organ, Dennis W., and Julie McFall. "Personality and Citizenship Behavior in Organizations." In *Personality and Organizations*, edited by B. Schneider and D. Smith, 291–316. Manwah, NJ: Lawrence Erlbaum, 2004.

Pearsall, Paul. *Toxic Success: How to Stop Striving and Start Thriving*. Makawao, Maui, HI: Inner Ocean Publishing, 2002.

Perlow, Leslie. *Finding Time: How Corporations, Individuals, and Families Can Benefit from New Work Practices*. Ithaca, NY: Cornell University Press, 1997.

Petrini, Carlo. *Slow Food Nation: Why Our Food Should be Good, Clean, and Fair*. New York: Rizzoli, 2007.

Pratt, Michael G., and Kurt T. Dirks. "Rebuilding Trust and Restoring Positive Relationships: A Commitment-Based View of Trust." In *Exploring Positive Relationships at Work*, edited by J. Dutton and B. Ragins, 117–36. Mahwah, NJ: Lawrence Erlbaum, 2007.

Rafaeli, Anat, and Robert I. Sutton. "Expression of Emotion as Part of the Work Role." In *Psychological Dimensions of Organizational Behavior*, edited by B. Staw, 106–20. Upper Saddle River, NJ: Pearson/Prentice Hall, 2004.

Ragins, Belle Rose, and Jane E. Dutton. "Positive Relationships at Work: An Introduction and Invitation." In *Psychological Dimensions of Organizational Behavior*, edited by B. Staw, 3–25. Upper Saddle River, NJ: Pearson/Prentice Hall, 2004.

Ramin, Cathryn Jakobson. *Carved in Sand: When Attention Fails and Memory Fades in Midlife*. New York: Harper, 2008.

Reich, Robert. *Supercapitalism: The Transformation of Business, Democracy, and Everyday Life*. New York: Alfred A. Knopf, 2007.

Ressler, Cali, and Jody Thompson. *Why Work Sucks and How to Fix It*. New York: Penguin, 2008.

Ricci, Monica. *Organize Your Office . . . In No Time*. Indianapolis: Que, 2005.

Robinson, Joe. "The Incredible Shrinking Vacation." In *Take Back Your Time: Fighting Overwork and Time Poverty in America*, edited by J. de Graaf, 20–27. San Francisco: Berrett-Koehler, 2003.

Roethke, Theodore. "Dolor." In *Approaching Poetry*, edited by Peter Schakel and Jack Ridl. Boston: Bedford/St. Martin's, 1997.

Rose, Mike. *The Mind at Work: Valuing the Intelligence of the American Worker*. New York: Penguin Books, 2004.

Rothlin, Philippe, and Peter Werder. *Boreout! Overcoming Workplace Demotivation*. London: Kogan Page Ltd., 2008.

Schneider, Benjamin, and D. Brent Smith. "Personality and Organizational Culture." In *Personality and Organizations*, edited by B. Schneider and D. Smith, 347–69. Manwah, NJ: Lawrence Erlbaum, 2004.

Smith, Adam. *An Inquiry into the Nature and Causes of the Wealth of Nations*. Oxford: Oxford University Press, 1993.

Staw, Barry. "Organizational Psychology and the Pursuit of the Happy/ Productive Worker." In *Psychological Dimensions of Organizational Behavior*, edited by B. Staw, 89–99. Upper Saddle River, NJ: Pearson/Prentice Hall, 2004.

Sutton, Robert I. *The No Asshole Rule: Building a Civilized Workplace and Surviving One That Isn't*. New York: Warner Business Books, 2007.

Tannen, Deborah. *You Just Don't Understand: Women and Men in Conversation*. New York: Quill, 2001.

Warr, P. "Well-being and the Workplace." In *Well-being: The Foundations of Hedonic Psychology*, edited by D. Kahneman, E. Diener, and N. Schwarz, 392–412. New York: Russell Sage, 1999.

Weber, Max. *The Protestant Ethic and the Spirit of Capitalism*, translated by Peter Baehr and Gordon C. Wells. New York: Penguin Books, 2002.

Wetmore, Donald E. *The Productivity Handbook*. New York: Random House, 2005.

Whyte, William H. *The Organization Man*. New York: Simon & Schuster, 1956.

Wilson, Sloan. *The Man in the Gray Flannel Suit*. New York: Avalon Publishing, 1955.

Winston, Stephanie. *Getting Out from Under*. Reading, MA: Perseus, 1999.

———. *Organized for Success*. New York: Crown Business, 2004.

Woodward, Bob, and Carl Bernstein. *All the President's Men*. New York: Simon & Schuster, 1974.

Zeer, Darrin. *Office Yoga: Simple Stretches for Busy People*. San Francisco: Chronicle, 2000.

Articles

"10 Tips for Weight Control for Office Workers." *Obesity*, December 17, 2006. http://www.associatedcontent.com/article/101165/10_tips_for_weight_control_for_office.html?cat=51 (accessed April 1, 2008).

Angliss, Carrie. "How Your Health Affects Your Job." *OfficePro* 68, no. 7 (October 2008): 14–17.

———. "What to Do When Your Job Is a Dead End." *OfficePro* 68, no. 6 (August/September 2008): 42–44.

Armour, Stephanie. "Day Care's New Frontier: Your Baby at Your Desk." *USA Today*, March 31, 2008.

"Asking for a Raise." *OfficePro* 68, no. 5 (2008): 9.

"Bad Office Behavior." *OfficePro* 68, no. 5 (2008): 7.

Balderrama, Anthony. "Six Signs Your New Job is Lousy." *CNN.com*, February 18, 2008. http://www.cnn.com (accessed July 21, 2008).

Bender, Jonathan. "Cubicle Land—How to Stand Out." *CNN.com*, July 18, 2008. http://www.cnn.com (accessed July 21, 2008).

Black, Elizabeth. "Meeting Nightmares." *OfficePro* 68, no. 5 (June/July 2008): 24–27.

Blain, Loz. "Developing a Viable Cure for Office Worker Obesity." *Gizmag*, April 21, 2007. http://www.gizmag.com (accessed April 1, 2008).

Britt, Robert Roy. "Conversational Black Holes Found in Workplace." *LiveScience*, February 16, 2005. http://www.livescience.com (accessed December 6, 2007).

Brynner, Jeanna. "Study: Office Bullies Create Workplace 'Warzone.' "

LiveScience, October 31, 2006. http://www.livescience.com (accessed December 6, 2007).

Carey, Bjorn. "Psychological Stress in the Healthy Human Brain." *LiveScience*, November 22, 2005. http://www.livescience.com (accessed December 6, 2007).

Carlson, Jessica and Steven Mellor. "Gender-Related Affects in the Job Design-Job Satisfaction Relationship." *Sex Roles: A Journal of Research,* August 2004. http://findarticles.com (accessed December 6, 2007).

Choi, Charles Q. "Your Boss Really Is Clueless." *LiveScience,* January 16, 2007. http://www.livescience.com (accessed December 6, 2007).

Cynkar, Amy. "Whole Workplace Health." *Monitor on Psychology* 38, no. 32 (March 2007). http://www.apa.org (accessed March 23, 2007).

Eaton, W. W., J. C. Anthony, W. Mandel, and R. Garrison. "Occupations and the Prevalence of Major Depressive Disorders." *Journal of Occupational Medicine* 32, no. 11 (November 1990): 1079–87. http://www.ncbi.nlm.nih (accessed December 11, 2006).

Ensminger, Aaron. "How Much Should You Be Making?" *OfficePro* 68, no. 5 (June/July 2008): 21–23.

"Finding the Right Fit." *OfficePro* 68, no. 6 (August/September 2008): 10.

"From Playground to Cubicle." *OfficePro* 68, no. 8 (November/December 2008): 9.

Garrison, R., and W. W. Eaton. "Secretaries, Depression, and Absenteeism." *Women's Health* 18, no. 4 (1992): 53–76. Available at *NCBI—PubMed.* http://www.ncbi.nlm.nih.gov (accessed December 11, 2006).

Goldberg, Richard J., and Steven Steury. "Depression in the Workplace: Costs and Barriers to Treatment." *Psychiatric Services* 52 (2001): 1639–43. http://www.ps.psychiatryonline.org.

Goodman, Ellen. "No Time to Think? Then Slow Down." *Ann Arbor News (Boston Globe)*, April 6, 2007.

Grobart, Sam. "Underpaid? How to Find Out Now?" *CNNMoney.com,* March 22, 2007. http://money.cnn.com (accessed July 21, 2008).

Haley, Jen. "Finding a Job after 50." *CNN.com*, August 20, 2007. http://www.cnn.com (accessed July 21, 2008).

Hallowell, Edward M. "The Human Moment at Work." *Harvard Business Review*, January–February 1989, 59.

"High Tech Job Matching Now Online." *OfficePro* 69, no. 6 (August/September 2008): 7.

"Internet E-mail Usage Update." *Braun Consulting News.* http://www.braunconsulting.com (accessed February 25, 2007).

Jones, Del. "Are You Proud of Your Job?" *USA Today*, May 23, 2005. http://www.usatoday.com (accessed January 7, 2008).

Kallestad, Brent. "Study: 2 of 5 Bosses Don't Keep Word." *LiveScience*, January 2, 2007. http://www.livescience.com (accessed December 6, 2007).

Kershaw, Sarah. "Family and Office Roles Mix." *New York Times*, December 3, 2008. http://www.nytimes.com (accessed December 4, 2008).

Kraft, Ulrich. "Burned Out." *Scientific American Mind* (June/July 2006): 29–33.

Lewis, Katherine Reynolds. "When 40 Hours Isn't." *Ann Arbor News*, September 3, 2007.

Lorenz, Kate. "Do You Have Job Burnout?" *CNN.com*, June 5, 2008. http://www.cnn.com (accessed July 21, 2008).

Murray, Stefanie. "A Look Inside Google." *Ann Arbor News*, September 23, 2007.

"Office in a Bucket." *Gizmag.* http://www.gizmag.com (accessed April 1, 2008).

Pfeffer, Jeffrey, and John F. Veiga. "Putting People First for Organizational Success." *Academy of Management Executive* 13, no. 2 (1999): 37–48.

Rhodes, Hillary. "Priority E-mail." *Ann Arbor News* (Associated Press), October 6, 2008.

Schlosser, Julie. "Cubicles: The Great Mistake." *CNNMoney.com*, March 22, 2006. http://money.cnn.com (accessed January 10, 2007).

"Solutions for Burnout in the Workplace." *OfficePro* 68, no. 6 (August/September 2008): 13.

Statistics Canada. "Depression and Work Impairment: Findings." *Health Reports.* http://www.statcan.ca/english/freepub (accessed June 9, 2008).

"Web Commuters." *OfficePro* 68, no. 5 (June/July 2008): 10.

"Web Surfing 'As Addictive as Coffee.'" *CNN.com International*, May 19, 2005. http://edition.cnn.com (accessed February 26, 2007).

"Web Surfing at Work: New Workplace Reality." *Braun Consulting News*

7, no. 3 (Summer 2003). http://www.braunconsulting.com (accessed February 26, 2007).

Weinstein, Bob. "Watch Out! You May be Working for a Corporate Cult." *Tech Republic*, March 8, 2000. http://articles.techrepublic.com (accessed October 10, 2008).

Whigham-Desir, Marjorie. "Strategies for Coping with Workplace Depression." *Black Enterprise* 9, no. 93. http://www.findarticles.com (accessed December 6, 2007).

Other References

All About Depression. "Environmental Causes of Depression." *All About Depression: Causes: Environment, Stress, Trauma, Childhood.* http://www.allaboutdepression.com (accessed December 11, 2006).

The Animals. "We've Gotta Get Out of This Place." Song recorded by MGM, 1965.

Berg, Justin M., Jane E. Dutton, and Amy Wrzesniewski. "What is Job Crafting and Why Does it Matter?" Working paper: Center for Positive Organizational Scholarship. Ross School of Business, University of Michigan, Ann Arbor, 2007.

"Clerk." *Wikipedia*. http://en.wikipedia.org (accessed June 30, 2008).

Esse, Juliana. "Environmental Causes of Depression." *Information Centre*. http://www.20002depression.org.uk (accessed December 11, 2006).

Fenner, Susan. "'A Rose by Any Other Name' Does Not Apply to Job Titles." International Association of Administrative Professionals. http://www.iaap-hq.org (accessed July 2, 2008).

"Industrial Revolution." *Wikipedia*. http://en.wikipedia.org (accessed July 1, 2008).

International Association of Administrative Professionals. "History of the Secretarial Profession." http://www.iaap-hq.org (accessed July 2, 2008).

International Association of Administrative Professionals. "Office of the Future: 2020." http://www.iapp.-hq.org (accessed July 2, 2008).

Lester, Greg. *Personality Disorders in Social Work and Health Care*. Cross Country Education (manual for presentation), 2005.

Mayo Clinic. "Job Satisfaction: Strategies to Make Work More Gratifying."

Adult Health. http://www.mayo-clinic.com (accessed December 5, 2007).

McManamy, John. "Is Work Driving Us Crazy?—Depression in the Workplace." *McMan's Depression and Bipolar Web.* http://www.mcmanweb.com (accessed December 10, 2006).

National Institute for Occupational Safety and Health. *NIOSH Publication: 99-101: Stress . . . at Work.* http://www.cdc.gov/niosh/docs/99–101/ (accessed March 21, 2007).

Scott, Elizabeth. "Job Satisfaction." *About.com.* http://www.stress.about.com (accessed December 5, 2007).

Snell, Melissa. "The Civilization of the Renaissance in Italy." *About.com: Medieval History.* http://historymedren.about.com (accessed September 2, 2008).

"Stress Management for Your Personality and Lifestyle." Presentation handout at Faculty and Staff Assistance Program, University of Michigan, Ann Arbor, 2008.

"Ten Tips for Computer Users." *Ergonomics Awareness.* Flyer by MHealthy, University of Michigan, Ann Arbor, 2007.

"U.S. Job Satisfaction Keeps Falling, The Conference Board Reports Today." *The Conference Board*, February 5, 2005. http://www.conference-board.org (accessed December 5, 2007).

Wooten, Lynn Perry. "Building a Positive Organizational Culture." Presentation handout at Institute for Social Research, University of Michigan, Ann Arbor.

Index

11479380R00221

Made in the USA
San Bernardino, CA
22 May 2014